Under Pressure

Under Pressure

Rescuing Our Children from the

Culture of Hyper-Parenting

Carl Honoré

HarperOne

An Imprint of HarperCollinsPublishers

HarperOne

Some names have been changed in this book to protect people's privacy.

HarperCollins books may be purchased for educational, business, or sales promotional use. For information please write: Special Markets Department, HarperCollins Publishers, 10 East 53rd Street, New York, NY 10022.

HarperCollins Web site: http://www.harpercollins.com
HarperCollins®, ✠ ®, and HarperOne™ are
trademarks of HarperCollins Publishers.

FIRST EDITION
Designed by Joseph Rutt

The Library of Congress Cataloging-in-Publication Data is available upon request.
ISBN 978-0-06-112880-6

08 09 10 11 12 RRD (H) 10 9 8 7 6 5 4 3 2 1

To my parents

That great Cathedral space which was childhood.
—Virginia Woolf

I wanted to do everything for my children: clear every
obstacle from their path, fight every battle, and take every
blow.

—John O'Farrell, May Contain
Nuts

Contents

INTRODUCTION	Managing Childhood	1
ONE	It's the Adults, Stupid	19
TWO	Early Years: When Milestones Become Millstones	37
THREE	Preschool: Play Is a Child's Work	57
FOUR	Toys: Just Push Play	73
FIVE	Technology: Reality Bites	89
SIX	School: Testing Times	113
SEVEN	Homework: The Sword of Damocles	145
EIGHT	Extracurricular Activities: Ready, Set, Relax!	161
NINE	Sports: Play Ball	181
TEN	Discipline: Just Say No?	199
ELEVEN	Consumerism: Pester Power and the Walking, Talking ATM	215
TWELVE	Safety: Playing with Fire	239
CONCLUSION	Leave Those Kids Alone	257
	Resources	265
	Notes	269
	Acknowledgments	279
	Index	281

Managing Childhood

*No matter how calmly you try to referee, parenting will
eventually produce bizarre behavior, and I'm not talking
about the kids.*

—Bill Cosby

In an affluent corner of London, in a primary school built more
than a century ago, a very modern parent-teacher evening is in
full swing. My wife and I are here for an interview about our
seven-year-old son. A few parents sit outside the classroom on
plastic chairs, staring at the floor or glancing at their watches.
Some pace the corridor, fiddling nervously with mobile phones.

The year-two workbooks are piled up like small snowdrifts
on a table. We flip through them, smiling at eccentric spellings,
cooing over sweet drawings, and marveling at the complexity of
the arithmetic. Our son's triumphs and failures are laid bare on
the page, and they feel like our own. I celebrate each gold star in
his workbook with a silent cheer.

Eventually, Mrs. Pendle invites us into the classroom. Our
son seems to be thriving, so we have high hopes for the interview.
Once we take our seats at a low table, Mrs. Pendle delivers her

verdict: Our son is very good at reading and writing. His math is solid. His science could be better. He is well behaved and a pleasure to teach.

It is a very good report, yet somehow not quite good enough. "She didn't mention his amazing vocabulary," says my wife, as we walk away from the classroom. "Or explain why he's not in the top group in every subject," I add. Our tone is jocular—we're making fun of the pushy parents you read about in the newspapers—but there is an edge to the irony. We partly mean it, too.

After my wife goes home to relieve the babysitter, I head off to visit the art teacher. "Your son really stands out," she gushes. "He always comes up with a different twist on things." *That's more like it,* I think to myself. One of his works is pinned to the wall of the art room as a model for other pupils. It is a sketch of a scraggy magician done in the style of Quentin Blake, who illustrated the books of Roald Dahl. Underneath the portrait, our son has depicted the old man's head from different angles. The teacher takes it down to show me. "Amazing for a seven-year-old to come up with something that plays with perspective like that on his own," she says. "He really is a gifted young artist."

And there it is, that magic word, the six letters that are music to the ears of every parent. *Gifted.* I walk home from the school already mapping out my son's ascent to the top of the international art world. Will his first exhibition be in London or New York? Does he need an agent? Are we raising the next Picasso? Suddenly, all those visits to the Tate Gallery, all those Sunday mornings spent dragging the children around the Turners and Titians, have paid off. My son is an artist.

My wife is delighted by the news, not least because the father of a classmate was present when the art teacher delivered her panegyric. After a late supper, I start sifting through parenting magazines and surfing the Internet, hunting for the right course to nurture our son's gift. The ad that catches my eye promises, "Unlock your child's genius!" My wife wonders if I'm going too far, but her words are no more than background noise to me now.

The next morning, on the walk to school, I float the idea of enrolling in an art course. But my son is having none of it. "I don't want to go to a class and have a teacher tell me what to do—I just want to draw," he says, firmly. "Why do grown-ups have to take over everything?"

The question stops me in my tracks. My son loves to draw. He can spend hours hunched over a piece of paper, inventing alien life forms or sketching Wayne Rooney dribbling a soccer ball. He draws well and it makes him happy. But somehow that is not enough. Part of me wants to harness that happiness, to hone and polish his talent, to turn his art into an achievement.

Of course, I am not the first parent eager to steer my child to the top. It comes with the territory. Two thousand years ago, a schoolteacher named Lucius Orbilius Pupillus identified pushy parents as an occupational hazard in the classrooms of ancient Rome. When the young Mozart helped make prodigies fashionable in the eighteenth century, many Europeans hot-housed their own children in the hope of creating a wunderkind. Today, however, the pressure to make the most of our kids feels all-consuming. We want them to have the best of everything and to be the best at everything. We want them to be artists, academics, and athletes, to glide through life without hardship, pain, or failure.

In its more extreme form, this brand of child rearing has different names around the world. Helicopter-parenting—because Mom and Dad are always hovering overhead. Hyper-parenting. Scandinavians joke about "curling parents" who frantically sweep the ice in front of their child. "Education mothers" devote every waking second to steering their children through the school system in Japan.

Yet parents are not the only ones curling, pushing, and helicoptering. Everybody, from the state to the advertising industry, has designs on childhood. In Britain, a task force of parliamentarians recently warned that too many children dream of growing up to be fairy princesses or soccer stars. Their solution: career advice for five-year-olds.

Wherever you look these days, the message is the same: childhood is too precious to be left to children and children are too precious to be left alone. All this meddling is forging a new kind of childhood. In the past, the Working Child toiled in the fields and, later, in the factories of the Industrial Revolution. The twentieth century saw the rise of the Free-Range Child. Now we have entered the age of the Managed Child.

Before we go any further, let's be clear about one thing: not all childhoods are created equal. You don't find many children being project-managed in the refugee camps of Sudan or the shantytowns of Latin America. Even in the developed world, millions of youngsters, especially in poorer families, are more likely to suffer from underparenting than overparenting. Let's be honest: most helicopter-parents hail from the middle class. But that does not mean this cultural shift only affects the well-to-do. When it comes to social change, the middle classes often set the tone, and over time their hang-ups and foibles trickle up and down the social ladder. Or at the very least they make everyone else feel guilty for failing to keep pace.

Look around and it's clear that children are already the target of more adult anxiety and intervention than at any time in history. A pregnant friend in New York e-mails to say that she spends one hour every evening pumping WombSong Serenades into her bump in the hope of stimulating her unborn infant's brain. On the other side of the world, ambitious parents are enrolling their children in an "Early MBA" program in Shanghai. Every Sunday morning, the pupils learn the value of team building, problem solving, and assertiveness. Some are barely out of diapers.

Many children now keep the kind of schedule that would make a CEO queasy. Infants are shuttled from baby yoga to baby aerobics to baby sign language lessons. In Corte Madera, California, Gail Penner bought a Palm Pilot for her son John's birthday to help him keep track of his extracurricular activities—piano, baseball, Spanish, basketball, soccer, tennis, swimming, and karate. "He's so busy he needs to learn how to manage his time," she says. John is ten.

Even when children do have spare time, we are often too afraid to let them out of our sight. The average distance from home British kids are permitted to wander by themselves has fallen nearly 90 percent since the 1970s. My son, like more than two-thirds of his peers, has never walked to the park alone.

Technology helps us keep tabs on children like never before. GPS devices embedded in their jackets and schoolbags and uniforms turn them into little red blips on our computer screens at home and at work. Mobile phones increasingly double as tracking devices: if a child drifts out of the designated "safe zone," Mom and Dad get an instant text message. Day-care centers and nurseries are installing Web cams so parents can view real-time footage of their toddlers from anywhere in the world. Even summer camp is no longer a refuge from the prying eyes of the twenty-first-century parent, with photos and video clips relayed from remote lakes and forests to in-boxes back home or uploaded to the Web. "People used to be happy leaving their kids with us for a week or two without hearing any news apart from maybe a postcard or the odd phone call," says one veteran camp counselor in Colorado. "Now, we get parents freaking out if their kid doesn't appear on the Web site every day. Or if he does appear and isn't smiling."

This is the first generation to star in its own version of the *Truman Show*. It starts with the printout from the ultrasound scan and moves on to eavesdropping on the womb with prenatal heart listeners. Actor Tom Cruise was so desperate to monitor his unborn daughter that he reportedly bought his own sonogram machine, despite warnings from doctors that his amateur spying could harm the fetus. After birth, every moment is then captured in digital and Dolby. Like paparazzi, modern parents are always lurking, finger on the shutter release or the record button, waiting for that perfect shot—or seeking to engineer it. I catch myself barking orders from the director's chair: "Just make that face one more time for the camera." Or: "Everybody stop playing for a second and look at me with a big smile."

The micromanaging no longer stops at the end of school. Many Britons now plan every detail of their children's "gap year" before university. Parents in China take on average a week off work to settle their offspring into college, with many moving into makeshift accommodations on campus. North American universities are assigning full-time staff to field the deluge of calls and e-mails from moms and dads who want to help pick courses, taste-test cafeteria food, proofread essays, and even screen Junior's roommates. The umbilical cord even remains intact after graduation. To recruit college students, blue-chip companies such as Merrill Lynch have started sending out "parent packs" or holding open-house days when Mom and Dad can vet their offices. "Our candidates and our interns look more and more to their parents when they're making career decisions," says Dan Black, director of campus recruiting in the Americas for Ernst & Young. Employers even find parents tagging along to their children's job interviews. One candidate recently turned up at a leading consultancy firm in New York with her mother in tow. "Mom asked all about the salary, promotion prospects, and vacation package," says one of the interviewers. "It was like she just couldn't hold back."

These days, nothing is too good for our children. I am amazed by how much stuff my own kids have. How did it happen? We are not a shopaholic family, yet their rooms are submerged in a river of toys—and that's just the ones we haven't carted off to the charity shop. What will happen when they discover information technology? Will they end up like Julio Duarte Cruz, who, like teenagers all over the world, rushes home from school to spend time with his gadgets. "My bedroom is my own virtual world," he tells me via e-mail from Seville, Spain. "And my parents like it because they know exactly where I am."

BY ANY YARDSTICK, we are raising the most wired, pampered, and monitored generation in history—and is that really such a bad thing? After thousands of years of trial and error, perhaps we have finally stumbled on the magic recipe for child rearing. Maybe all that micromanaging pays off in the end. Maybe we are bringing up the brightest, healthiest, happiest children the world has ever seen.

Reports of the death of childhood have certainly been exaggerated. There are many advantages to growing up in the developed world in the early twenty-first century: You are less likely to suffer malnutrition, neglect, violence, or death than at any point in history. You are surrounded by material comforts that were unthinkable even a generation ago. Legions of academics, politicians, and companies are striving to find new ways to nurture, feed, clothe, school, and entertain you. Your rights are enshrined in international law. You are the center of your parents' universe.

Yet childhood today seems a far cry from the "nest of gladness" imagined by Lewis Carroll. And parenthood is no walk in the park, either. In many ways, the modern approach to children is backfiring.

Let's start with health. Cooped up like battery hens, with little exercise and a high-calorie diet, children are growing dangerously fat. In the United States, manufacturers are supersizing car safety seats to accommodate the nation's tubby toddlers. Nearly a fifth of American children are overweight, and the rest of the world is following suit. The International Association for the Study of Obesity estimates that 38 percent of under-eighteens in Europe and 50 percent in North and South America will be obese by 2010. Already the extra pounds are condemning children to heart disease, type 2 diabetes, arteriosclerosis, and other disorders once confined to adults.

Athletic kids suffer as well. Too much training too young is wearing them out. Injuries like ACL (anterior cruciate ligament) tears, formerly only seen in college and professional athletes, are now rife in high school and increasingly common among nine- and ten-year-olds.

And where the body goes, the mind follows. Depression, self-harm, and eating disorders are on the rise among children around the world, as are cases of stress-induced illnesses, such as stomach pain, headaches, and chronic fatigue. Even allowing for overzealous diagnosis, the numbers are alarming: the United Nations warns that one in five children already suffers from a psychological disorder, and the World Health Organization estimates that by 2020 mental illness will be one of the top five causes of death or disability in the young. In Britain, a teenager tries to commit suicide every twenty-eight minutes. Rather than end it all, Japanese teens retreat into their bedrooms and refuse to come out for weeks, months, or even years at a time. Experts estimate that over 400,000 of the country's adolescents are now *hikikomori,* or full-time hermits. Elsewhere, university students are cracking up like never before. A decade ago the most common reason for visiting the campus counselor was boyfriend or girlfriend trouble; today it is anxiety. Steven Hyman, a professor of neurobiology, former director of the U.S. National Institute of Mental Health, and current provost of Harvard University, says that the mental health of U.S. college students is now in such a parlous state that "it is interfering with the core mission of the university."

Much of the malaise is caused by a culture that leaves everyone pining for the fame, fortune, and physical beauty of an A-list celebrity. Yet the burden falls most heavily on children higher up the social ladder, where the pressure to compete is more intense. Research from around the world suggests that child depression and anxiety—and the substance abuse, self-harm, and suicide that often go with it—are now most common not in urban ghettos but in the smart downtown apartments and leafy suburbs where the go-getting middle classes project-manage their children. In *The Price of Privilege,* Madeline Levine, a clinical psychologist in an upmarket part of San Francisco, reports that children in homes with an annual income between $120,000 and $160,000 are three times more likely to become depressed or anxious than are their less affluent peers. A recent survey found that nearly 40 percent of fifteen-year-old girls from well-off families in

Britain suffer from the sort of psychological distress that puts them at risk of mental illness. In Brittany, France, anxiety and suicide rates have risen in tandem with rising marks in the tough baccalauréat exams and greater access to higher education. The Japanese *hikikomori* are almost always from middle-class families.

To keep pace, or even just to get by, more children than ever before—over six million in the United States alone—are taking medication to alter their behavior and mood. Even infants are now washing down antidepressants with their bedtime milk. Worldwide, prescriptions for Ritalin, Attenta, Focalin, and other drugs designed to help curb hyperactivity in children have tripled since 1993. Experts fear that many families are now using psychotropic medication as a parenting tool. One physician in a well-to-do suburb of New York now puts a question to every parent who approaches him for a Ritalin prescription: "Do you want this to make life easier for your child or to make it easier for yourself?" Underlying this pill-popping boom is a tart irony: a generation of adults who used drugs to hang loose and free the mind is now using them to keep their own kids on a tight leash.

The urge to upgrade our children has taken on a Frankenstein edge. Inspired by research showing that taller people tend to be more successful, some parents now pay to inject growth hormone into their healthy, normal kids, with every extra inch of height costing $50,000. Others prefer a little nip and tuck to create the perfect look. These days, plastic surgeons have to keep a watch out for teenage patients being pressured by their parents to get that nose job or ear-pinning procedure. A doctor in Sao Paulo, Brazil, tells how a sixteen-year-old girl recently broke down on his operating table just before the anesthetic was administered. "She was sobbing and asking why her parents couldn't accept her face the way it was, so we sent her straight home," he says. "Her mother was furious."

The tragedy is that all this micromanaging, all this pampering, hothousing, and medicating is failing to produce a new race of alpha children. Teachers across the world report that pupils now find it hard just to sit still and concentrate. Employers complain that many new recruits are less flexible, less able to work in teams, and less hungry to learn.

Micromanaged children can end up struggling to stand on their own two feet. Academic advisers tell of university students handing over the mobile phone in the middle of interviews and saying: "Why don't you sort this out with my mom?" Large numbers of middle-class children now choose to live at home well into their twenties, and not always because of college debt and soaring house prices: many simply cannot bear to leave behind a place where they are the center of the universe. One father I know in Oxford is amazed that his twenty-four-year-old daughter, who possesses a glittering résumé, has moved back into her old bedroom. "She even wants me to drive her to the cinema," he says. "It's as if she's twelve again." The Japanese refer to twenty-something stay-at-homes as "parasite singles."

Raised on a pedestal, children come to expect the world to fall at their feet—and get angry when it doesn't. Is it a coincidence that *Supernanny, Brat Camp,* and other television programs showing how to tame unruly kids now fill the airwaves across the world? Later in life, the tantrums can give way to narcissism. A 2006 personality survey found signs of "elevated narcissism" in nearly two-thirds of the 16,000 U.S. college students interviewed, a 30 percent jump from 1982. The *Wall Street Journal* recently reported that instead of buying flowers or chocolates for Mother's Day, many American twentysomethings now prefer to indulge in a bit of self-improvement, going on diets, fixing their own teeth, getting haircuts, cleaning their apartments, or joining dating services. Why? Because the best way to make a twenty-first-century mom happy is to upgrade her children.

Reared on someone else's definition of success, with failure not an option, children can also end up with narrow horizons. At a time when the global economy is crying out for risk takers, we are teaching our children to play safe, to follow the path handed down by others. Of course, young people still rebel, but where are the campus protests that rocked the political establishment and reshaped popular culture in the 1960s and 1970s? Many college students seem more interested in burnishing their résumés than brandishing placards. Professors describe a new generation of worker bees who are masters at playing the system but devoid of personal spark. "There's no real fire there, no rough edges, no burning passion to go out on a limb or challenge the status quo," says one Ivy League professor. "A lot of kids now seem to be speaking from a script."

William Blake famously summed up childhood thus:

To see a world in a grain of sand,
And a heaven in a wildflower,
Hold infinity in the palm of your hand,
And eternity in an hour.

Today, many children are too busy racing to violin practice or Kumon tutoring to hold infinity in the palm of their hand. And that wildflower sounds a little scary—what if it has thorns, or the pollen triggers an allergic reaction? When adults hijack childhood, children miss out on the things that give texture and meaning to a human life—the small adventures, the secret journeys, the setbacks and mishaps, the glorious anarchy, the moments of solitude and even of boredom. The message sinks in very young that what matters most is not finding your own way but putting the right trophy on the mantelpiece, ticking the box instead of thinking outside it. As a result, modern childhood seems strangely bland, packed with action, achievement, and consumption, yet somehow empty and ersatz. The freedom to be oneself is missing—and kids know it. "I feel like a project that my parents are always working on," says Susan Wong, a fourteen-year-old in Vancouver, Canada. "They even talk about me in the third person when I'm standing right there."

We all suffer when children become projects. Instead of bringing families together, too much striving and rushing around can end up pulling them apart. Just ask Connie Martinez, a mother in Los Angeles. On a recent visit to the cinema, her five-year-old son suggested sitting in the seat behind her. "He said it would be like being in the car together," she explains. "We spend so much time driving around to his activities that he feels most comfortable staring at the back of my head. I was horrified."

Bubble-wrapping children drains the life from public spaces. In my old neighborhood in Edmonton, Canada, streets that once hummed with the sound of kids playing road hockey, shooting baskets in the driveway, or just running through sprinklers are now eerily quiet. Instead, the children are parked indoors in front of the PlayStation, or riding in cars to their next appointment. An obsession with our own children can also make us less committed to the welfare of other people. Even in countries famous for their social solidarity, a me-first edge has seeped into the playground. "More and more I hear parents talking about 'My child this, my child that,'" says a schoolteacher in Gothenburg, Sweden. "Their child is the messiah and they don't seem to care about other children at all." Everywhere, parents are lashing out at anyone who stands in the way of their offspring. A thirty-three-year-old woman recently knocked down and kicked the referee at a youth basketball game in Cedar Rapids, Iowa. She was furious that several calls had gone against her son. The referee was five months' pregnant. In Toronto, a couple threatened to sue a Brownie Girl Scout leader when she urged them to stop obsessing about how many badges their eight-year-old daughter was earning. At a coveted primary school in Paris, a mother recently pinned the principal to a wall after he refused to admit her son because his birthday fell too late in the year. "If I had known, I would have induced labor and had him a month earlier!" she shrieked. Other parents are seeking advantage by taking the opposite tack. Spurred by studies showing that the oldest children in a class are more likely to thrive in the long run, parents in the United States, Britain, and other countries are "redshirting" their kids, or holding them back a year so that they start kindergarten in the top age group.

This bubbling panic, this sense that only an alpha child stands a chance anymore, can have an ugly effect farther down the social ladder. Blue-collar parents start wondering if they should sell the car or cut back on groceries to hire a tutor. A recent survey in the United States found that many children from lower-income Latino families had not bothered to apply to their local state college because they assumed the tuition fees and the grade requirements were on a par with those at Ivy League schools. Three-quarters said they would have applied had they known this was untrue.

The same panic also clouds judgment in better-off homes. Deep down, most of us know that hyper-managing children is absurd. The trouble is that it is very easy to get caught up in the frenzy.

With everyone so wound up, and with so much at stake, is it any wonder that around the world you find parents moaning about the burden of child rearing, or that novels and Web sites exposing the dark side of being a parent (and especially a mother) have mushroomed in recent years. Of course, children have always been hard work. But today, with expectations soaring, the burden is enough to put people off altogether. Birth rates have tumbled in much of the industrial world, and the childless even talk of being "childfree," as if kids were a nasty form of herpes. A recent magazine headline in Italy, a nation famous for its love of *bambini,* says it all: "Are children worth it?"

The answer, of course, is yes—and that is why we have to do better. This book is not a nostalgia trip or an attempt to turn back the clock. I doubt there has ever been a golden age for children—every generation makes mistakes. Yet now there is hope for change. Across the world, the frenzy surrounding children is coming under review. The media bristles with warnings and mea culpas. *Newsweek* columnist and mother of three, Anna Quindlen, spoke for many when she apologized to the graduating class of 2004. "You were kicked into high gear earlier," she wrote. "How exhausted you must be." One hundred British scientists and other intellectuals signed an open letter in 2006 calling for a campaign to save childhood from the toxic effects of modern life. A few weeks later, the American Academy of Pediatrics warned against the scourge of overscheduling and putting too much emphasis on schoolwork. Across Asia, political leaders have talked about the need to ease the burden on the young. Chen Shui-bian, the president of Taiwan, wrote of his hope that children will have "fewer tests, lighter satchels, and more sleep." *Confessions of a Slacker Mom* and other books that make the case against parental competition are selling briskly.

And from words comes action. Governments, even in the hard-toiling Far East, have started to make more room for creativity, play, and rest in their school systems. Families everywhere are fighting to loosen the grasp that advertisers hold over their children. Youth sports leagues are reforming to allow kids to play without letting adults spoil the fun. Across North America, whole towns now hold days when homework and extracurricular activities are canceled.

The young are also sending a message that they want adults to back off. When Britain held its first annual conference for head boys and head girls in 2006, the theme was "pupil power" and the delegates called for less hothousing and testing. Leading academic institutions are starting to send a similar message. Not long ago, Marilee Jones, a former dean of admissions at Massachusetts Institute of Technology, noticed that the MIT campus had lost some of its creative luster. She decided that the application process was weeding out the mavericks, the Bill Gates types, the rebels who pursue an idea for the sake of it rather than to please parents or potential employers. "The kid who grinds a telescope in his bedroom to satisfy his own curiosity rather than to take it to a fair to win an award—that kid is the true scientist and observer," she says. "Give me that kid any day."

After nearly three decades at MIT, Jones was forced to resign recently when it emerged that many years ago she had falsified her own résumé—the ultimate sin for a dean of admissions. But despite her fall from grace, she helped to fuel the groundswell against the idea that childhood must be a mad dash to get into a blue-chip college. Toward the end of her tenure, Jones rewrote the MIT application form, halving the space devoted to extracurricular activities and including more searching questions about what really gets a candidate's blood pumping. She also crisscrossed the United States, talking to auditoriums full of teachers, high-school counselors, and families. I caught up with her at a conference in Silicon Valley, a hotbed of hyper-parenting. Clad in a black dress and a jaunty silk scarf, she cut straight to the chase. "We are raising a whole generation of kids to please us, to make us happy and proud, to be what we want them to be," she told the 350-strong crowd. "I know because I did the same thing to my own daughter for years and I almost lost her as a result."

Her prescription was bracingly subversive: children thrive when they have the time and space to breathe, to hang out and get bored sometimes, to relax, to take risks and make mistakes, to dream and have fun on their own terms, even to fail. If we are going to restore the joy not only to childhood but to parenthood, too, then the time has come for adults to back off a little, to allow children to be themselves. "This is the beginning of a revolution," Jones called out, and the auditorium erupted with applause.

Finding a new recipe for childhood in the information age will not be easy. The first step is to take a collective time-out, which means stepping away from the hype and the panic long enough to see that many children are getting a raw deal. Then we have to tackle some hard questions: When is it right to push children and when is it best to back off? How much freedom do they need? How much technology? What risks should children be allowed to take?

There are certainly dangers in writing a book like this. One is that any plea to be less anxious about children can end up making everyone feel even more anxious. Another is the old-fogey trap. Every generation has despaired of its youth, sometimes in apocalyptic terms, and I know I am reaching an age when the words "When I was young . . ." can trip easily off the tongue. Yet the risks are worth taking.

This book is not another parenting manual—there are enough of those already. You won't find a box with favorite tips or a pop quiz at the end of each chapter. My aim is to find a way to tame the anxiety surrounding children. That entails rethinking what it means to be a child and what it means to be an adult—and finding a way to reconcile the two in the twenty-first century.

Our investigation will take us around the world. In the coming pages, we will visit classrooms from Finland and California to Italy and Hong Kong. We will drop in on an outdoor nursery where three-year-olds live dangerously in a Scottish forest. We will visit a U.S. town that jumps off the overscheduling treadmill once a year, then go to a sports clinic in New York that aims to reinvent youth basketball for children. We will attend a toy fair in London and a toy experiment in Buenos Aires. At every step, of course, we will hear from the experts, but we will also hear from those engaged most deeply in this battle to redefine childhood for the twenty-first century: parents and children themselves. Many of the people who feature in the coming chapters will tell their story in the rumpus room or across the kitchen table, or by e-mail from the home computer.

This book is also a personal journey. As the father of two children in London, I am on the front line. Like most parents, I want my kids to be happy, healthy, and successful. But I also want parenting to feel less like Mission Impossible. I want to ditch the itch to take over.

In the end, what I really want is for my children to look back on their youth with joy, to remember seeing the world in a grain of sand. I want them to have a childhood worthy of the name.

It's the Adults, Stupid

On these magic shores, children at play are forever beaching their coracles. We too have been there. We can still hear the sound of the surf, though we shall land no more.
—*J. M. Barrie,* Peter Pan

On a summer afternoon toward the end of exams, the ancient colleges of Oxford are a playground for gilded youth. Sunshine warms the stone buildings as a breeze riffles the ivy clinging to the eaves. At Magdalen College, students from around the world hang out on lawns of putting-green perfection, reading newspapers, chatting on mobile phones, listening to iPods. A croquet game starts up, sending laughter echoing round the old quad. This is a snapshot of the new elite at rest. To paraphrase Cecil Rhodes, father of the Rhodes Scholarship program, these young people have won first prize in the lottery of life.

Or have they? George Rousseau, codirector of Oxford University's Centre for the History of Childhood, is not so sure. We meet in the old smoking room of Magdalen College. Faded paintings of rural scenes hang on the paneled walls. Professors chat donnishly over cups of tea and coffee beneath a beamed ceiling. From our worn leather armchairs we can see students ambling across the courtyard below. Rousseau, who has spent thirty-five years teaching at elite colleges on both sides of the Atlantic, kicks off by telling me that twenty-first-century children get a raw deal.

"I feel sorry for many young people today, particularly those in affluent families," he says. "They don't face the threat of death and disease that earlier generations did, and they have many advantages, but they are also nannied, pressured, and overprotected to the point of suffocation. They are left with no sense of freedom."

If that is going to change, then we must first understand how childhood evolved into its present form. This is not an easy task, Rousseau tells me. Generalizations are hard to make because children's lives vary so widely, not only across time but also across social classes and cultures. The history of childhood as an academic discipline only really took off in the 1960s, and even now our knowledge of adult-child relations in the premodern era remains patchy. "The result is a lot of speculation and guesswork," says Rousseau.

One common myth is that childhood did not exist at all in the past. This idea entered conventional wisdom in the 1960s when Philippe Ariès, a French historian, argued that children in medieval Europe were treated as miniature adults from the moment they were weaned—wearing the same clothes, enjoying the same entertainment, working the same jobs as everyone else.

Ariès was right that the distant past was a very adult place, but his claim that our forebears had no conception of childhood and therefore never treated children differently was wide of the mark. Two thousand years before NetNanny, Plato insisted that a society should monitor what its young see, hear, and read. Even the Rule of Benedict, the leading monastic guide in medieval Europe, stipulated that child monks be granted extra food and sleep, as well as time to play. "Ariès came up with a compelling narrative for his time but it was partly wrong, or at least incomplete," says Rousseau.

Another misconception is that, hardened by high death rates, parents in earlier times avoided forging an emotional bond with their offspring, treating them instead like disposable servants. Families often recycled the name of a dead child by giving it to a sibling. In the first century A.D., the Roman philosopher Seneca recommended mutilating children to make them more effective beggars. Not long after, a Greek gynecologist named Soranus published a book with a ruthlessly Darwinian title: *How to Recognize the Newborn That Is Worth Rearing*. Killing or abandoning unwanted babies was surprisingly common in the West right up until the nineteenth century. As late as the 1860s, a third of all infants born in Milan were dumped in doorways or left at the foundling hospitals set up to handle the deluge. Plenty of evidence suggests that beatings, neglect, and sexual abuse of children were endemic in many cultures. Lloyd deMause, an American psychotherapist-cum-historian, famously concluded in 1974 that "the history of childhood is a nightmare from which we have only begun to awaken."

But there is another side to the story. Even if life in the past was harsh, the parents of yesteryear did not necessarily regard their children as chattel unworthy of sentiment. Mothers who abandoned babies often left them with keys, brooches, and other tokens in the hope of being reunited one day, even if in heaven. Across the ages, diaries, letters, and journals reveal parental love and tenderness flourishing when life was at its cheapest. Just listen to Gregory of Tours lamenting the fallout from a famine in sixth-century France: "We lost our little ones, who were so dear to us, whom we cherished in our bosoms and dandled in our arms, whom we fed and nurtured with such loving care. As I write, I wipe away my tears."

And yet much has changed. Even if our ancestors were no strangers to parental love or the idea of childhood, even if they felt a similar instinct to cosset, control, and burnish the young, most of them were not obsessive about children. "This constant pushing, monitoring, and nannying of the young is very much a feature of the modern world," says Rousseau.

The shift began after the Middle Ages, as new ways of thinking took hold. The Puritans declared that all babies were born with the stain of original sin and that only vigorous adult intervention could save their souls. The philosopher John Locke, whose views carried enormous weight across Europe, cranked up the pressure by publishing in 1693 a book called *Some Thoughts on Education,* which argued that a child enters the world as a tabula rasa, or blank slate, just waiting to be filled up (by adults, of course).

Later, Jean-Jacques Rousseau, one of the philosophers who inspired the Romantic movement, which swept across Europe from the late eighteenth century, told adults to back off. He argued that childhood—"its games, its pleasures, its amiable instinct"—should be cherished for itself rather than exploited as the means to an end; that children were born pure, spontaneous, and joyful and should therefore be left to learn and create at their own pace. Fired by this Romantic ideal, artists like Joshua Reynolds and Thomas Gainsborough began painting children as little angels at play, while writers like William Wordsworth and Johann Wolfgang Goethe exalted the child as a quasi-divine creature possessed of a special bond with nature.

Even today we remain torn between the Lockean and the Romantic approaches to childhood: should we mold kids like putty, or relax and let them be children? Either way, both philosophies, together with rising prosperity, helped nudge children up the agenda. This change came first to the upper and middle classes, which gradually paved the way for a broader cultural shift. Etiquette manuals started giving advice on how to educate and groom the young in the seventeenth century. The market for clothes, books, toys, and games designed especially for children took off soon after. Around the same time, doctors began exploring how the young might benefit from specialized medical care, thus laying the foundations for pediatrics to emerge later as a separate field of medicine. And as the focus on children intensified, so, too, did parental worry. In the late eighteenth century, long before SATs and "stranger danger," an English clergyman named John Townsend wrote of "fond and anxious parents, who have sacrificed your ease, your rest, your worldly property, your health, your all, for the comfort and prosperity of your offspring." By the nineteenth century, child welfare was an important subject of debate among intellectuals, reformers, charities, and bureaucrats, with the first movements for child rights springing up and states enacting laws and creating welfare programs to protect the young.

The real revolution, however, was the demise of child labor, which gathered pace from the mid-nineteenth century. In Britain, for example, school attendance quadrupled between 1860 and 1900. This was largely driven by the Romantic belief that putting children to work and profiting from their toil was immoral and by the growing need for an educated workforce. As their earning power fell, children's value rocketed in other ways. They came to be seen as a precious national resource. A British doctor named Margaret Alden warned in 1908 that "the nation that first recognizes the importance of scientifically rearing and training the children of the commonwealth will be the nation that will survive." The twentieth century was dubbed the "century of the child," with the League of Nations declaring in 1924 that "mankind owes the child the best it has to give."

The shift in public attitudes was mirrored in the home. Historians have found evidence that, as early as the seventeenth century, family relations took on a warmer, more sentimental tone. Parents started celebrating their children's birthdays and using terms of endearment such as "my dear child" in letters and diaries. Once derided as self-indulgence or even a challenge to God's will, grieving the death of a child became commonplace in the nineteenth century. By the early 1900s, U.S. courts were awarding compensation to the parents of children killed in accidents— not for lost wages but for emotional anguish.

As birth and death rates fell, the family evolved, too, shrinking, turning inward, and increasingly building itself around the needs of the child. Instead of struggling to keep a large brood of children alive, parents in the twentieth century could concentrate on honing and enjoying a small number of them. "There is a huge difference between saying 'my children are precious to me' and saying 'I have three children but only one of them is likely to survive,'" says Rousseau, the Oxford historian. Studies around the world show that parents in smaller families are more inclined to micromanage their offspring. They have more time to invest per child and may feel they have fewer chances to get it right. Parents in larger families are also more likely to recognize that each child is born with a particular temperament and abilities— and that there are therefore limits on how much you can shape development.

The net effect is that the family has come to revolve around the child in a way never seen before. I see this in my own life. We tape our children's schedules to the refrigerator and bend our own around them. We arrange our holidays and weekends to please them. We are even thinking about moving house to be near the right school. If the statistics are right, we will soon be consulting them on which car or computer to buy for the family. Is it any wonder that after all that effort, all that sacrifice and self-abnegation, our children's accomplishments start to feel like our own? Or that children have become, more than ever before, an extension of the parental ego—a mini-me to eulogize round the watercooler or on Web sites? Parents have always boasted about their children's exploits, yet today the average Christmas "brag letter" reads like a college application form, a brazen catalogue of Junior's academic, social, and sporting prowess. Some parents even talk about their children using the first person plural: "We are taking the International Baccalaureate" or "We won a scholarship to the Sorbonne." What children eat and wear, the music they listen to, the school they attend, their hairstyles, the sports they play, the gadgets they use—everything is now worn as a parental badge of honor. How else do you explain Baby Gucci slip-on shoes at $230 a pair?

As the family has grown more childcentric, parents have turned to their children to meet more of their emotional needs. This seems a natural response to a world where nearly half of all marriages end in divorce and kids offer the only relationship guaranteed to last till death do us part. It may also explain why we so often talk about what our offspring can do for us, rather than vice versa. The slogan from *Supernanny,* which airs in forty-five countries, says it all: "How to get the most from your children."

Falling birth rates have reinforced children's status as a scarce, and therefore valuable, commodity. Spain, France, and other countries have begun paying "baby bonuses" to encourage procreation. Interviews with women yearning to start a family, with or without a partner, are now a media staple, as are tales of couples undergoing expensive fertility treatment. "I will sacrifice everything to get pregnant," thirty-eight-year-old Anna tells *Bild,* a German magazine. "I feel empty and incomplete without a baby." Fecundity is the new black. Celebrity dads from David Beckham to Brad Pitt flaunt their kids like fashion accessories, while pregnancy, once career suicide for an actress, has become the fastest route onto the front page of *Hello* or *People,* with the paparazzi scrambling to snap the latest A-list baby. In several countries, surveys suggest that the very wealthy have started having larger families. Kids are now a status symbol, the ultimate homage in a consumerist culture. Never mind the trophy wife. This is the age of the trophy child.

It is also an age of insecurity—and history shows that when people feel uncertain about the future, they plow more energy into their children. The launch of Sputnik by the Soviets in 1957 shattered the illusion of Western superiority and sparked calls to push kids harder in the classroom. The oil crisis of the 1970s had a similar effect. By turning up the competitive thermostat in the workplace and beyond, globalization has cranked up the pressure to maximize every shred of our children's potential. Science has played a part, too. From the 1990s, research showing that babies begin forming complex neural webs at birth has turned every second of the early years into a potential teaching moment. Just listen to this warning from *Newsweek:* "Every lullaby, every giggle and peek-a-boo, triggers a crackling in his neural pathways, laying the groundwork for what could someday be a love of art or a talent for soccer or a gift for making and keeping friends." Talk about pressure.

The media has helped to foster the rat-race atmosphere. Each time another ten-year-old novelist, teenaged entrepreneur, or pre-pubescent pop band hits the headlines, the bar is raised, making "average" look a lot less acceptable. In the past, prodigies were often portrayed as a bit freakish. Today they are hailed as the gold standard, proof that all that pushing and polishing actually works—and that if you weren't such a slouch you could have a superchild, too. Advertisers have made an art form of playing on the fear that our children will be left behind. A popular market-ing slogan in Taiwan is "Do not let your child lose at the starting line!" The BBC regularly sends me publicity for Muzzy, a furry toy animal that comes with DVDs that promise to set toddlers on the road to bilingualism. The brochure is stuffed with smiling teenagers wearing Harvard T-shirts or showing off their Fulbright scholarships. Every time it arrives I feel a jolt of panic that my monolingual children are headed for a future flipping burgers at McDonald's.

With so much at stake, parenting itself has evolved into a competitive sport. Mom and Dad of the Year contests have been around since the Second World War, but today the pressure is really on to be the best parent you can be. Maybe the best ever. This is particularly true for women. With celebrities like Catherine Zeta-Jones and Gwyneth Paltrow setting the pace, the twenty-first-century mother feels obliged to be everything at once: domestic goddess, yummy mummy, soccer mom, dietician, academic adviser, personal secretary, Florence Nightingale and Mother Teresa, and maybe even breadwinner too.

Of course, most of us know deep down that ticking all those boxes is impossible. The problem is that in a competitive culture, where every aspect of childhood is under the microscope, the natural instinct to do the best for our children kicks into overdrive. Even when we poke fun at overzealous parenting—the mother who corrects all the spelling in her daughter's homework, the father who berates the soccer coach for not playing his son more—part of us wonders, *What if they're right? What if I'm letting my children down by not parenting harder?* Racked by guilt and terrified of doing the wrong thing, we end up copying the alpha parent in the playground.

Jo Shirov knows the feeling. A slim, stylish fortysomething, she combines a career as a human-resources manager in Toronto with bringing up seven-year-old twins. On my visit, the Shirov family home looks like a photo shoot from *Elle Décor,* all neutral colors, wood floors, and ethnic cushions. The twins, Jack and Michael, are doing their homework at the kitchen table. There is even a carrot cake baking in the oven (organic ingredients, of course). Beneath the smooth veneer of twenty-first-century parenting perfection, though, Shirov is paddling like a duck on steroids. "If you think the corporate world is competitive, you should try being a mother today," she says. "You feel like everyone is judging you, and—this a horrible thing to admit, I know—but sometimes you end up doing stuff just to impress other moms rather than for the sake of your child." For example? She pauses a moment, lowers her voice, and then adds: "I enrolled the boys in a Mandarin class because everyone was saying how important it was, but they totally hated it," she says. "We dropped it pretty soon after, but it still took me a month to tell the other mothers we'd given up."

Sometimes the pressure on parents is more explicit. At one private school in Taiwan, boys hit the books for up to eighteen hours a day. When Hsiou-mei Wang withdrew her burned-out son, family friends were scandalized. "They told us that being in this school was like winning the lottery and that we were crazy and irresponsible to leave," she says. Her son graduated from a less intense school and is thriving at university, but the same friends are now chewing on sour grapes. "They tell us he is just lucky or that it is unfair that he has done so well," says Wang. "The pressure to do what every other parent is doing is incredible."

You can say that again. Enrolling the kids in extracurricular activities has been a barometer of parental performance for at least a century, but today many children are more tightly scheduled than ever before. One reason is cultural momentum. A friend of mine is bemused to find his two small children enrolled in five extracurricular activities apiece. "I don't really know how it happened," he says. "It just seems to be what you do as parent nowadays." Another reason is that many of us can now afford to give our children experiences—fencing lessons, math tuition, tennis camp—that we never had. The rise of the dual-income household, combined with longer working hours in many professions, has also put the modern family in a time squeeze. Outsourcing the kids to extracurricular activities is one way to pick up the slack. Marian Schaeffer, a copyright lawyer in Boston, keeps her two elementary-school children in activities most days of the week. "It's fun and enriching for them," she says. "But, you know, to be honest it's also a very handy form of child care."

Keeping the kids busy also promises to keep them safe—another modern obsession. Rooted in the eighteenth century, the idea that children are fragile creatures in need of protection has become deeply entrenched in our culture, amplified endlessly in the echo chamber of the media. Even if the kidnapping or murder of children is rare, twenty-four-hour news coverage, with its rolling updates, slow-motion photo montages, and tearful press conferences, turns every isolated case into a tragedy that feels like our own. Just look at the media furor triggered by the 2007 disappearance of three-year-old Madeleine McCann from her hotel room in Portugal. No wonder research shows that the more news people consume, the more anxious they feel about their own children. The other day I heard a radio report about a seven-year-old girl who had been knocked over and killed by a 4x4 jeep in northern England. My first thought was: my children can forget about walking alone to the corner shop until they're ten. Or maybe twenty-five.

As the panic over child safety has grown, so, too, have efforts to corral the young. In the early twentieth century, traffic fatalities sparked a clampdown on street games and the emergence of fenced-off playgrounds. Today, children are herded into vast entertainment complexes to play under the watchful eye of trained staff and closed-circuit cameras.

One reason for this mollycoddling is the threat of lawsuits. In 2006, the Chesterbrook Swim Club in Fairfax County, Virginia, removed the high diving board from its pool, not because anyone had ever been injured jumping from it but to cut its ballooning insurance premiums. Most pools in North America are now shorn of diving boards for the same reason. As a culture, we have simply forgotten how to handle risk. Many twenty-first-century parents had free-range childhoods. When I was ten, my mother would usher me out the door in the morning and not expect to see me home again till lunch or dinnertime. Today, that kind of laissez-faire approach is seen as a dereliction of duty. A recent Baby Blues cartoon strip poked fun at the new aversion to risk by comparing parenting past and present. It featured a little boy nursing a scraped knee after falling from a tree. The mom from yesteryear takes it in her stride: "I guess you learned a lesson about climbing trees," she says. The modern mother is in a panic: "We need to pass legislation to make trees safer!"

Technology encourages us to take that protective impulse to Orwellian lengths. Sally Hensen, an insurance adjuster in London, calls herself Big Mother. On her computer at work, she checks the Web cam at her daughter's nursery every few minutes, and when the boss is away she keeps the pixelated video feed permanently open in a small window on the corner of her screen. "After I got a pedometer I became obsessed with counting my steps," she says. "It's the same with the Web cam: because it's there, I expect to be able to check on my daughter at any moment of the day."

Expect is the key word. In this competitive, consumer culture, everything connected to childhood is subject to spiraling expectations. We already choose sperm and egg donors like garments from the Bergdorf catalogue: "I'll take the tall, athletic one with a master's degree—and blue eyes would be nice, too." Or listen to Angelina Jolie musing on how to assemble the perfect family by adopting babies from across the Third World: "It's, you know, another girl, another boy, which country, which race would fit best with the kids?" If we can have perfect teeth, the perfect house, and the perfect holiday, then why not a perfect child? Parenting manuals have a long history, but they took on a more prescriptive tone in the nineteenth century, with a new breed of bossy experts issuing commandments on feeding times, toilet training, bathing techniques, and sleep patterns. Today, the belief that parenting is a skill to teach, practice, and perfect sustains a global army of pundits who lay down the law through magazines, books, courses, Web sites, radio phone-ins, and television shows. As their power to influence the economy has waned, politicians have joined the chorus with state-sanctioned pointers on how to raise our children.

This avalanche of advice, along with TV shows like *Little House of Horrors* that "fix" dysfunctional families in a single one-hour episode, reinforces the idea that raising a child is like baking a cake or nurturing a Tamagotchi, the handheld digital pet: follow the recipe and you'll end up with the child of your dreams. Older and better educated than ever before, modern parents are also more inclined to take a "best practice" approach to child rearing, convinced that the right management, expertise, and investment will deliver optimum results. This is particularly true for women, who can end up channeling into motherhood the same professional vim that once went into their careers. If stay-at-home mothers turn parenting into a Big Job to justify leaving the workforce, those who carry on working do the same to prove that motherhood is as important to them as the office. The upshot is the professionalization of parenting on a scale never seen before in history—and a heavy blow to parental self-confidence. Perhaps that is why some parents now hire consultants to coax their toddlers into eating vegetables or using the potty, to teach their five-year-olds how to ride bikes, and to take their teenagers shopping for clothes. Or why some families hold regular corporate-style meetings round the kitchen table to assess performance and evaluate their long-range goals.

By comparison, traditional parenting has come to look amateurish, second-rate, or just plain lazy. How can a game of catch in the backyard compete with a baseball clinic run by certified coaches? When every birthday party has a professional magician or face-painter, can you really get away with pin-the-tail-on-the-donkey and a slice of cake? And who can read *The Goblet of Fire* as well as Jim Dale does in those audiobooks? You may know in your heart that the best things in life are free, but when everyone else is spending money to upgrade, the pressure to follow suit can be hard to resist. The other day I caught myself wondering if I should hire a coach to teach my kids how to swing a cricket bat.

At the same time, the pressure is on to make children happy. The Romantic idea that childhood should be a time of play gradually evolved into a belief that happiness was the birthright of all children. Ask any parent today what they want for their offspring and "being happy" is usually near the top of the list. One strategy for achieving this is to tell children at every turn how beautiful, clever, and wonderful they are. Another is to buy them stuff. As well as making us feel good or less guilty, spending is also an easy way to avoid conflict. Nearly half of us now tell pollsters we want to be our "child's best friend," and nothing ruins a friendship like saying no. In a busy, stressful world, why spoil precious family time by arguing over whether to buy a Kit Kat from the display at the supermarket checkout? It's so much easier, so much more peaceful, to give in to Pester Power. I know because I do it myself. A lot. Every family car journey is punctuated by pit stops to buy chips or candy or drinks or whatever it takes to win some peace.

All this spending has helped jack up the price of parenting. The estimated cost of raising a child now ranges up to $300,000, which covers clothes, housing, food, transportation, health, day care, and schooling—college fees not included. A professional woman can expect to forgo more than a million dollars in income by putting motherhood before career. A line in a recent BBC report likened parenthood to financial suicide: "Couples could become millionaires by avoiding the *parent trap* [my italics] and investing the money elsewhere." Is it any wonder that when we do have kids we seek to maximize the return on our investment?

Over the last generation, this yearning to get the most out of our children has reached its ultimate conclusion: we no longer just want to supply the best childhood money can buy; we want to live it, too. In a world where youth is the Holy Grail, adults carry on like latter-day Peter Pans, reading *Harry Potter*, scootering to work, listening to 50 Cent on the iPod, clubbing into the wee hours. Just look at the way we dress. My father has never owned a hoodie or jeans or sneakers. He wore a suit and tie to work and a collared shirt on days off. My son and I are often indistinguishable in our cargo shorts, T-shirts, and sports sandals. I've even worn a baseball cap back to front. In my thirties. Okay, it was my early thirties, but even so. The generation gap has been replaced by the Gap.

This blurring of lines can be fun for everyone, but it also leaves the young less space in which to be children. The skate parks near my home in London are overrun with men in their twenties and thirties, all kitted out in Tony Hawk–approved skater gear, showing off their ollies, kickflips, and grinds. Children who turn up with their skateboards are given the cold shoulder.

When adults lay claim to the trappings of childhood, the scope for rebellion narrows. The historical evidence suggests that children grow up healthier in societies that allow them a few years to experiment and even go off the rails. But how do you rebel when Dad knows the charts inside out and plays the Kaiser Chiefs or Snow Patrol so loudly that the house shakes? Or when Mom has a pierced navel and attends pole-dancing classes? You have two solutions. You seek out a more extreme form of rebellion, like drugs, an eating disorder, or self-cutting. Or you do not rebel at all—you conform, you settle into the role of the Managed Child, you become another brick in the wall.

Underlying this melting of the generational lines are the envy and nostalgia that have always made it hard for adults to keep their hands off childhood. Convinced that youth is wasted on the young, we roll up our sleeves and set about showing them how it should be done, or how we wish we had done it in our time. That is why each culture, each generation has reimagined childhood to suit its own needs and prejudices. The Spartans exalted the warrior child. The Romans encouraged valor in the young. The Puritans dreamed of pious and obedient children. The Victorians hedged their bets, hailing the resilient, working child from the slums while at the same time sentimentalizing the innocent stay-at-home child from the middle classes.

Today, we have ended up with a mess of contradictions. We want childhood to be both a dress rehearsal for a high-achieving adulthood and a secret garden full of joy and free of danger. We tell our children to "grow up" and then bristle when they do. We expect them to fulfill our dreams and yet somehow remain true to themselves.

The common thread, of course, is that through the ages children have never chosen their own childhood. Adults have always called the tune. "It's never really about the children," says George Rousseau, the Oxford historian. "It's always about the adults." Today it seems to be more about the adults than ever. The question now is: how can we make childhood be more about the children?

TWO

Early Years:
When Milestones
Become Millstones

*If things could come from nothing, time would not be of the
essence, for their growth, their ripening to full maturity.
Babies would be young men in the blink of an eye, and full-
grown forests would come leaping out from the ground.
Ridiculous! We know that all things grow, little by little, as
indeed they must, from their essential nature.*
—*Lucretius, first century* B.C.

On a windy afternoon in early spring, as Taipei dashes through
another business day, the most anxious place in the city may just
be the parenting section of the Eslite Bookstore. When I arrive,
more than a dozen people, mostly women, are browsing the hundreds of titles. Apart from the odd whispered exchange, a nervous
silence reigns. Raising children is a very serious matter in the
capital city of Taiwan.

Eslite stocks books by both Western and Asian experts, and the titles reflect the pressure felt by parents across the world to put their child ahead of the curve. A manual called *Prodigy Babies* is selling briskly, as is a slim volume called *The Genius in the Crib*. Another popular choice is *Sixty Ways to Ensure Success for Your Gifted Child*. In one corner, I notice a chic mother-to-be leafing through a chunky volume. She pauses to stroke the cover, closing her eyes to utter what looks like a silent prayer. Then she slips the book into her black Fendi bag and strides off to the checkout.

I wander over to inspect the tome that has caught her fancy. The title is calculated to send any parent into a panic: *Children's Success Depends 99% on the Mother!* The back flap has a photograph of the Korean author looking smug, and no wonder: she has two daughters doing undergraduate studies at Harvard and Yale and a son at Harvard Business School.

The scene takes me back to when my wife announced that she was pregnant with our first child. Once the euphoria had subsided, we did what parents all over the world do when a baby is on the way: we headed to the local bookstore and started assembling our own library of child-rearing manuals. Like everyone else, we wanted to give our baby the best start in life.

I remember one book in particular. It charted month by month the developmental milestones for newborns: moving head from side to side, smiling, tracking objects with the eyes, grasping hand toys, experimenting with cause and effect, and on and on and on. I kept a close eye on that graph. If our son fell behind schedule, it was panic stations. What's wrong with him? Are we failing as parents? Should we consult the doctor? By the same token, nothing made my day more than finding my son ahead of the curve, especially if another parent noticed. (He rolled over very early, since you ask.)

Our ancestors would have been amazed. Through most of history, infant development was not a pressing concern. Newborns were often farmed out to wet nurses or simply strapped to their mother while she went about her work. The death of a baby was often considered less tragic than that of an older child. Michel Eyquem de Montaigne, the great Renaissance essayist, famously wrote: "I have lost two or three children in infancy, not without regret, but without great sorrow." Okay, Mrs. Montaigne probably felt a little more strongly, but all the same, such talk today would be enough to trigger an investigation by Social Services.

That is not to say that our ancestors did not feel the temptation to make infants grow up just a little faster. Some parents in medieval Europe used strings and wooden frames to encourage babies to walk earlier. From the late seventeenth century, European surgeons tried to hasten the arrival of speech by cutting the ligaments in infants' tongues. But even a hundred years ago, most parents were still more worried about whether their baby would survive than whether it would clear developmental hurdles ahead of schedule. As infant mortality fell and expectations soared, however, the emphasis gradually switched to getting babies off to a flying cognitive start.

Today, the pressure to hit the ground running is stronger than ever. Science has shown that a baby is the world's most powerful learning machine—even more powerful than was thought a generation ago. Using puppet shows featuring vanishing ducks, researchers have shown that infants can grasp the idea of "object permanence"—that when Mom leaves the room she does not cease to exist—as early as ten weeks, not at nine months as previously believed. A 2007 study concluded that babies can distinguish between languages simply by looking at the speaker's face.

In a Canadian experiment, four-month-old infants watched a video of an adult speaking English or French with the sound turned off. Each time the speaker switched languages, the babies perked up and paid close attention.

Every infant experiences a neural Big Bang that establishes the network of synaptic connections that will then be ordered and pruned over the coming years. To make the most of this early phase of brain construction, babies need stimulation. The same holds true in the animal kingdom. In one series of well-known studies, rats raised with other rats in a large cage filled with toys developed brains of greater neural richness than those reared alone in small, empty cages.

The problem is that this type of research has entered the cultural bloodstream in the shape of a stark diktat: the more stimulation your baby gets and the earlier he gets it, the smarter he will be. And if you fail to make the most of this early neural development, the window of opportunity will slam shut at the age of three and you can forget about college. From there it is a short step to handheld tummy speakers that fill the womb with "neurally enriching" music or to the I'coo Pico stroller whose built-in iPod dock allows baby to listen to songs or Mandarin vocabulary on the move, turning that stroll in the park into a "multisensory experience."

Whether this barrage of stimulation actually works is less clear. The latest neuroscience suggests that all the enrichment the human infant needs is built into the everyday experience of your average baby—and that instead of being a tabula rasa waiting passively to be filled up by adults, babies are programmed to seek out the input needed to build their brains. That is why mankind managed successfully to rear children for thousands of years without electronic mobiles and Baby Einstein DVDs. What about those clever rats raised in enriched environments? Well, before you race off to fill up the nursery with flash cards and plasma screens, consider the least reported finding from that research: no amount of enrichment ever produced rats with better brains than those raised in nature.

Of course, some children grow up in a family environment that leaves them underequipped for school. A major study by the University of London tracked 15,500 children born between 2000 and 2002 into a range of social backgrounds. By the time the kids turned three, the offspring of graduate parents, who are more likely to fill the home with books, stories, and conversation, were ten months ahead of those of less qualified parents in vocabulary, and a year ahead in their grasp of shapes, sizes, colors, letters, and numbers. Early enrichment programs can help children from less privileged homes bridge that gap. But that does not mean everyone else needs to sign up, too—or that piling on the stimulation can upgrade the basic wiring of the brain. John Bruer is the author of *The Myth of the First Three Years* and president of the James S. McDonnell Foundation, which funds research into brain science. He dismisses outright the belief that more stimulation yields a better brain: "The idea that you can provide more synapses by stimulating the child more has no basis in science."

That does not stop us trying. When researchers found in the 1990s that listening to Mozart enhanced college students' spatial reasoning, an entire industry sprang up based on the claim that flooding the nursery with piano concerti could boost a baby's brain. So alluring was this idea that in the late 1990s and early 2000s, hospitals in the state of Georgia sent every newborn home with a CD entitled "Build Your Baby's Brain Power Through the Power of Music," featuring works by Bach, Handel, and Mozart. Today, you can still buy albums and DVDs trumpeting the so-called Mozart effect. The only problem is that the Mozart effect is nonsense. In 2007, the German research ministry finally commissioned a crack team of neuroscientists, psychologists, educationalists, and philosophers to investigate all the research done on the phenomenon. Their conclusion: even if listening to Mozart does boost spatial-temporal reasoning (and not all studies have shown this), the effect lasts no more than twenty minutes. What's more, the German team found zero evidence that listening to classical music does anything at all to hone the infant brain.

A misreading of science, coupled with those soaring expectations, also fuels a lot of doomed attempts to teach foreign languages to infants. Research in the 1990s showing that babies possess a unique ability to learn any tongue sent parents scampering off to buy Berlitz tapes in the hope of turning their newborns into minipolyglots. It did not work. Why? Because babies only tune in to a language when it is spoken to them regularly by a real person. In more recent experiments, infants exposed only to foreign-language DVDs or audiotapes or bilingual toys absorbed nothing at all—not one word or phrase, not a single sound. Nor did they arrive at school with more appetite for conjugating French verbs or identifying Mandarin symbols. Conclusion: babies need a human, hands-on connection, not artificial stimulation, to learn.

Does that mean foreign-language classes with real-life teachers are the answer? Around the world, ambitious parents are enrolling their children in English lessons earlier and earlier. Across Asia, children not yet fluent in their native tongue are spending hours slaving over their ABCs. In the other direction, Western parents are shelling out for Chinese-speaking nannies and Mandarin classes for their toddlers. My neighbor takes his two-year-old to Mandarin lessons every Saturday morning. "Chinese is the future," he says. "The sooner she starts, the better."

Again, that depends. Research shows that in order to become bilingual, children need to be exposed to a foreign language for at least 30 percent of their waking hours. That means taking proper immersion classes or spending a big chunk of the day speaking the other language with a parent or nanny, or with other toddlers in a nursery. It does not mean stuffing an hour of Mandarin instruction between gymnastics and the Saturday-morning shopping trip. "The truth is that there is no easy way to pick up a language—you have to live it, study it, read it, eat it, and breathe it," says Ellen Bialystock, an expert on bilingualism at Canada's York University. "You should always give a child the richest language experience you can, but it has to make sense in the home; it can't be contrived, it can't be just another chore on the parental to-do list." It also turns out that not learning a second language in the early years does not mean a lifetime of monolingualism. "Learning languages gets a bit harder as you get older but there is no evidence of a window of opportunity that closes forever at a certain age," says Bialystock. "People can learn languages throughout their lives. How you learn them is more important than when." Nor is this just the case with languages. The latest research shows that the brain goes on developing long after the early years, and that for most knowledge and skills there is no "critical window" that closes forever on the third birthday.

The bottom line seems to be that infant cramming is often pointless, and may even backfire. Skills gained through force-feeding often have to be relearned later. One London music teacher tells of a girl driven by her parents to master the violin from the age of three. She surged ahead of her peers, yet by the age of six her technique was so distorted that she had to spend months relearning the basics. "The worst part was that the other children, who had been playing to their ability level, hit their stride and left her behind," says the teacher. "It was a classic case of the tortoise and the hare."

Too much stimulation can interfere with sleep, which babies need to process and consolidate what they have learned during the waking hours. When parents get anxious about milestones, when they spend more time cultivating than comforting their baby, the infant can get stressed, too. If a baby's brain becomes flooded with stress hormones like adrenaline and cortisol, the chemical change can become permanent over time, making it harder to learn or to control aggression in later life and increasing the chance of depression.

So what is the right way to treat an infant? Well, the question itself is flawed. However much we may want science to provide a step-by-step guide to the early years, our patchy knowledge of brain development makes this impossible. What's more, every child and every family is different, which means that there can never be a single recipe for raising a baby.

Yet there are some clear guidelines. One is that all infants thrive on one-on-one interaction with plenty of eye contact. Study after study has shown that babies are fascinated by strong contrasts and colors, which is precisely what they get from the human face, with its complex, shifting landscape of wrinkles, curves, crevices, and shadows. A baby scrutinizing her parent's face, deciphering the emotions and expressions flickering across it, is doing the neural equivalent of the Jane Fonda workout. An educational video, an electronic mobile with flashing lights, or a poster with white, black, and red patterns simply cannot compete. Just look at how, in the absence of gadgets and gizmos, a parent interacts with her baby: gazing into his eyes, smiling, nuzzling, adopting exaggerated facial expressions, tickling, pronouncing words v-e-r-y slowly, kissing, imitating sounds back and forth. This may not look like much compared to the showier thrills of baby sign language, but it is actually a rich and stimulating conversation—and you don't need a specialist to teach you how to do it because it comes naturally to all of us. As well as being a source of joy and wonder, this elemental chat, this loving interplay, between parent and infant helps to build the latter's prefrontal cortex, the "social" part of the brain that governs empathy, self-control, and the capacity to read nonverbal signals from other people—the very skills that teachers identify as the most important for thriving in kindergarten and beyond. Experts agree that forming a strong bond with one or more carers is the cornerstone of all child development and all later learning. It can also immunize children against stress throughout their lives.

And perhaps this message is slowly starting to sink in. Around the world, child-development experts are issuing the same advice to anxious, impatient parents: Every baby develops at a different speed. The early years are important, but they are not a race. Spend less time trying to enrich your baby and more time getting to know her. Trust your instincts instead of mimicking whatever the alpha mom in the playground is doing.

Some parents are learning those lessons the hard way. June Thorpe spent more than a decade as a high-flying events planner in Miami, Florida. After giving birth at the age of thirty-six, she tackled motherhood as if organizing a conference. She devised a rigid schedule of eating, sleeping, yoga, massage, and interactive play for her baby, Alexia, and pinned it to the fridge door. "I wanted to get her into a routine as soon as possible to get her off to a good start," Thorpe remembers. The problem was that the routine did not suit Alexia, who carried on waking up several times a night and took longer than usual to sit up by herself. At coffee mornings, Thorpe felt like a failure listening to other mothers boast about how well their children slept, how early they had started crawling, or how well they were taking to solid food. She began to regard motherhood as a dreary, demoralizing, dead-end job.

Then everything changed when she discovered the blogosphere. Thorpe found writings from scores of moms caught in the same rut—and many who dug themselves out by forging their own path. The message she took away was that mothering comes in all shapes and sizes, and that trying to follow someone else's rules or timetable can make it tedious and frustrating, and ultimately crowd out the most fascinating and rewarding part of being a parent: getting to know your own child. In other words, you don't have to rush off to that baby yoga lesson or spend hours making the house look like a photo spread in *World of Interiors*. To hell with the Joneses. It's okay to spend the afternoon lying together on the bed, cuddling, breast-feeding, drifting in and out of sleep. Sometimes you'll spend most of the night failing to get your child to stop crying, and that's okay, too.

"When I looked outside my own social circle, I suddenly realized that I wasn't alone in feeling that the pressure to be a so-called supermom was making motherhood a chore," says Thorpe. "And I think that Alexia was probably picking up on my anxiety, too." So she changed tack. She decided to go with her instincts. That meant putting away the schedules, the developmental charts, and the interactive DVDs, and letting Alexia breast-feed and sleep whenever she felt like it. Instead of baby yoga classes, mother and daughter now take a nap together on the large sofa in the sitting room, surrounded by soft cushions and stuffed animals.

Thorpe loves the new regime. It seems less like work, and she feels much closer to Alexia, more able to read her moods and needs. Alexia has started sleeping through the night. "She seems more contented now that I'm not trying to force her into being my idea of what a baby should be," says Thorpe. "And I'm more contented knowing I don't have to fit into someone else's idea of the perfect mom. The most important thing is what's right for Alexia and me."

New father Edward Hardy came to the same conclusion with his son, Emmanuel. From the start, he and his wife said no to developmental wall charts, structured activities, and infant stimulation devices. Instead, they kept their parenting small and simple. Brochures offering baby yoga and baby sign language classes and catalogues stuffed with Baby Einstein DVDs went straight in the bin.

In the early months, Hardy, who works as a technical writer in London, spent a lot of time doing the basic stuff with Emmanuel—bathing, dressing, diaper changing, soothing, massaging, and feeding. Day trips to a soft play area in Watford turned out to be more trouble than they were worth—thanks to the cost, travel, stress, and disruption to Emmanuel's napping routine. Instead, Hardy took his infant son in a sling to the local playground or park. The pair also spent long hours sitting in a nearby cafe, where Emmanuel played with his toys, gnawed on bits of toast, and flirted with the waitresses. "To some people that may all seem very dull and predictable, but it actually gave him a changing environment with lots of things to see and different stimuli," says Hardy. "And it gave us lots of time just being together, getting to know each other."

Hardy admits that there were moments of tedium, that there were times when a trip to the Victoria and Albert or some other museum in central London sounded pretty appealing. But riding out the boredom has paid dividends. "Before we had Emmanuel, I used to think babies were dull," says Hardy. "But when you really spend time with them and get to know them, you notice every tiny change that they go through, every detail of their evolution and development, and you realize that they're fascinating."

Hardy has a very warm, easy relationship with Emmanuel, who is now a bright, happy, inquisitive four-year-old. He puts this down to all that time spent just being together instead of striving to reach development milestones. "Could it be that what drives parents to these ambitious lengths is guilt? That somehow a child playing in a sandbox in the local playground is not good enough anymore?" he says. "What I learned is that there is an inverse correlation between the effort you put in—money, organization, stress—and the gains you reap. Actually, now I believe that local sandboxes are quite magical." The moral of the story: for babies, less is often more.

Of course, this is not to say that developmental milestones have no role to play. They can be crucial in identifying the small minority of children who need early intervention. The key is to treat them as general guidelines instead of as a daily timetable written on tablets of stone. Research shows that parents have a reliable instinct for knowing when something is genuinely wrong with their infant, especially when they step back from the competitive frenzy.

When it comes to what children should be doing in the early years, play is more important than chasing milestones. *Play* is a loaded word these days. In a workaholic, get-ahead culture, it sounds almost heretical—a guilty pleasure, an excuse for indolence or wasting time. Yet play is so much more than what happens when we stop working. In its purest form, it is a profound way to engage with the world, and the self. True play is spontaneous, uncertain—you never know where it will take you. It is not about winning or losing, or reaching a destination or milestone. It defies all the tools of our high-achieving culture: targets, timetables, and measurable outcomes.

Artists have always understood that a playful mind can unlock the richest secrets—and that children understand play better than anyone else. Pablo Picasso talked of his need to remain childlike in order to paint. Henri Matisse observed that the most creative people always have "a tremendous spirit of adventure and a love of play." Even in the more rigorous world of science, a playful testing of the boundaries, an acceptance of childlike uncertainty, a refusal to be boxed in by someone else's idea of the right way to do things, is often the first step toward the eureka ideas, the lightning bolts of genius that turn the world inside out. Sir Isaac Newton once noted that "to myself I seem to have been only like a boy playing on the seashore, and diverting myself now and then finding a smoother pebble or a prettier shell than ordinary, while the great ocean of truth lay all undiscovered before me." Albert Einstein spelled it out even more clearly: "To stimulate creativity, one must develop the childlike inclination for play and the childlike desire for recognition."

If adults can let the mind soar by playing like a child, then what does play mean to children themselves? Quite a lot, as it turns out. The latest scientific research suggests that free play is an essential part of growing up, and not just in humans. Mammals do it, too. All that frolicking, wrestling, and chasing that wolf cubs and baby lions get into in nature documentaries seems to have a purpose. Young mammals expend around 2 to 3 percent of their energy on playing—that may not sound like much, but

evolutionary biologists say it is too large an outlay not to have
some payback. And play can be dangerous, too: nearly 80 percent
of deaths among young fur seals occur when pups are too busy
cavorting to notice a predator.

So what do animals get in return for all that exertion and
risk? Well, it seems that play may be Mother Nature's way of
making us clever. Research shows that mammals that play the
most, such as dolphins and chimpanzees, have the largest brains.
One theory is that bigger brains are more sensitive to environmental stimuli, and therefore need more play to knock them into
shape for adulthood. Studies of cats, rats, and mice have found
that play peaks precisely at the moment when their brains are at
their most elastic. "Animals at play are most likely directing their
own brain assembly," says John Byers, a leading play expert at the
University of Idaho. Scans also show that the human brain lights
up much more intensely and widely than expected during play.

Does that mean that depriving children of play hampers their
creativity and ability to learn? The short answer is that no one
knows for sure because not enough research has been done yet.
Studies done on animals suggest that a play deficit takes a toll.
Researchers have found that baby rats deprived of play grow
smaller neocortices, the part of the brain that controls higher func-
tions like sensory perception, spatial reasoning, motor commands,
and (in humans, at least) language. They are also less socially adept
later in life. Children diagnosed with Attention Deficit/Hyperac-
tivity Disorder (ADHD) display similar symptoms.

What does seem clear is that play is a basic impulse for children. They invest a whopping 15 percent of their energy in play,
and seem almost to have a physical need for it. I remember my
son racing home from nursery at lunchtime to continue a make-
believe story he had been forced to interrupt in the morning.

Even when circumstances militate against it, children still find a way to play. Records of life in Victorian factories tell of child workers sneaking away from their machines to kick a ball around, tell stories, or indulge in a little hide-and-seek. I spent a year working with *meninos de rua,* or street children, in Fortaleza, a coastal city in the impoverished northeast of Brazil. These were kids for whom a typical Western childhood was something only glimpsed on television. They lived in favelas, or shantytowns, where food was scarce and violence simmered just below the surface. At four and five they would take to the streets to earn a living shining shoes or washing cars. Much of the time the *meninos* kept up a streetwise, world-weary façade, but sometimes the instinct to play broke through. They would suddenly down tools to play soccer with an empty Coke can or indulge in a game of tag. They even played bingo using makeshift cards and stones. It was in those moments of play, of leaving behind the responsibilities and ravages of the adult world, that the *meninos* were happiest—it was when they remembered that they were children.

At the moment, the evidence seems clear that play is good for children in many ways. It allows them to create imaginary worlds where they can tackle fears and rehearse adult roles. Like little scientists, children come up with theories about the world—the earth is flat or all men with beards are wizards—then test and revise them. Playing in groups without adults running the show helps children learn how to divine other people's feelings and how to handle the frustration and compromise that are a part of relationships. Just watch a couple of three-year-olds building a house from sticks in the garden. They gather material, negotiate how to assemble it, devise rules, tussle over who puts what where. In free play children also begin to discover their own interests and passions, strengths and weaknesses.

Nigel Cumberland is a former headhunter-turned-coach for high-fliers in Hong Kong. He finds that many new recruits look stellar on paper but lack spark, social awareness, and gumption in person. They would rather be told what to do than take a problem by the scruff of the neck and solve it with a flash of brilliance. Cumberland thinks this is because they were starved of play as small children. "If little kids could play more you'd have better engineers, better managers, and more inspiration in the workplace," he says. "If you deny a baby or a toddler the chance to play, and then put him in a preschool where he is always competing and being measured, you get fear, and that leads to an unwillingness to take risks. You end up with boring adults."

Play is just a natural version of the more structured learning that occurs in the classroom—and it may even lay the foundations for reading, writing, and numeracy. In one study, Herbert Ginsberg, a professor of psychology and education at Columbia University, observed eighty children. He found that they devoted 46 percent of their free play to counting, exploring shapes, and patterns, and sorting objects into sets—basic mathematics, in other words.

To become properly literate and numerate, a child must first grasp that numbers and letters are symbols denoting quantities and sounds. You don't gain that from tracing letters out in Kumon notebooks; you do get it from play and the social intercourse that goes with it. "If we ask a child to set the table and talk about it," says Anna Kirova, an expert in early childhood education at the University of Alberta, "one plate for each person, one fork for each person, how about another spoon to go with the fork—well, this is one-to-one correspondence. Or they could be matching rocks to sticks, it doesn't matter. The whole concept of matching is what stays with them." The next step is then to make the leap to connecting numbers to quantities and letters to sounds.

The chief drawback of children's play is that, to an adult eye, it looks too much like slacking. This prejudice goes back a long way. When the world's first kindergarten (literally "children's garden") opened in Germany in 1840, its founder, Friedrich Froebel, was ridiculed for suggesting that play was an essential part of childhood development, and his book was burned by critics. Today, even as we pay lip service to the importance of play, we often shrink from giving it full rein. We want to corral and quantify it, bend it to fit our targets and timetables, make it more like work. This is not to say that grown-ups should have no role in children's play. Our input is crucial, but mainly as a sounding board or a source of gentle suggestions. That means letting small children play on their own terms.

More parents are heeding that call. Martha Hoffman, a former lobbyist turned stay-at-home mom in Washington, D.C., started off playing with her baby son, Theo, as if he were a toy. She got down on the floor, just like the experts advise, but could not resist the urge to take over. If Theo was building a tower with wooden blocks, Hoffman was right by his side, picking up fallen bricks and straightening out the final structure so it looked like the one on the box. On the beach, she was always filling up his bucket with water and refurbishing his sand castles. "I knew it was ridiculous but I just couldn't help myself," says Hoffman. Everything changed when she called in a family therapist to investigate why Theo, then nearly three, was having trouble playing with children his own age. While he worked on a wooden puzzle of farm animals, she guided him to all the right pieces. She then chose another puzzle for him to do. The therapist was appalled. "He just stared at me and said, 'Who's actually playing here, you or your son?'" says Hoffman. "It was the wake-up call I needed."

Hoffman decided to ease off. She still gets down on her hands and knees to play with Theo, but not every time he reaches for a toy. And when she does play with him, she checks the urge to guide his every move and tidy up his handiwork. "It's tough because I'm a perfectionist and I want the best for him, but basically I had to lighten up," she says. "A child needs to play in his own way without his mom jumping in all the time." A few months later, Hoffman e-mailed me to say that Theo is getting along better with his peers, and she enjoys playing with him much more now that she is no longer striving to optimize their every moment together.

In so many ways, science is telling us to stop sweating the small stuff. Just because infancy is a time of unparalleled brain plasticity does not mean that a baby needs round-the-clock stimulation, or that he will be damaged for life if left to cry for a bit in the crib while you answer the door. Such moments of frustration can actually be the first step to learning that being alone is not the end of the world and that things do not always go as planned. Being bored gives children the space to notice the details of the world around them—the fly buzzing at the bedroom window, the way the wind ruffles the curtains—and teaches them how to use and fill time. What's more, we now know that, contrary to what John Locke believed, babies are not lumps of putty whose entire future depends on how they are parented. Each of us is born with a unique genetic blueprint that plays a big part in shaping our intelligence, temperament, and abilities. In other words, a child who learns to speak early may do so not because his parents have spent long hours working the flash cards but because his genes predisposed him to conquer speech at a young age. Some experts now argue that peers, teachers, and the community play a larger role in shaping children than once thought. Others suggest that what parents are—their education, income, age, intelligence, attitude to reading—has a far greater bearing on how children turn out than what parents do. After sifting through piles of data and longitudinal studies for their book *Freakonomics,* Steven Levitt and Stephen Dubner concluded that often nurture cannot trump nature: "In this regard, an overbearing parent is a lot like a political candidate who believes money wins elections, whereas in truth, all the money in the world can't get a candidate elected if the voters don't like him to start with."

Bottom line: it is wrong to assume that every single thing we do as parents leaves an indelible mark, for good or ill, on our children, even in the early years. Parents are hugely important, of course, but a child's success does not depend 99 percent on the mother—or the father, for that matter.

There is an old marketing adage that half of advertising works; we just don't know which half. To some extent, the same may be said of parenting. The question is what to do with this knowledge. You can use it as a reason to obsess about every twist and turn of your child's life and development, just in case. Or you can relax a bit, knowing that moments when your child is not being enriched or basking in your attention, moments of boredom even, are a natural part of growing up. And that pouring all your energy into reaching the next milestone as fast as possible is often a waste of time and may even be harmful.

That is how Hoffman now sees her role. "It's a weight off the shoulders to know that you don't have to be working on your baby all the time," she says. "Now I have to find a preschool that thinks along the same lines."

THREE

Preschool:
Play Is a Child's Work

The most important part of education is proper training in the nursery.

—Plato

Not so long ago, the preschool years seemed like a pretty sweet deal. At home, and even at nursery, children did what comes naturally. I spent my early years listening to stories, dressing up, making anarchic works of art, and singing songs. I messed around with toys and built castles in the sandbox; I bickered and played with my friends. For the most part, I had the freedom to explore the world on my own terms. And my goal, if that is the right word, was a modest one: to arrive at the first day of school happy, confident, and able to get along with my peers.

How quaint that all seems now. Over the last generation, the preschool years have turned into an academic rat race. Who has time for finger painting or puppet shows when there are letters to trace and numbers to learn? Forget the paddling pool—it's time to rehearse for that kindergarten interview. Gymboree, a toy

chain in the United States, runs a twelve-week course that promises to turn two-year-olds into "global citizens" by exposing them
to art, dance, and music from cultures around the world. The
Hualan International Village Kindergarten, an elite boarding preschool in the Chinese port city of Tianjin, now accepts three-
year-olds.

With so much pressure to master the three Rs at younger
ages, tutoring companies have launched preschool divisions.
Tokyo cram schools already enroll two-year-olds. At Junior
Kumon branches around the world, three-year-olds now study
the alphabet, addition, and basic phonics. They also learn to
write numbers and count to two hundred. Nurseries, especially
in the private sector, have cut back on art, music, and drama to
make room for literacy and numeracy lessons. And then when
children finally do reach school, worksheets and homework start
piling up from the very first week. To cram in all the formal
learning, many kindergartens in the United States have abolished
morning and afternoon recess altogether. Even lunch break is
more for eating than playing.

Why so much toil at such a young age? Why all the hurry?
One reason is that we live in an impatient, hyper-competitive
culture. Around the world, preschool teachers are coming under
pressure to rank their pupils. Is my daughter in the ninety-fifth
percentile? If not, why not? And what can we do to boost her
ranking? If a child can read *The Cat in the Hat* at four, just imagine what he will be tackling at ten. Or thirty-five. Of course,
many of us suspect that turning the early years into an academic
treadmill is misguided: is sitting at a desk really the natural habitat for a three-year-old? But once again, when the competitive
whirlwind starts to blow, our judgment sometimes goes out the
window.

At the same time, politicians have pushed early learning up the agenda. In the 1960s, governments began introducing programs to help underprivileged children keep up academically, the Head Start scheme in the United States being one example. Today, with businesses clamoring for better-trained workers and parents pushing for higher educational standards, officialdom has reinvented the early years as the time to instill basic literacy and numeracy in every child.

Like world peace, "early education" sounds like a no-brainer—how can anyone quibble with getting children off to a flying start? The problem is that academic hothousing is subject to the law of diminishing returns. True, it can sometimes yield the sort of results that make teachers gawp and parents crow: children who arrive at kindergarten already reading chapter books, writing their names, or in full command of the times tables. But what about the longer term? Does all that early learning pay off later? Well, no, actually. The latest research suggests that reaching learning milestones early is no guarantee of future academic stardom. One study in Philadelphia found that by the age of seven or eight there was no discernible gap between the performance of children who spent their preschool years in nurseries that were rigidly academic and those who came from laid-back, play-based ones. The only difference was that the hothoused kids tended to be more anxious and less creative.

While many believe that knowing letters, numbers, shapes, and colors is the best preparation for school, teachers take a very different view. They say that the child who arrives at Year 1 socially adept, who knows how to share, empathize, and follow instructions, will stand a better chance of mastering the three Rs later on.

The truth of the matter is that human beings are hardwired to learn from birth, and are best served reaching the academic milestones when they are emotionally and psychologically ready. Some develop more slowly than others, but most get there in the end; yesterday's bumbler might be tomorrow's bookworm. This demands patience, a rare commodity in our hurry-up culture. I remember when my son first came home with reading homework at the age of five. He struggled to string the sounds together into words and to remember how to pronounce the more testing letter combinations. It was frustrating, and I wondered if he was dyslexic. But then, all of a sudden, as though a switch had flicked inside his head, his reading took off. Pretty soon he was falling asleep every night with a book on his chest.

Experts agree that formal learning is more productive from around age six, when children are better able to handle abstract ideas and differences in early development have largely evened out. Pushing the three Rs too soon may even turn them against learning, making them harder to teach later on. A study conducted in 2003 found that children in Denmark and Finland, where formal schooling starts at ages six and seven, concentrate better than do their counterparts in Britain, where it starts two years earlier.

What children seem to thrive on most in the preschool years is the freedom to explore the world around them in a safe, relaxed environment with plenty of stories, rhyming, songs, chat, and play. They need to strive and struggle and stretch themselves but not in the way many adults imagine.

When it comes to preschools that break the mold, many look to the town of Reggio Emilia for inspiration. This small city in northern Italy began carving out its place on the early education map just after the Second World War. Returning to find his hometown in ruins, a young teacher named Loris Malaguzzi decided that the best way to rebuild was to start at the beginning, by reinventing preschool. Malaguzzi was more than just a pedagogue, though; he was a charismatic social reformer with a big idea. Marshalling a crack team of like-minded teachers, he set out to create preschools that would "change the culture of childhood." What that meant in practice was tapping into children's natural curiosity and giving full rein to their impulse to express themselves. "Today, the mainstream view is that the child needs constant adult guidance and input in order to reach standards set by adults themselves," says Claudia Giudici, a local Reggio teacher and spokeswoman. "We think that adult involvement should be kept to a minimum so that kids can build their own knowledge and relationships."

Reggio preschools do not teach the three Rs. Nor do they have a fixed curriculum. Instead, pupils delve into projects that spring from their own interests. If they observe a flock of birds flying across the autumn sky, they might spend the next two or three months learning about different bird species, building nests of their own from material gathered outdoors, and investigating the phenomenon of migration. Art is treated as the natural medium through which children explore, analyze, and understand the world, rather than as an optional extra. Or as the launchpad to a glamorous career.

In a Reggio preschool, children are not ranked, and learning is very much a group endeavor. If one child is absent, the others discuss how he might have reacted to the day's activities or what sort of questions he will raise tomorrow. There is no competition to produce the best picture or the neatest booklet. Nor is there any hurry to finish a project—the timetable establishes itself as the children go along.

Reggio does not publish teacher manuals because its approach is always evolving, and each child, like each group of children, is unique. The one article of faith is that a Reggio teacher does not take over. She throws new ideas and materials into the mix but always in a way that permits the children to make discoveries on their own. Mistakes are allowed to happen, and projects begin without a clear of idea of where they might lead. At the end of the day both teachers and students reflect on and document what they have learned. This can take whatever form comes most naturally—words, drawing, painting, sculpture, collage, music, movement. Documenting allows teachers to learn more about the children in their care and about the learning process itself; it gives children a chance to deepen their learning by revisiting their findings and explaining them to others.

The aim of Reggio is to create children who can think, dream, analyze, play, speculate, and socialize. And it seems to work. Today, half the children under six in Reggio Emilia attend Reggio-style schools, which are all funded by the municipal government. Many of today's pupils are the offspring of Reggio graduates. In the 1990s, *Newsweek* declared Reggio preschools the best in the world, turning the Italian town into a mecca for teachers, academics, and politicians from all over the planet. Nearly twenty thousand foreign observers have come on fact-finding missions since 1994.

To see the Reggio approach in action, I join the flow in early spring. The town itself is pretty unremarkable by Italian standards, with 140,000 residents living in postwar tenement blocks huddled around a medieval core. My visit coincides with that of nearly four hundred observers from the United States and the Nordic countries. Like pilgrims visiting the stations of the cross, they shuffle between the local schools, clutching not Bibles but notebooks and folders bearing the logo of Reggio Children, the body set up to handle the international deluge.

To escape the crowds, I drive out to Pratofontana, a hamlet eight kilometers away. The Reggio preschool here is called Prampolini, and it is a fine example of the Reggio creed that beauty lifts the spirits and fires the imagination. The grounds are a feast for the senses. The rosebushes are covered in white and pink blooms. Butterflies flicker across a herb garden bulging with sage, rosemary, mint, thyme, and basil. A wooden bird-watching hut looks out across flat farmlands that stretch as far as the eye can see. This part of Italy is known for its milk and cheese, and for its red Lambrusco wine, so the surrounding fields are dotted with vineyards and grazing cattle. On the side of the school facing the town, there is a splendid tree house with tables, chairs, and place settings. When the wind dies down, you can just about hear the sound of water trickling through the small stone fountain at the foot of the garden.

The school itself is a delightful brick structure with shuttered windows and terracotta roof tiles, the inside all white walls and high ceilings. Everywhere you look there is something to get the creative juices flowing: a dressing up area with a vast wardrobe of costumes here, a corner with painting easels there. The shelves groan with containers full of pens, pencils, brushes, rulers, feathers, bolts, dried pasta, plastic hooks, scrap metal. The dining room looks like a bistro, the little blue tables adorned with potted plants, clay figures, and ceramic bowls full of walnuts. At lunchtime, the smell of homemade lasagna wafts from the kitchen.

The children, aged three to six, clearly love it here. One group is making clay figurines under a trellis in the garden, chatting all the while about where the material comes from and how its texture changes in different temperatures. Nearby, a team of three-year-olds is using strips of copper and old wiring to dress an eagle made from scrap metal.

Giulia and Marco are busy painting the rosebushes. A teacher checks in from time to time, but the pair are essentially on their own. Standing behind large easels, brushes in hand, they seem lost in the act of creation. Giulia picks a rose, smells it, and holds it up to inspect from all angles. She then places it on her easel and photographs it with a camera. "To remember for later," she explains. "And to compare it to my painting." From time to time, Giulia and Marco chat about the rosebush—the shades of color, how the light falls on it, the way the wind changes the shape of the leaves. This is what Blake meant when he talked about seeing a world in a grain of sand. It's hard to believe the pair are only five years old.

Another girl comes up to show off a ladybug on her finger. The three children hand it back and forth. Marco compares the red of the ladybug's wings to the roses. Giulia says the insect will bring good luck. And then they return to the easels. After about forty-five minutes, the children tell the teacher they have finished. Their paintings, especially Giulia's, are remarkably accomplished. Marco is delighted with his. "This is exactly as I saw it in my head," he says, beaming.

The other work at Prampolini is just as sophisticated. On the second floor, a group of four- and five-year-olds is winding up a project about water that started when one of their number visited a nearby aqueduct and came back full of questions. Over the last six months, they have visited local rivers, canals, and irrigation channels, exploring how the color, depth, and movement of water varies and talking about the ways that water shapes our lives. To help explain their findings to the other pupils, they have taken scores of photographs. When I arrive, two boys are arranging the images on a computer. A boy and a girl are using wooden blocks to reconstruct their memory of a boat passing through a lock thirty kilometers from here. "Where was the motor that moved the doors?" asks the teacher. The children think for a moment. "It was hidden in the walls," says the boy, "which are made of concrete." This sparks a spirited discussion of how water might affect an engine, and how the fumes from an engine might affect water.

In the next room, the fruits of another project are already on display. It began when some of the children decided that one of Pratofontana's traffic circles needed sprucing up. They each drew their own plan, then they pooled ideas and built intricate models of their shared vision. In one, the traffic circle is a colorful garden made of real pebbles, grass, and flower petals, with lots of paper people and cars stationed around it.

The newest project is getting underway upstairs in the attic. It started when some of the children suggested giving a gift of sound to the fountain in the garden, which fell quiet during the cold winter. Five four-year-olds huddle round a low table covered with a menagerie of objects: tiles, stones, pieces of wood, buttons, seashells, different types of paper. There is also a sound system with a microphone. "The project is in embryonic stage so we don't yet know what we want to document or learn," says Alessandro, the teacher. "We don't impose things on the children; we prefer to leave space for experimentation and see how they approach the subject first."

The children are searching for materials that reproduce the sound of water trickling through a fountain. Lorenzo ruffles a sheet of tissue paper. "That sounds more like rain," he says. Claudia nods beside him. She then runs a strip of wire along a dried corn on the cob. "That's not right either," she says.

Dario, who has a tangle of curly brown hair and a cheeky smile, picks up the microphone. "When it's windy it sounds like this," he says, blowing into the mike. Then he flicks his tongue round the inside of his mouth to make a sound surprisingly like that of dripping water. The other children clap and roar with laughter.

Alessandro lets the children go, but he also steers gently from time to time. He points to a plastic bottle filled with sand. "What kind of sound do you think that makes?" he asks. Claudia picks up the bottle and shakes it. "It sounds more like the wind, like the wind you hear in the field behind my house," she says. Then Dario shakes it more vigorously. "Now it sounds like a storm."

Alessandro is pleased. "I hope they will learn about music and the world of sound, which could lead to talking about the senses, but we'll see where their imagination takes us," he says. "Amazing things happen when you let kids follow their instincts."

The first thing most people notice in a Reggio school is the respect shown the children. That doesn't mean a *Home Alone* free-for-all where the kids tear the place apart and swear at the grown-ups. It means that instead of patronizing the pupils by speaking to them in silly voices or filling the classrooms with stuffed animals from Disney, instead of force-feeding them an academic curriculum, the teachers encourage them to interact with the world on their own terms.

But what strikes me most about Prampolini School is the way childlike excitement goes hand in hand with serious work. The children knuckle down to their projects with a concentration that is both touching and inspiring, yet there is as much laughter here as you find anywhere under-sixes gather. Long before brain scans began proving its value, play was a central part of the Reggio philosophy. The project work is all conducted in the spirit of fun. One of Malaguzzi's guiding principles is to "do nothing without joy." In between the serious projects at Prampolini, there is plenty of time for just messing about. During my visit, I see four children absorbed in a complicated role-playing game in the wooden tree house outdoors. Others dash around one of the play areas dressed up as medieval knights.

At the end of my visit, I chat to some of the foreign observers in Reggio. All are impressed by the sophistication of the children's work and their ability to concentrate. They also admire the teachers' knack for guiding the work projects without taking over.

Mary Hartzell, director of a Reggio-inspired preschool in Santa Monica, California, returns to Italy every few years to keep in touch. Back home, her pupils go on to thrive in schools of all types. "They leave us as creative thinkers and extremely capable learners," she says. "With their excellent social, communication, and problem-solving skills, they work well together in groups, but they are also individuals with a strong sense of themselves."

Of course, the Reggio approach is not without critics. Some say it only works for affluent children, and that kids from working-class families often need more—not less—guidance in their lives. Others say it is too rooted in the Italian experience, with its strong emphasis on links to the wider community, to travel well. Supporters refute both arguments, asserting that Reggio schools cater successfully to children of all social classes. Prampolini takes kids from low-income groups, as well as immigrants and even Gypsies.

The Reggio philosophy is also traveling very well. I visited one Reggio-inspired nursery in Manhattan that is like Prampolini without the lush farming fields. Reggio techniques, from project work to documentation, are popping up in non-Reggio preschools, too.

At the same time, other educational philosophies that let children be children are gaining ground in preschools around the world. Montessori and Steiner Waldorf are two examples. Like Reggio, both eschew testing, grades, and formal academics to unleash the child's natural curiosity and playful spirit. As Maria Montessori said, "Play is a child's work."

And again that approach seems to work. Studies of children from similar family backgrounds show that those who attend Montessori preschools arrive at primary school better prepared to tackle reading and mathematics, and to handle complex problems. Montessori kids are especially good at playing and working with their peers.

After visiting Prampolini, I travel to the other side of the world to see a Waldorf preschool in action. Highgate House sits on a hill overlooking the island of Hong Kong. It is a breathtaking view, with the sea stretching into the distance and smart villas nestling in the wooded slopes below. Hong Kong's storied skyscrapers are hidden away on the other side of the island.

Highgate House is the only Waldorf preschool in a state where early academic learning is almost a fetish. When I arrive, the scene could not be more different from what you see in other nurseries around Hong Kong. Play rules here. Instead of hunching over desks studying Chinese script, some of the children are sitting in a circle watching a teacher light a candle and play a few notes on a xylophone as a prelude to story time. Others are playing alone outside on the terrace, which has a climbing frame, a large basket of pinecones, wood blocks, car tires, a sandbox, and a rabbit hutch that is home to Holly, Thumper, and Fluffy.

Julie Lam, the educational coordinator, tells me that children who transfer here from other nurseries often arrive exhausted or ill from the academic hothousing. Some just stand still in the middle of the room because they do not know how to play or make friends. Hong Kong is, after all, the sort of place where children are often fluent in the times tables before they can tie their own shoelaces. "Deep down everyone knows what's right and wrong for their kids," says Lam. "But when everyone else is doing one thing, it takes a lot of courage to do the other."

Wisdom Chan can vouch for that. As the owner of an investment company, he is very much a part of the Hong Kong professional elite. But unlike most of his fellow high-fliers, he decided to resist the pressure to put Beatrice, his two-year-old daughter, on the academic fast track. While many of her peers spend long days in classrooms with blackboards, Beatrice plays at Highgate House for a couple of hours three days a week.

I meet Chan when he comes to collect Beatrice. As we chat, she scrabbles around in the sandbox with a friend. The two argue over a shovel, but without an adult stepping in to mediate, they eventually find a way to share. Together they dig a hole and refill it several times.

"What I like about this school is that it is very easygoing; they don't push them to do this and that, or to learn things before they are ready, or to conform to a single idea of what a child should be," says Chan. "I've read a lot of books on child development, and the priority at this stage is for Beatrice to have fun, to be interested in what she is doing and interact with other children. The formal teaching comes later."

It was not easy opting out of the hothouse nursery system. Friends and family warned that Beatrice would stagnate. Even Chan had his doubts. "I was worried at first that she'd come here and have a good time but fall behind, so I gave it two months as a trial," he says. "She enjoyed it so much and in the process learned all kinds of things, like the names of animals and the difference between an airplane and a helicopter. She now speaks better than most of her peers who go to academic nurseries, and seems to know a lot more about the world. She has better social skills, too. When it comes time for her to go to school she will be more than ready."

Local principals agree. Some complain that children emerge from the hothouse nurseries of Hong Kong burned out and socially inept. By contrast, the Highgate kids, like Waldorf, Reggio, and Montessori graduates around the world, arrive full of energy and with a hunger to learn. A group of local parents is now campaigning to create a Waldorf primary school in Hong Kong to which children can move on from this hilltop enclave.

Nevertheless, old habits die hard. To ease entry into the island's more academic primary schools, Highgate House now offers optional literacy and numeracy lessons from four years of age. The sessions are full of art and movement—the children walk out the letters on the floor—but Lam regards it as no more than a necessary evil at such a young age. "It shows how deep the prejudice runs," she says, with a sigh.

Yet many parents at Highgate House are sticking to the school's original ethos. Wisdom Chan has no interest in pushing Beatrice to tackle literacy before she starts school. Seeing how his daughter has flourished and how happy she is, he and his family are now Waldorf converts. Friends who were skeptical at first now talk of enrolling their own children.

As I gather my things to leave, Beatrice runs up to her father. She is breathless with excitement about something in the sandbox. "Spider," she says, wreathed in smiles. "With many legs."

Chan laughs and throws his arms around her. "These are the moments you remember for the rest of your life," he says. "My son, Albert, will be starting here next term."

The push to free small children from the tyranny of formal academics is also fueling the rise of an even more radical kind of preschool. It has no books, coloring pads, or crayons, no jungle gyms, swing sets, or boxes of plastic and wooden toys, no surveillance cameras, computers, or rubberized playgrounds. It does not even have a roof or walls. That is because everything happens outside in Mother Nature, much as Jean-Jacques Rousseau prescribed in the eighteenth century. A fixture in Scandinavia since the 1950s, "outdoor nurseries" are now spreading across Europe and beyond.

Anyone who has ever watched children while away an afternoon in the woods knows that nature is the ultimate playground. But it is also the original classroom: long before whiteboards and blackboards, the outdoors was where the young learned how to observe, manipulate, and take pleasure from the world around them.

The private Lakeside School in Zurich decided to open an outdoor nursery in 2003. The spark was falling standards. Teachers had noticed that children arriving at kindergarten had poorer motor skills and preferred to wait to be told what to do by adults rather than seize the initiative. They also struggled to concentrate, to notice small details, to enjoy the moment, because they were always itching to move on to the next structured activity. The Lakeside solution was to go back to nature.

Twice a week, whatever the weather, a dozen three- and four-year-old preschoolers now trek off into the woods on the outskirts of Zurich. The nursery started with set assignments, as a way to placate the parents, but very soon ditched the idea as counterproductive. With no fixed curriculum, the children choose what to explore each morning. In a recent week in early spring, they spent a day investigating the buds erupting on the trees and bushes. Then it suddenly snowed, and the class decided to build an igloo. After a storm at the end of the week, the children spent a day helping local rangers cut up fallen trees using miniature saws. Along the way, almost by osmosis, they pick up the rudiments that others get drummed into them in the classroom. They learn shapes by comparing stones, counting by gathering twigs and flowers. They learn the colors by inspecting the feathers of birds or studying the way leaves change through the seasons. They learn about sounds by listening to the noises local fauna make. By the time they reach kindergarten, they are confident, focused self-starters with a thirst for knowledge.

As in a Reggio, Waldorf, or Montessori classroom, teachers at an outdoor nursery cultivate a light touch. The priority is to give the children space and time to do their own learning. Liz Blum, director of the Lakeside nursery, thinks being in nature makes this easier. "When you see children out in the woods, exploring, playing, taking responsibility, making mistakes and learning from them, doing their own thing, you just know that is what children are meant to do."

What can we take from all this? That formal academic training can wait. That free play is an essential ingredient of early childhood. That there are many different ways to learn, which implies that there is more than one way to parent.

Watching his daughter thrive at Highgate House has certainly helped Wisdom Chan take some of the heat out of his own parenting. "You have to take that philosophy of giving children time and space and apply it outside the nursery," he says. "I want Beatrice to live her life for her, not for me."

FOUR

Toys:
Just Push Play

You think a wooden animal is a simple thing; it's not.
—Hilda Doolittle, poet 1886–1961

Hamleys is the largest toy shop in the world, and also one of the oldest. When it opened in London in 1760, its founder hoped to create a place where children could escape from the adult world, and much of that Neverland spirit survives today. With forty thousand different toys spread over seven floors, the modern Hamleys is a tourist attraction to rival Buckingham Palace and the Tower of London, drawing millions of families every year. Many come to buy, others just to soak up the atmosphere.

Flanked by the grown-up boutiques of Regent Street, Hamleys still feels like a refuge from adulthood. The ground floor is a shrine to stuffed animals of every species—lions, bears, frogs, pigs, dogs, hippopotami. Staff wearing costumes and demonstrating toys lend a carnival atmosphere. When I arrive on a gray Monday morning, a clown is blowing bubbles from a plastic gun at the hordes of children streaming through the entrance. Inside, a young man with a goatee sends a small Styrofoam airplane swooping above the crowds like a boomerang. Nearby, children huddle around a stall where another staffer is making stacks of coins vanish and reappear beneath little brass cups.

That feeling of wonder and escape, of adult anxiety put to one side, of childhood given free rein, pervades the shop—until you reach the second floor. This is the preschool department, and play is a serious business here. The space is dominated by toys that promise to turn your bundle of joy into a superchild. The brand names speak volumes: Brainy Baby, Clever Clogs, Amazing Baby. Even the atmosphere is more sober. Every other floor vibrates with the sound of children laughing and whooping; here, most of the customers are adults, and an uneasy quiet reigns. It reminds me of the parenting section of the Eslite Bookstore in Taipei.

I have come to Hamleys to buy a Madeline doll for my daughter's third birthday, yet find myself drawn to the preschool department. It is hard to resist, not least because most of the toys promise to harness cutting-edge technology and the latest brain research to help get any child off to a flying start. There are DVDs that claim to teach the alphabet and foreign languages to infants, plastic farms that make animal noises, and electronic books with sound effects and characters' voices. Designed to hang from the back of a car seat, the Tiny Love Wonder Wheel keeps baby entertained and stimulated on the road with a symphony of sounds and lights—and it even comes with an infant-friendly remote control. For a moment, I wonder how this might have changed those long journeys-from-hell when our son oscillated between sleeping and crying in the backseat.

Most of the wording on the packaging is calculated to get the heart of the modern parent racing. The Leapfrog Hug and Learn

Animal Globe, a soft ball that plays songs and emits animal sounds, promises "a world of learning with every roll or press!" Many companies publish charts trumpeting the cognitive benefits of each toy. Tiny Love has seven categories: senses, gross motor skills, fine motor skills, object recognition, cognition, communication and language, and Emotional Intelligence. Suddenly, a low-tech Madeline seems horribly inadequate.

It turns out I am not the only parent wandering the aisles in a miasma of guilt and panic. A straw poll suggests that many of the shoppers in the preschool department are torn between wanting toys that are fun and wanting toys that build better brains. Anything that combines the two, of course, is catnip. Angela Daly, a physiotherapist, came in looking for a wooden train set for her three-year-old son. She found one, but is also taking home a VTech Tote and Go Laptop Plus, which promises to "program your preschooler for early learning."

"Part of me feels toys should be simple things to have fun with, like we had when we were growing up," she says. "But then another part thinks: 'There's a lot of new technology and scientific research out there, and if my son is going to be playing anyway, why not play with toys that will make him more intelligent?'"

Such thinking would have been alien to parents in the premodern era. Children have had toys since before written history—and many have barely changed through the ages. Archaeologists excavating the Indus Valley civilization found small carts and whistles shaped liked birds dating back nearly five thousand years. Persian parents gave their children wagons made of limestone and equipped with wooden axles in 1100 B.C. In ancient Greece and Rome, kids played with balls, clay rattles, hobbyhorses, and spinning tops. Yet it never occurred to earlier civilizations that toys could help build better children. Our ancestors bought or made objects to keep their kids amused and distracted, or left them to fashion their own from sticks, stones, or whatever turned up. The notion that the right toy could eventually help them marry into a better family or win a place at court never entered the equation.

That began to change in the seventeenth century. With children moving up the cultural agenda and a toy industry taking off in Europe, toys came to be seen as more than just playthings. They could be tools for honing young brains, a means to an end. Intellectuals like John Locke encouraged parents to buy toys that delivered education as well as entertainment, and manufacturers responded. First came playing cards with the alphabet on them. The first jigsaw puzzles, which appeared in England not long after Hamleys opened, were touted as a tool to teach history and geography, while early board games, such as Arithmetical Pastime, promised to help with sums.

Yet designing toys specifically to boost intelligence and enhance specific motor or cognitive skills is a more recent phenomenon. Though its roots stretch back to the 1920s, the market for educational toys really took off in the 1990s, just as the competitive pressure on children switched into hyper-drive. Today, around half of all the money spent on toys in the industrial world is spent on preschoolers, with most of that going for products claiming to enhance brainpower. In his 2007 State of the Union address, U.S. president George W. Bush saluted three citizens for extraordinary acts of public service. One of them was the founder of the Baby Einstein Company.

Of course, many "educational" toys are just traditional toys rebranded. Hamleys' xylophone is pretty much the same instrument that children have been tapping on for nearly four thousand years, yet the box sports a checklist of cognitive benefits ranging from stimulating the senses to honing social skills.

More controversial are those toys designed to use sounds, lights, and other bits of interactive wizardry to entertain and educate children. The question, though, is: do they actually do what it says on the box?

Let's start with the question of entertainment. In this age of generational blur, we assume that children have the same tastes that we do, that faced with a choice between a Madeline doll that does nothing and a gadget that beeps, whistles, and flashes, the twenty-first-century child will opt for the latter. But would she?

To find out, I drop in on an experiment in Buenos Aires. With sales of electronic toys soaring in the Argentine capital, local parents are starting to wonder if going high-tech is worth the money. On a lazy Sunday morning, the local headquarters of the International Play Association has decided to stage its own version of the old Pepsi-versus-Coca-Cola taste test. A dozen children aged from three to eight will be shown a range of toys to see how they react.

The room is large and airy, with polished wood floors and industrial shades draped over naked bulbs hanging from the ceiling. Finger paintings dot the walls. Each toy is set on its own mat, with all the usual suspects here: piles of mixed Lego, wooden bricks, and dominos; dolls and stuffed animals; puzzles and Jenga; miniature tents; and a cluster of electronic gadgets.

A young man named Leo, who reminds me of Che Guevara without the beret, introduces each toy, and then the experiment begins. Two boys instantly make a beeline for the Lego. A trio of girls start attacking Leo with a stuffed octopus. A five-year-old wearing a backwards baseball cap heads straight for the electronic toys. He opens up the laptop and starts typing the letters that appear on the screen; each time he gets them right, a bell rings. At first he seems thrilled, but then, after a few minutes, he wanders over to the Lego. A four-year-old girl then picks up a brightly colored electronic box and starts punching the symbols on it, each of which calls out the corresponding word in English. "Tree," "house," "car," says a tinny voice. Leo sits beside her and tries to make the game more entertaining by asking questions and making funny noises, but the girl soon loses interest. "It's more fun speaking to a person," she announces, before getting up and walking over to play with the dolls.

Most of the fun, along with the richest play, seems to be happening with the simplest toys, the ones that leave more room for the child's imagination. Kneeling on a mat, an eight-year-old boy in a blue tracksuit assembles wood bricks into a complex series of towers. "I'm not sure what it is yet," he says. "It might be a castle or a jail or a boat—or it might be a spaceship. Yes, it's a spaceship." He then embarks on a long and winding narrative involving astronauts setting off to find a special rock on the other side of the galaxy and fighting aliens along the way.

As the hour winds down, more than half the children are huddled around the Lego. Brows furrowed in concentration, they sit building cars and spaceships and houses in companionable silence, sometimes stopping to show off their handiwork, or search for an unusual brick, or help a younger child snap two awkward pieces together. Occasionally one of the children launches into a short story about her invention. On the neighboring mat, the electronic toys lie discarded and forgotten. When Leo announces that the hour is up, groans of protest echo around the room.

After a short break, the children sit in a circle on the floor to talk about the experiment. Leo asks which toys they would like to take home. Most votes are for the Lego, the puzzles, and the wooden bricks. When he asks about the electronic toys, the children shake their heads. "We have lots of toys like that at home, but they get boring after a while because they're always the same," explains a six-year-old girl. "I like toys you can make things up with."

Obviously the IPA experiment is not a definitive study—only a limited range of toys was used and the most popular high-tech goodies, such as video games, were not featured at all. But it does raise some intriguing questions. For a start, it challenges the assumption that in this electronic age children naturally favor electronic toys.

Most parents have some experience of this. On Christmas morning, your toddler tears the wrapping off a gift to reveal a very expensive high-tech toy. You grapple with the instructions, insert the batteries, and then hand over the gadget, fully expecting it to be the star attraction for the day. But your child has other ideas. She casts the toy aside and instead starts playing with the box, making it a character in her own story, or pretending it is a helmet or a house.

Even the high priest of high-tech, Bill Gates, understands children's need to direct their own play rather than have it dictated by a toy: "If you've ever watched a child with a cardboard carton and a box of crayons create a spaceship with cool control panels, or listened to their improvised rules, such as 'Red cars can jump all others,' then you know that this impulse to make a toy do more is at the heart of innovative childhood play. It is also the essence of creativity."

After the IPA experiment, the parents come together to discuss the findings. Some are surprised the high-tech toys got such short shrift. "It makes you wonder if the electronic stuff is actually aimed at parents rather than at children," says one mother.

"Maybe we're buying these toys to show off or make us feel like better parents."

Others still feel the pull of the "educational" tag. "Children don't find vegetables attractive, but that doesn't mean they shouldn't eat them," says a father. "Maybe educational toys are like vegetables—less fun, but good for your development."

But are they really? After all the research, design, circuitry, testing, manufacturing, and marketing that goes into them, do these educational gadgets live up to the hype by making children smarter? The short answer is that no one really knows.

Neuroscience is at too embryonic a stage to prove how different toys affect the brain. When it comes to standing by the grandiose claims made on their packaging, even toy companies send out mixed signals. Some argue that modern children are somehow different from earlier generations in that they need props, prodding, and guidance to get the creative juices flowing, and educational toys channel play in a way that builds better brains. "While other toys leave children to make their own discoveries about what happens when they interact with them, ours spark a learning moment with every touch and turn," says Scott Axcell, marketing manager for Leapfrog. "This gives children a taste for learning, so when they finally get to school, their minds are open to the fact that learning can be fun." Others are more cautious, mindful that there is no solid evidence that educational toys deliver a cognitive boost. Dr. Kathleen Alfano, director of child research at Fisher-Price Company, admits point-blank, "There is no proof that this type of toy helps children become smarter."

If that is the case, then the question is: do we really need electronic toys at all? Critics argue that whatever benefits flow from early exposure to interactive DVDs or high-tech learning centers can be supplied just as well, if not better, by simple play with old-fashioned toys. Many experts dismiss the educational tag outright as a marketing ruse. In Britain, the Good Toy Guide has resisted pressure from the industry to include a separate "educational section" in its prestigious annual survey of new products coming on the market. "An educational tag on a toy means nothing, and parents really don't need to be spending extra money buying these products," says Carole Burton, editor of the guide and a toy appraisal manager for Britain's National Association of Toy and Leisure Libraries. "If parents bought the product sitting next to a so-called educational toy on the shelf, they would find it does exactly the same thing at a fraction of the price."

The Stockholm-based International Toy Research Centre takes a similar line. "I question the whole concept of an educational toy," says founder and director Krister Svensson. "It is the setting of play that is educational, not the toy itself. You can make a complex toy that forces children to manipulate it in a certain way, but children can learn just as much from repeatedly taking the lid off a shoebox and putting it back on again."

A more controversial view is that electronic toys are not just a waste of money but may also be harmful. That by doing too much they turn the child into a passive observer, a Pavlov's dog who learns to follow a recipe ("push this button and that will happen") rather than how to imagine or solve problems. Even some traditional toys have become more prescriptive, leaving less room for children to invent their own play. Just look at Lego. The company once made most of its money selling boxes of mixed bricks that children used to build whatever their imagination conjured up. Today, more than half Lego's revenues come from themed kits designed to assemble a single structure—a Star Wars Imperial Destroyer, say, or a Bionicle Inika. My son has several of these kits, and in each case he built the model only once and never used the specialized pieces to make his own design. "The danger is that children might become addicted to the imaginative input from others," says Svensson. "What children really need is more time without input, more time to process their own experiences."

Toy makers counter that the twenty-first-century child needs more preset storylines and branded characters, more adult input, in order to play. Nonsense, say the experts, children have the same play needs today as they did five hundred years ago. Dr. Michael Brody, who teaches Children and the Media at the University of Maryland and chairs the Television and Media committee of the American Academy of Child and Adolescent Psychiatry, is one of many who think modern toys are often too highly structured. "Play is the work of kids, and for that, the basic toys—blocks, baby dolls, pull-toys, clay, crayons, and paper—are best," he says. "[Many modern toys] superimpose someone else's story on the kids, so kids don't develop their imaginations."

As in every other field of childhood, such warnings should be taken with a pinch of salt. After all, critics have been fretting that toys would bring about the end of civilization at least as far back as the nineteenth century. Maria Edgeworth, the Anglo-Irish novelist, dismissed dolls and action figures as a barrier to physical exercise and imaginative play. Ralph Waldo Emerson attacked all man-made playthings as a pernicious distraction from the teachings of the natural world. "We fill the hands and nurseries of our children with all manner of dolls, drums, and horses, withdrawing their eyes from the plain face and sufficing objects of nature, the sun, and moon, the animals, the water, and stones, which should be their toys," he wrote. Long before Brainy Baby videos and interactive learning centers, critics warned that overactive toys would produce underactive children. "The more imagination and cleverness the inventor has put into the toy, the less room there is for the child's imagination and creativity," noted one observer in the 1890s. Despite such fears, however, the world has continued to produce generations of healthy, creative children.

Yet maybe those fears are not so fanciful today. The toys now on display on the second floor at Hamleys certainly do a lot more than anything on sale there in the 1800s. A VTech Magic Moves Baby Ball is more likely to turn a child into a passive observer than is a hobbyhorse or a rag doll. In a wired world, electronic toys have a role to play, but even manufacturers warn against gorging on their gadgets. "One of our biggest challenges is making parents understand that when it comes to electronics, the principle that 'if a little is good, a lot must be better' does not apply," says the director of educational development at one well-known toymaker. "Parents need to use their common sense to find the right balance." At the same time, there is mounting evidence that simple, low-tech toys that allow children to play on their own terms may deliver a boost to learning. In a recent experiment, the International Toy Research Centre placed Brio wooden train sets and other basic toys in a number of primary schools in Sweden. Children were encouraged to play with them during recess breaks. The result: calmer, more focused pupils. "The teachers were amazed by the effect on the children," says Svensson. "Instead of taking an hour to settle down, they now arrive at the door ready to learn."

Some parents are reaching similar conclusions at home. In San Diego, California, Michael and Lucy Noakes spent a small fortune on electronic educational toys when their son, Sam, was born. "The house was so full of beeps and animal noises and Spanish words and other sounds that it felt like a pinball arcade," remembers Michael. But Sam did not blossom into the uber-child his parents had hoped for. He was restless and aggressive, took a long time learning to speak, and showed little imagination in his play. On his third birthday, a psychologist friend suggested that Sam might be overstimulated, so as an experiment the Noakes put away the gadgets and gave him simple wooden toys to play with. Within weeks, Sam started to change. He began inventing stories, using anything he could get his hands on—chopsticks, hairbrushes, pens—as characters. He was also less edgy. Now four years old, Sam is thriving at nursery. "I think by giving him toys that did everything, we left him with nothing to do," says Michael. "Once he had toys that let him explore and express himself without steering him to do this or think that, he began to develop." Lucy nods her head. "As a parent you think that the latest, most expensive toy, especially if it claims to be educational, is going to be the best thing for your child, but it's not always true," she says. "Children need toys that actually let them be children."

Are toy makers listening? Some industry watchers detect the beginnings of a shift away from toys that do too much. To see how far the pendulum has swung, I spend a day wandering around the 2007 British Toy Fair. Nearly three hundred exhibitors from across the world have set up stalls in a vast, modern conference center in the East End of London. The household names like Fisher Price and VTech are all here, as are a slew of unknown entrepreneurs hawking what they hope will be the Next Big Thing. With armies of buyers and sellers stalking the displays, the fair has the brisk, slightly joyless feel of your average trade gathering. It reminds me of the second floor at Hamleys.

Many manufacturers at the fair are beating the educational drum. Stalls are festooned with slogans like "Learning Through

Play" and "Play to Learn." It is also clear that technology is king. Even Brio has launched a "Smart Track" line with microchips that make the train engine emit noises and stop at the station. One young inventor, Imran Hakim, has come to the fair to promote his new iTeddy, a cuddly bear with a personal media player embedded in its chest. It can download stories, cartoons, and online computer tutorials.

"Parents want to give their children a head start in the brain race," Hakim tells me.

"That may be true," I say. "But what about the children? Are you sure they want to turn Teddy into a multimedia platform?"

Hakim answers with the zeal of the true believer. "Toddlers want technology, too," he says. "This way they can take their audio and video with them wherever they go, even to bed."

A week later, I happen to catch Hakim on the *Dragon's Den,* a BBC TV show where entrepreneurs pitch their inventions to five ruthless investors. One of the quintet, Duncan Bannatyne, tears into the iTeddy. "Reading bedtime stories is a father's job—I don't want to be replaced by a teddy," he says. "I hope this business fails." He may not get his wish, however. Two other Dragons agreed to put money into iTeddy, and Hakim says leading retailers are knocking on his door.

Back at the fair, others are taking a stand against the technological takeover of toys. The stall next to the iTeddy is run by Dave Pateman, an affable sixtysomething from Bournemouth, a sleepy town on the southern coast of England. A carpenter and kitchen designer by trade, Pateman has reinvented himself as a low-tech David taking on the high-tech Goliath of the toy industry.

It all started as a reaction to the sight of his two grandchildren, then aged five and nine, glued to their Game Boys. "They were always punching buttons or in front of a screen," says Pateman. "And when they weren't, they were moaning about being bored." One summer afternoon, the whole family was sitting in the yard when the boys complained that there was nothing to do. Pateman snapped. He strode off to the garage to find something to entertain them and returned with an old bit of tubing and a frayed tennis ball. He stood the tube upright on the ground and challenged everyone to bounce the ball into it, which turned out to be far harder—and more amusing—than it sounds. Two hours later, amid much roaring and raillery, the whole family was still taking turns trying to land the ball in the tube. On their next visit two weeks later, the grandsons asked to play the ball game again. "I'd completely forgotten about it, but the boys hadn't, and that got me thinking," says Pateman. After doing some market research, he decided to turn his makeshift game into a marketable toy. He drew up some designs and flew out to China to find a manufacturer. The result is the £9.99 Frog in the Hole: a tube made of sturdy weatherproof plastic and two spongy rubber balls, all adorned with pictures of frogs.

When I first arrive at Pateman's stall, a brother and sister aged four and six are playing the game. They are the only children I've seen all day, and they're having a ball, laughing and cheering each other's near misses. Eventually their parents manage to drag them away. That means it's my turn. After several hours of testing cutting-edge electronic toys around the fair, I find Frog in the Hole hugely addictive. "It's such a simple thing—bouncing a ball into a hole—but children love it," says Pateman. "It's good for developing hand-eye coordination, of course, and we stress that in our advertising, but basically it's just a lot of fun. And it gets them away from the Game Boys and the TV." Frog in the Hole has attracted strong interest from buyers and toy chains.

Other entrepreneurs have come to the fair to peddle toys that do less so the child can do more. Tina Gunawardhana tells me that the West can learn a lot from poor countries like her native Sri Lanka, where children spend hours inventing imaginary worlds and complex games with only sticks, stones, or bits of discarded materials as props. "Western children are spoon-fed everything, including play," she says. "The result is that their imagination closes down and they get bored easily, always looking for the next electronic stimulus or experience to be handed to them on a plate."

Gunawardhana sells handsome wooden toys that encourage children to be creative. Among her top sellers are brightly painted animals and fish that fit like jigsaw pieces into shallow boxes. "We could have made an ark or an aquarium to go with them but we chose not to so that the child could come up with his own idea," says Gunawardhana. "They can make an ark, a zoo, or an aquarium from an old shoebox or a discarded plastic bottle. We want their imagination to run riot."

It is not just the mavericks and the mom-and-pop firms that are making toys that leave more room for the child to invent. Some industry giants are also looking at ways to build products that are less bossy and more likely to spark real play. At the Lego stand, I find several buyers checking out the latest additions to the Creator series, which was launched in 2003. Each box comes with diagrams for building three different models—the Fast Flyers kit yields a jet, hovercraft, and helicopter—as well as a dozen photographs suggesting other ways to use the bricks. The pieces are also more generic to encourage children to toss them into a general Lego box and use them for any construction they can think up. "I like the fact that this range is less restricting," says one buyer. "You don't just build a single model and that's it—the child is really inspired to go on inventing new things using the same pieces."

As I leave the Lego stand, my spirits begin to sag. There is something a bit tawdry about mixing toys with big business. What's more, I have just spent a whole day talking about children rather than to them. I feel like an observer at a conference on multiculturalism where every delegate is white. But then I stumble on the fair's day-care center. The first surprise is that there are actually some real children inside it. The second is that instead of being stuffed with all the latest electronic toys, the room is stocked with the sort of old-fashioned props that leave plenty of room to imagine and invent: wooden building blocks, picture books, dress-up costumes, stuffed animals, a climbing frame, Play-Doh, crayons, and paper. Apart from a PlayStation unit, which sits unused in a corner, the center is an electronics-free zone.

And you know what? The kids are loving it. Two six-year-old girls are huddled round the art table, dressing princesses they have cut out from sheets of colored paper. A little boy is marching around dressed as a Roman soldier. Two others are poring over a book about a dragon.

When a man comes to collect his daughter from the art table, she is reluctant to go. He insists. She digs in her heels. "Come on, Olivia, you can see all the lovely new toys in the fair," says Desperate Dad. "Maybe we can even buy one for you to take home."

Olivia shakes her head, and then delivers a rebuke to warm the heart of every parent who has ever been the victim of Pester Power and to send a chill through the sales teams working the stands that surround the day-care unit.

"I don't want any lovely new toys," she cries, dashing back to the art table. "I just want to stay here and play."

FIVE

Technology: Reality Bites

Technology . . . the knack of so arranging the world that we don't have to experience it.

—Max Frisch, architect, 1911–91

On a warm summer day in 2005, a man in his twenties walked into an Internet cafe in Taegu, the fourth largest city in South Korea. His name was Lee Seung Seop. He logged on to a computer and began playing Starcraft, an online battle simulation game with zippy graphics and a nifty storyline about human exiles fighting for survival on the edge of the galaxy. Mr. Lee hunkered down for a marathon session. Over the next fifty hours he only rose from his chair for toilet breaks or to take a short nap on a makeshift bed. He sipped mineral water but hardly ate at all.

Eventually, friends tracked him down to the cafe and pleaded with him to stop playing. Mr. Lee told them he would finish soon and then go home. A few minutes later his heart failed. He collapsed to the floor and later died.

To hardcore gamers, Mr. Lee was a martyr, or just plain unlucky. But to others his death was a cautionary tale, proof that the electronic gadgets that populate our world should come with a health warning. Spooked by his heart attack, some South Korean parents rushed to ban computer games at home. An understandable reflex, perhaps, but a wise one?

There is no escaping the fact that we live in a high-tech culture, or that IT has changed the world in lots of wonderful ways. How many of us would now choose to live without e-mail, cell phones, or the World Wide Web? Compared to Asteroids, Pac-Man, and the other clunky computer games of yesteryear, Starcraft and some of its rivals are subtle, sophisticated, and hugely entertaining.

Like the world around them, children sway to an electronic beat more than ever before. Surveys suggest that eleven- to fifteen-year-old Britons spend over seven hours a day in front of a screen, up 35 percent since 1994—and that does not even include the time devoted to chatting and texting on mobile phones. U.S. children under six now spend the same amount of time gazing at screens as they do playing outdoors. Once a chance to explore the woods and splash around in a lake, some summer camps have been reinvented as an IT retreat, with children spending five to six hours a day at the keyboard. Babies are wired, too. In many countries, special channels now offer all-day viewing for infants six months and up. A quarter of American under-twos have a TV in their bedroom. Perhaps you've already bought an iTeddy for your newborn.

Technology seems like the perfect gift for a child. We want our kids to have the best of everything, and we feel the pressure to supply them with the gear that everyone else is showing off in the playground. High-tech gadgets promise to prepare them for life in a high-tech world. They also promise to keep them safe. You can always reach your child if she has a cell phone. And your nine-year-old cannot be run over by a car, abducted by a pedophile, or given a free sample of crack cocaine when he is rooted in front of his Nintendo at home. As any busy parent knows, electronic media also offer a very tempting form of babysitting on tap. Who among us has not plunked the children down in front of Teletubbies or a Game Boy to win a few minutes of peace to answer e-mails, cook supper, or just read the newspaper? I know I have.

Yet even as we outsource the care of our children to the flickering screen, one question remains unanswered: is all this technology a good thing? For some high-tech gurus, the answer is a resounding yes. Like toy makers claiming that the modern child needs lots of props and stimulation in order to play, they hail the arrival of a new generation unlike any that has come before it. Twenty-first-century children, we are told, are "digital natives" who thrive on spending long hours interacting with screens, keyboards, and joysticks. They are the vanguard that will carry humanity into a brave new world of virtual relationships, multitasking, and round-the-clock availability.

But you don't have to be a Luddite to query that vision, or to ask if we are all spending too much time with our technology. There are growing signs that the IT revolution is leading to digital overload, for adults as well as children. In the age of the CrackBerry, e-mails, phone calls, and text messages follow us everywhere, to the dinner table, to the bathroom, into bed. According to one recent survey, one in five adults will now interrupt sex to take a call. Even high-tech companies are starting to question the wisdom of being plugged in all the time. A 2005 study by Hewlett Packard concluded that the relentless bombardment of e-mails, phone calls, and instant messages causes the IQ of the average office worker to dip ten points—double the fall caused by smoking marijuana. A more recent study found that a sample of Microsoft workers took an average of fifteen minutes to return to a demanding task, such as writing computer code or a report, after stopping to deal with an incoming e-mail or IM. Most first drifted off to answer other messages or to do a little surfing through cyberspace.

Another fear is that too much screen time, especially when it involves fast-paced imagery, can rewire young brains into a permanent state of overstimulation. In a landmark study published in *Pediatrics* in 2004, U.S. researchers concluded that every hour of TV watched per day between the ages of one and three increased by nearly 10 percent the chances of being diagnosed later with attention deficit/hyperactivity disorder (ADHD). That means a toddler taking in three hours of Baby Channel daily is almost 30 percent more likely to have attention problems in school. While studies have shown that violent TV encourages violent behavior in some children, new research suggests that violent video games may promote aggression and inure players to shocking images. One study found that playing violent video games for thirty minutes lowered activity in a child's frontal lobe, the region of the brain linked to concentration and impulse control.

And then there is the myopia epidemic. Unusual half a century ago, shortsightedness now affects a quarter of the world's population—and the rate is still rising. Southeast Asia leads the way, with up to 80 percent of teenagers in Singapore and Taiwan affected, but parts of the West are moving in the same direction. Half of all twelve-year-olds in Sweden are now myopic, with experts predicting the figure will top 70 percent by the time they turn eighteen. Some blame the surge partly on children spending too many hours sitting indoors peering at screens.

What are we to make of such warnings? Once again the lesson from history is that we should first reach for a large pinch of salt. Every new technology unleashes a fresh wave of anxiety. Plato warned that reading would bring about the end of civilization by killing off memory, argument, and the oral tradition. In the early days of cinema, critics feared that the barrage of moving images might damage audiences' eyesight, and possibly drive them insane. Radio was vilified for turning children into zombies with no inner life, or even for making them "psychopathic." Then it was the turn of TV and video recorders. Perhaps information technology and video games are just the bogeyman du jour. Maybe we are simply projecting onto our children our own anxieties about the upheaval caused by the IT revolution.

Certainly, the jury is still out on many of the jeremiads. The evidence linking screen use to myopia is not conclusive. Nor has the video game boom sparked an epidemic of juvenile violence. Other research casts doubt on the claim that television causes ADHD. In 2006, two years after publishing the study affirming a link, *Pediatrics* published new research showing no link at all. The researchers reached the same conclusion that others have: ADHD is a neurological condition that people are born with, not an illness caused by parents handing the remote control to their small children.

Evidence is also mounting that the right sort of technology in the right doses can actually be beneficial. Studies suggest that watching small amounts of well-made children's television, especially alongside an adult, can teach children about the world and help develop literacy and numeracy. It can also spark imaginative play. My son uses TV as a source of material for his own stories.

He watches a *Star Wars* video for a while and then runs off upstairs to make up his own adventure involving Darth Vader and Han Solo.

Scientists are even showing that playing computer games can deliver a cognitive boost. One recent study found that playing all-action video games enhanced the ability to discern small objects in a cluttered space and to switch attention quickly between tasks. A recent study in Barcelona suggested that computer games can stimulate mental function in patients with Alzheimer's disease. Even the slower, less adrenaline-soaked games may help, too. These days, the top sellers are not the shoot-'em-up, instant-gratification bloodbaths that get newspaper columnists so hot under the collar. They are the simulation games that take many hours to complete, obliging players to decipher rules, weigh evidence, solve problems, analyze data, form hypotheses, and make both snap and considered judgments—just the sort of skills to help in the classroom or the workplace.

Around the world, the average IQ has been rising steadily for decades, a phenomenon known as the Flynn effect. While scores for verbal and numerical skills have remained the same, those measuring visual and spatial intelligence, as well as the ability to complete sequences of shapes, have soared. Scientists are not sure how to explain this, with theories ranging from better nutrition and smaller families to growing familiarity with IQ tests and changes in the tests themselves. But some put the Flynn effect, which already seems to have peaked in the industrial world, down to the extra visual and intellectual stimulation delivered by the multimedia culture. In *Everything Bad Is Good for You,* Steven Johnson makes a compelling case that our multi-layered high-tech environment is making us smarter in some ways.

Yet even if technology has benefits, there is clearly a danger that too much screen time squeezes out other elements of a healthy childhood. A major study published in 2006 by King's College, London, found that British eleven- to twelve-year-olds are now two to three years behind their peers of the 1970s when it comes to grasping concepts like volume and density, an ability that has been linked to general intelligence and the capacity to handle complex new ideas. The researchers speculated that part of the blame may lie with the trend for the young to spend less time playing outside with sand, mud, and water and more time plunked in front of Xboxes and TV.

And is it any wonder that the digital generation is the fattest in human history? You don't need to be a dietician to work out that sitting on your arse watching reruns of *OC* or playing Maelstrom does not burn many calories. Britain's Institute of Child Health estimates that for every extra hour of TV a five-year-old child watches on the weekend, his risk of obesity in adulthood rises by 7 percent. Research from the U.S. suggests that children who watch over two hours of television a day are more than twice as likely to suffer from hypertension linked to weight gain. A recent study of Mennonite communities in Canada turned up similar findings. Instead of slouching in front of screens, Mennonite children spend their days outdoors, walking, cycling, and performing farm chores. Researchers found that they were stronger, leaner, and fitter than their mainstream Canadian peers, even though the latter play organized sports and attend physical education classes. In a similar vein, the Central Council for Education in technology-mad Japan has noticed a steady decline in basic motor skills since the mid-1980s: Japanese children no longer run, jump, catch, and throw as well as did earlier generations. They have weaker muscles, slower reflexes, and less stamina.

Other studies suggest that playing sports, which involves focusing on distant objects, and spending time outdoors, where better light relieves the need to focus precisely for near vision, make children less prone to myopia.

Too many screen hours can deny young children the real-life, hands-on interaction with people and objects that is essential for their development. It also eats into time for reflection and rest. Sleep deprivation can stunt physical growth as well as impair concentration and memory, yet studies around the world show that on average kids are sleeping up to two hours less per night than a generation ago. A key reason for this is that so many children's bedrooms now resemble the flight deck of the *Starship Enterprise,* stuffed with noisy TVs, game consoles, telephones, and computers. Many other studies link electronic media in the bedroom with lower academic scores.

Even though it promises to bind us together in a nirvana of broadband connectivity, technology can also come between us, walling us off in our own digital bubbles. These days it's often quicker and easier to read about what your mates are up to on their blogs or online profiles than to meet and talk about it in person. And even when we occupy the same physical place, the gadgets can divide us. The Cole family in Phoenix, Arizona, bought a new minivan recently, complete with cell phone and iPod docks for the adults up front and embedded TV screens in the back for the two children. Their first expedition was to the Grand Canyon, 250 miles away. No one uttered a single word during the four-hour trip. "The technology stopped us bickering about stuff and getting on each other's nerves," says mother Julie. "But it also cut us off from each other. We were like a bunch of strangers traveling together on a Greyhound. It was weird, and not very nice." The Coles now ration their technology use on long journeys: twenty minutes of unplugged time for every forty minutes of electronic media. "This way we get the best of both worlds," says Julie. "We have our entertainment, but we also talk."

Even fans of the IT revolution are starting to warn that children need more than just a USB connection to the outside world. As the editor of *Children's Technology Review,* a United States–based monthly magazine that analyzes new software and gadgets aimed at the youth market, Warren Buckleitner is a card-carrying technophile. Over the years, he has exposed his two daughters to all the latest electronic gizmos—"You could say they've grown up in the candy store"—and today both girls love instant messaging, talking on their mobile phones, and surfing the Net as much as the next teenager.

But the Buckleitner home in Flemington, New Jersey, is not the high-tech free-for-all you might expect. There are strict limits. Mobile phones and TV are switched off for family meals. The only computer with Internet access is placed near the kitchen so the parents can monitor their daughters' use.

Buckleitner believes that much of the latest technology can be both entertaining and educational, but he also worries that overuse can lead to social isolation. Over thousands of years, mankind has evolved a complex, nuanced, and instinctive arsenal of physical communication—body language, facial expressions, pheromones—that dwarfs broadband in its ability to transmit meaning and forge emotional bonds. What happens when those eye-to-eye connections are displaced by rapid-fire virtual exchanges?

"Electronically, children may be connecting with other people on some levels, but they're not really exercising their social muscles when they're sitting alone in a room," says Buckleitner.

"In the overall ecology of childhood, a kid one hundred years ago, today, or one hundred years from now needs the same things—and that includes a certain number of minutes using their interpersonal skills in real-life situations. Otherwise you end up with a culture with little social lubrication."

Some evidence already points in that direction. In the past, study after study has shown that when presented with a range of objects and a human face, infants and young children tend to look first at the face. This is how they learn to communicate. In a series of experiments carried out in British primary schools in 2006, however, researchers found that instincts may be shifting. Most children still chose a human face over a doll's house, a plastic boat, or a toy train. But when a blank TV screen appeared alongside the face, most six- to eight-year-olds turned first to the screen, just as alcoholics in similar studies home in on a pint of beer or a glass of wine. The researchers found that most five-year-olds still have the face bias, which suggests that the problem does not lie with nature—the instinct for social interaction remains hardwired into the human brain. It is the nurture that is getting in the way.

Across the world, teachers report that the new generation of digital natives seems less articulate and less able to get along with their peers. Bullying in the playground and online is growing in many countries. In Britain, a major survey found that between 1986 and 2006 the number of teenagers who say they have no best friend in whom to confide rose from under one in eight to nearly one in five—and that at a time when any self-respecting teen lists dozens, or even hundreds, of "friends" on his MySpace page.

By making the unsayable so easy to say, and by encouraging everyone to click the Send button first and ask questions later, information technology can certainly be a social handicap. Teenagers and college students use their personal blogs to make bitchy comments about teachers and roommates, and are then stunned when the victim reads the attack and confronts them. Others fall into the flaming trap—saying things in e-mails, texts, and instant messages that they would never dream of saying face-to-face, and then finding that relations are strained in the real world. Fifteen-year-old Adam Turner sees this awkwardness all the time in his high school in Boise, Indiana. "Things can get pretty tense sometimes when you meet up afterward," he says. "You don't say anything about it, but it's still there, hanging in the air." Already some of the leading lights of the Internet boom, such as Jimmy Wales, the founder of Wikipedia, and Tim O'Reilly, the man who coined the phrase Web 2.0, have proposed a code of conduct that includes never saying anything online "that we wouldn't say in person."

Does the new technology also reinforce the narcissism that can be a by-product of micromanaged childhood? The danger is certainly there. Social networking sites like Bebo send the message that even the most banal details of our private lives are worth broadcasting to a global audience. What's more, with RSS feeds supplying bulletins from news and gossip sites that reflect our own views, online stores tracking our spending and sending us customized ads, and Google doing the same by monitoring our searches, Web content is now so personalized that it is less a window on the world and more an echo chamber of our own prejudices. This is especially limiting for children, who thrive on exposure to a range of views.

A decade into the IT revolution, two things are becoming clear. The first is that not all technology is created equal: many computer games, for instance, give the brain a better workout than you get from watching television. The second is that when it comes to screen time, less is often more.

The battle to build a more balanced relationship with technology is on. With their usual heavy-handedness, authorities in China have taken steps to bar under-eighteens from cybercafes. In South Korea, possibly the most wired nation on earth, the government has set up over two hundred counseling centers and hospital programs to tackle "Internet addiction" among the young. In 2007, it opened what may be the world's first boot camp for cyberjunkies, the Jump Up Internet Rescue School, where computers are banned and children spend the day completing outdoor obstacle courses and studying drumming and pottery. Elsewhere, others are using the technology itself as a way to lure kids away from the screen. Witness the rise of *LazyTown*, the Icelandic children's television show that broadcasts in more than a hundred countries. Its hero, the spandex-clad Sportacus, has had remarkable success inspiring children to lead more active lives. His healthy eating drive persuaded cinemas in Iceland to sell baby carrots instead of ice cream and popcorn, and boosted sales of vegetables in the country by 22 percent. Most Icelandic children now go to bed at exactly 8:08 p.m. because that is when Sportacus turns in. Everywhere, *LazyTown* is inspiring kids to get up off the sofa and run outside to dance, perform jumping jacks, kick a ball around, or explore their neighborhood on foot. "We live in a high-tech world, so you have to use the technology to reach children," says Magnus Scheving, the show's creator and the man who plays Sportacus. "Television can be inspirational for healthy living. Remember Jane Fonda's workout videos?"

Even the high-tech industry is looking for ways to get children off their bottoms. New game consoles like Nintendo Wii make players use their own body movements to box, dance, or play tennis on the screen. Others are using technology to lure children out of the house and away from the screen altogether. A new generation of high-tech toys that fly, walk, drive, and roll with extraordinary realism is hitting the market. The hope is that children will spend less time navigating an electronic car through Full Auto 2 and more time chasing a state-of-the-art ornithopter around the backyard. Gene Khasminsky is director of design at Interactive Toy Concepts, a Canadian firm that makes a palm-sized, radio-controlled helicopter called the Micro Mosquito. "I think, right now, that there is a push back from our industry to get kids off the couch where they're playing video games," he says.

Even so, many parents find that the only way to stop their children from becoming couch potatoes is to impose a moratorium on technology. Take the Hydes, who live in a suburb of Sydney, Australia. Their two children, twelve-year-old Jasmine and ten-year-old Lachlan, used to spend hours every day either online, playing with their Xbox, or watching TV in their own rooms. The family was so wired that mother Maureen sent e-mails to call people down to the kitchen for supper. Though worried that their children were spending too much time in front of screens and not enough time running around outdoors, the Hydes had given up the battle to make them switch off. But then one night everything changed. At around 9 p.m., Maureen e-mailed Lachlan asking him to come downstairs to tidy up his school things before going to bed, but he did not answer. She shouted up the stairs and still not a peep. When she finally went up to his room, she found him slumped over his desk, a game of FIFA Soccer idling away on the Xbox. Her first thought was that he had suffered the same fate as Mr. Lee during his Starcraft marathon. "I got such a shock because I honestly thought he was dead, that he'd gone and died playing that bloody game," she remembers. It turned out Lachlan had just fallen asleep, but the episode was a wake-up call for the Hydes. The next day, the family sat down to rethink the place given to technology in their home. The parents decided to ration gadget time with a set of tough new rules: No more cell phones at meal times. No more eating in front of the TV except on special occasions. No screen use during homework unless an assignment entails Internet research. The Hydes also moved all the gadgets out of the children's rooms and into the basement play area. The kids howled, but the parents stood firm.

To fill the time freed up by switching off the high-tech gizmos, the Hydes set up a badminton net in the backyard and painted a court on the grass. It was an instant hit. Now the whole family plays almost every day: dad versus son, mom versus daughter, mixed doubles. The children spend hours knocking the birdie back and forth, chatting, joking, competing.

Maureen thinks that going on a high-tech diet has been a breath of fresh air. Dinner conversations are more lively now that the children aren't furtively texting under the table. Both Jasmine and Lachlan finish their homework more quickly and are doing better at school. They are also less lethargic: with no electronic beeps and whistles to distract them in their bedroom, they sleep more. Lachlan springs out of bed on weekend mornings instead of reaching for the Xbox console.

The children like the new balance, too. "I still love my computer, but it's good to leave it behind and do something else," says Jasmine. Her brother agrees. "I used to prefer Xbox to going outside," he says. "But I think it's cool to do both things."

Other parents have gone even further, turning their homes into technology-free zones. Alessandro Basso, who lives with his parents in Philadelphia, got hooked on PlayStation at the age of eleven. He would spend five or six hours a day in his room, eating meals on his lap and neglecting his homework. Once an avid sports player, he began choosing PlayStation soccer over kicking a ball around outdoors with his friends. He also began to put on weight. The Basso parents were worried enough to intervene, but every attempt to rein in his PlayStation habit met with angry defiance. When they imposed time limits, Alessandro ignored them. When they moved the PlayStation into the living room, he sneaked in to play in the middle of the night. Eventually, they decided that the time had come for a firm clampdown. One morning, while Alessandro was at school, they sold the Play-Station console on eBay. Alessandro threw a tantrum and remained in a foul mood for weeks, but eventually he got over it. He began going out to play soccer with his friends again, he lost weight, and his school marks improved. Today, he talks about PlayStation like a recovering alcoholic might about liquor. "I really hated my parents at first for getting rid of it, and I really missed it, but I have to admit my life is better now without it," he says. He pauses for a moment, runs his fingers through his dark, curly hair, and looks down at the floor. "I still play computer games at my friends' houses but I wouldn't want to have them at home," he says. "If we had PlayStation here I'd probably go back to playing it all the time."

Alessandro is an extreme case. Some people are more prone than others to addictive behavior. For most children, a total ban on technology is over the top. The best policy is to set limits that offer them a blend of low-tech and high-tech. But where does that balance lie? How many hours of screen time is right for children? Unfortunately there is no clear-cut answer. Some experts, including the American Academy of Pediatrics, recommend zero screen time for babies under two. But anyone who has ever looked after children, especially in a country where the weather is bad or with older siblings around, knows that this is almost impossible to arrange. That is why others take a less draconian view. The Canadian Pediatric Society recommends no more than thirty minutes a day for children under two.

Later the picture gets more blurry. While older children should be free to use computers for school assignments, learning, and creative work, they need limits on screen entertainment such as TV and video games. The best guide is common sense. If a teenager spends more time socializing online than in the real world, then something is out of kilter. Buckleitner urges parents to follow their instincts. "It's partly a gut thing," he says. "Just as you know when your child has eaten too much candy, you know when he's spending too much time in front of a screen."

That may sound glib, but it strikes at the heart of what we need to do in every sphere of child rearing nowadays: learn to trust our instincts and then take a stand.

We know our own children better than anyone else, so the first step to striking the right balance with technology is to watch them. After unplugging from the gadgets, are they touchy and aggressive, tired and withdrawn? If so, then it's probably right to limit their screen time. Start by removing high-tech gadgets from the bedroom, or by leaving them at home during vacations, which are a good time to break old habits and broaden horizons. Consider holding screen-free days. It also helps to set a time limit on screen entertainment that feels right for the family—two hours a day works for many. You may not always hit the target, but at least a line has been drawn in the sand.

The best way to quell the inevitable protests and withdrawal symptoms is to offer alternatives to the technology: sports, games, a bedtime story, baking, more freedom to play outdoors, more friends round to visit, more talking and doing things together as a family. Some of these require time, effort, and imagination from parents, but isn't that what we sign up for when we have children?

Certainly, parents need to put up a united front, agreeing, for instance, how much screen time is permitted when visiting friends' houses. We also need to rethink our own relationship with technology. If we slump in front of the TV for hours at a time, or constantly check e-mail and yak on the mobile phone, what kind of message does that send to the children?

We also need to revisit our own addiction to multitasking. These days, children are getting even more bang per minute for their high-tech buck. A 2005 survey by the Kaiser Family Foundation revealed that Americans aged eight to eighteen spend 6.5 hours a day using electronic media but manage to cram in 8.5 hours' worth of media exposure by juggling various things at the same time—think IMing friends and downloading music while checking e-mail, watching *Big Brother,* and playing the Sims. We all know from experience that this high-tech juggling act can deliver an adrenaline rush, but the impression it gives of productivity turns out to be no more than an illusion. In laboratories around the world, scientists are using the latest brain-scan technology to work out how we think when performing different tasks—and it doesn't look good for young multitaskers.

The simple truth is that the human brain, and that includes the brains of children reared in the Information Age, is not very good at multitasking. Of course, certain well-rehearsed actions, such as cycling or chopping carrots, can be performed on autopilot while thinking about other things. But researchers have shown that the moment you decide to tweak the action—by steering your bicycle to the left, say, or adding another carrot to the recipe—you need the full attention of your brain. Once you decide on your next course of action, however, the action itself—turning the handlebars or slicing the extra carrot—can be performed at the same time as planning another action. So there is some overlap.

The bottom line, though, is that much of what passes for multitasking is nothing of the sort: it is sequential. When your son has five windows open on his computer screen and is tapping away at his mobile phone while watching TV, what he is really doing is performing one task for a few seconds, stopping, switching to another for a bit, then stopping again, switching to a third task, stopping, and so on. And just as you might expect, this toggling turns out to be a very inefficient use of both time and brain power. When people flit back and forth between tasks, they make more mistakes and take much longer—sometimes double the time or more—than if they had performed each task from start to finish before moving on to the next one. That may explain why that history essay takes your teenage daughter two hours to finish instead of one or less.

David E. Meyer, director of the Brain, Cognition, and Action Laboratory at the University of Michigan, believes that nothing, not even a steady diet of early learning DVDs or computer summer camps, is likely to make multitasking anything other than a waste of time. "The bottom line is that you can't simultaneously be thinking about your tax return and reading an essay, just as you can't talk to yourself about two things at once," he says. "If a teenager is trying to have a conversation on an e-mail chat line while doing algebra, she'll suffer a decrease in efficiency, compared to if she just thought about algebra until she was done. People may believe otherwise, but it's a myth. With such complicated tasks, you will never, ever be able to overcome the inherent limitations in the brain for processing information during multitasking. It just can't be, any more than the best of all humans will ever be able to run a one-minute mile."

When it comes to the neurological limits on multitasking, children may actually be more handicapped than most. Using functional magnetic resonance imaging (fMRI), scientists have identified a region of the anterior prefrontal cortex that stores information about tasks in progress. This allows us to stop doing something and then pick up where we left off when we return to it seconds, minutes, or even hours later. This is the part of the brain that helps us "multitask," in the sense of toggling back and forth between tasks. Yet this region of the brain matures late, meaning that young children are even less well equipped to juggle tasks than are adults. In other words, all that hype about how the new generation of multitasking digital natives represents an evolutionary great leap forward is just that: hype.

Chronic multitasking is inefficient in ways that go beyond a poor use of time. Research suggests that the human brain needs moments of quiet and rest to process and consolidate ideas, memories, and experiences. It also needs to be in a relaxed state to slip into the richer, more creative mode of thought. How can any of that happen when every second is filled with electronic chatter? Endless channel hopping, Web surfing, and IMing also militate against the slower art of delving into a topic, staying with an argument long enough to unravel its nuances and complexities. University professors increasingly complain that twenty-first-century students balk at reading whole books, preferring much shorter excerpts and articles. They also seem impatient with ambiguity, demanding instant answers that are black and white. This is a serious handicap when exploring topics such as terrorism or immigration, which come in many shades of gray. Can democracy function properly if young voters want every issue wrapped up in text-message-style sound bites? Today's children are very good at finding and manipulating information, and at analyzing visual data, but even the apostles of the IT revolution now worry that too much electronic toggling is making it harder for them to concentrate or think deeply. At a recent conference on the future of technology, Dipchand Nishar, director of wireless products at Google, sounded a note of caution. "We had Generation X and Generation Y," he said. "Now we have Generation ADD."

How do you wean a child off multitasking? Simon Blake, a software engineer in California, put a limit on the number of programs his twelve-year-old daughter, Chrissy, could run on the family computer while doing homework. She can use the Internet for research but not to swap messages with friends on MySpace. She is only allowed to check her e-mail every thirty minutes, and her cell phone stays switched off throughout. The upshot is that homework now takes nearly 50 percent less time than before, and Chrissy's teachers have praised the higher standards in her work. "You can just tell she is more focused now, even when she's away from the technology," says Blake.

Chrissy resented the new rules at first but has come round to them. "To start with, it was kind of annoying having to wait for e-mails and IMs, but you get used to it," she says. "I definitely notice that I'm less distracted now."

To be sure, the classroom is now a key front in the battle to define the place of technology in children's lives. The traditional chalk-and-talk model of education, where the teacher stands in front of the blackboard and lectures the pupils, looks stale and outdated in a wired, interconnected world. In educational circles, the consensus is that schools need to adapt to the new technology. There is a strong case to be made that children today need more than just facts. They need to learn how to solve problems together in groups, how to distinguish good information from bad, how to connect and share ideas with peers in other countries, how to think across disciplines. IT can help with all of this. Pupils at a school in Vancouver can use e-mail or a Web cam to exchange ideas about global warming with peers in tsunami-ravaged Indonesia. A classroom discussion about slavery is enriched by students pulling down news reports about modern-day people-trafficking from a wireless Internet connection in the classroom. Even high-tech video games can be used to teach the low-tech basics. At Chew Magna, a small primary school in Bristol, England, Tim Rylands teaches English to ten- and eleven-year-olds with the computer game Exile. The children do not actually play the game. Instead, Rylands uses a whiteboard to steer them round its mystical landscapes, through ornate doors, into rooms bathed in golden light. The graphics are dazzling, almost otherworldly, and the children sit enrapt. Rylands then asks them to write what they have seen and how it made them feel. The children turn away from the whiteboard, pick up their pens, and start scribbling away. Chew Magna, a state school, delivers some of the highest English test scores in Britain, and Rylands has won awards for using new technology to teach old-fashioned literacy. "I am just using the technology to do the basic things in an off-the-wall way," says Rylands. "I am trying to create the magic, the enjoyment rather than just the basic skill."

Yet even Rylands accepts that technology is not a magic bullet. Research on the impact of IT on academic performance shows that sometimes it helps and sometimes it doesn't. Critics say that is because we are not yet using technology in the right way, but it is also clear that digital media has its limits as a learning device, that in many scenarios hands-on, real-life instruction will never be bested. This is especially true for smaller children. One study set out to teach two groups of twelve- to fifteen-month-olds how to use a puppet. The first group watched a video demonstration while the second watched a real person act out the same instructions. The latter learned to manipulate the puppet after a single lesson. Those parked in front of the screen needed six viewings to master it.

In an increasingly wired world, schools are already taking steps to help children strike a balance with technology. Many have already banned mobile phones in the classroom. Universities have blocked wireless Internet access in lecture halls to encourage students to listen rather than while away the hour updating their Bebo page.

Another way for schools to combat technology overload is to anchor part of the curriculum in Mother Nature. We have already seen how preschoolers thrive in outdoor nurseries; the same applies to older children. Venturing outside allows kids who normally spend so much time cooped up indoors to blow off some steam; it can also deliver rich, hands-on learning. A 2002 study of 150 elementary and middle schools in sixteen U.S. states found that using nature to teach some of the curriculum boosted marks in science, languages, social studies, and math. It also noticeably improved student behavior. After one school introduced an outdoor program, disciplinary referrals fell by 90 percent.

Exposure to nature, even if that means spending just an hour a week in a vegetable patch behind the school, also gives children an understanding of how the earth works and how mankind has a role in preserving it. It teaches them that chicken breasts do not come from plastic-wrapped polystyrene trays and French fries are made from potatoes that grow in the soil. If we are going to save the planet, then future generations need to make room for nature in their high-tech urban lives.

Tucked away in the mountains of northern Taiwan, the Forest School is a low-tech oasis in a society in thrall to electronic screens. As the name suggests, the pupils, aged six to twelve, spend a lot of time outdoors, climbing trees, rooting around in swamps, and studying nature close up, rather like the children at the Lakeside School in Zurich. Many class projects and home-work assignments are conducted in the forest. Though teachers sometimes use video in lessons and the school screens a weekly movie, television, video games, and computers are all banned.

I arrange to meet some of the Forest parents and pupils in an office in downtown Taipei. When I arrive, the children are racing around, hiding behind desks, laughing about a character they have invented. There is not a single Nintendo in sight. Ching-lan Lin, the director of Forest School, tells me that her graduates have earned a reputation for being articulate team players who love to learn, know their own strengths and weaknesses, and have a strong environmentalist sensibility. They are also completely at ease with technology because most of them have computers and TV at home. The Forest School now has a long waiting list.

One of the boys here tonight, Hong, is nine. Blessed with darting eyes and an infectious laugh, he seems to belong to a different species from the children you see plugged into Game Boys around town. He tells me how much fun he has at the Forest School. "We are free to go outside and play any time," he says. Does he feel shortchanged by the ban on technology? Not at all. He uses the computer and watches TV at home. "At the school we have fun and learn a lot without computers," he says, before bowing and rejoining his mates.

A smile creeps across his mother's face. "Hong has his whole life to sit in front of screens," she says. "Why should he spend his whole childhood doing the same thing?"

SIX

School: Testing Times

Education is what remains after one has forgotten everything he learned at school.
—Albert Einstein

Not too long ago, Marilee Jones was going through the mail at her office at the Massachusetts Institute of Technology. It was a few weeks after the college had sent off the annual fusillade of acceptance and rejection letters, and as dean of admissions, she was braced for the usual blowback from disappointed candidates. Some phone up in tears, others send poison-pen letters. On this day, though, one missive stood out for its sheer nastiness. The father of an applicant had scribbled three short sentences beneath his corporate letterhead: "You rejected my son. He's devastated. See you in court."

After nearly three decades in the job, Jones had developed a thick skin, so the threat of a lawsuit did not keep her up that night. Next morning, the promise of legal action looked even more hollow when a letter written by the son of Furious Father arrived. It contained just two sentences: "Thank you for not admitting me to MIT. This is the best day of my life."

Jones told me this story over breakfast in Palo Alto, California. She had come to address a conference on how an obsession with academic achievement is squeezing the lifeblood out of schools—and the children who attend them. Jones held up Furious Father as a cautionary tale of what happens when test scores and acceptance by the "right" college become an end in themselves. "It has reached a point where it's not about the kids or what's good for them anymore; it's about what the parents want; it's about Mom telling her friends that her daughter aced her SATs, or Dad boasting about how his kid got into MIT or Harvard," she said. "What happened to education for its own sake? When did our children's passion for learning, for finding a subject that really excites them, get pushed aside by the race to build the perfect résumé?"

A similar lament can be heard in homes, schools, universities, and think tanks around the world. At the dawn of the twenty-first century, the academic stakes seem higher than ever. Schools push children to master the three Rs earlier and earlier, ditching art, music, and even recess to clear space for extra cramming. Educating a child costs more money than ever before. From Manchester to Montreal to Melbourne, parents take on colossal mortgages to buy homes near the most coveted state schools. Private tutoring is a booming global industry. Families in China now spend a third of their income on education.

Treating exam scores as a matter of life and death is an old tradition in the Far East, where local cultures traditionally put a high premium on toil and competition. More than a millennium ago, the Chinese began forcing their children through a punishing steeplechase of exams, awarding the elite jobs to those who finished the race with top marks. And the Chinese model, with its stress on rote learning, spread across East Asia, condemning many of the region's children to long hours in the classroom and cram school, and a life of what has come to be known as "exam hell." In Korea, university entrance exam day is a national event, with television news broadcasting live from school gates and special police patrols escorting students to testing stations. Korean mothers start praying for straight As a hundred days before the exams, which is nothing compared to the superhuman studying their children put in. Korean pupils spur themselves on with a chilling mantra: "Sleep four hours and pass, sleep five hours and fail."

The West has traditionally been less frantic. Academic success only really became a matter of parental concern in the twentieth century. As recently as the 1960s and 1970s, many Western schools cleaved to the Rousseauesque ideal of freedom and child-centricity, stressing creativity, spontaneity, and nonconformity over discipline, rote learning, and tests. But then came the backlash. In the 1980s, governments across the English-speaking world began imposing heavier workloads, more testing, and longer hours in the classroom.

This back-to-basics shift was partly driven by the fear that hard-grafting East Asian children were pulling ahead in international test scores. Growing parental anxiety mixed with worries about economic competitiveness also played a role, as did the modern penchant for measuring and benchmarking. In 2000, the Organization for Economic Cooperation and Development (OECD) began publishing the results of the Programme for International Student Assessment (PISA), which puts around a quarter of a million fifteen-year-olds across the industrial world through the same reading, math, and science tests. Despite heavy skepticism from academics, PISA results have become a talisman, making headlines and sending low-scoring nations into a panic about falling standards. In Denmark, for instance, middling PISA scores have sparked fears that Danish schools place too much emphasis on the happiness of the pupils. In countries like Britain, meanwhile, the vogue for publicly ranking individual schools has fueled a scramble to gain entry into the top seeds.

In the rush to yank up academic standards, however, some fundamental questions have been brushed aside: Does all this pushing, testing, and benchmarking actually work? Does it make children happier, healthier, and smarter? Does it create better workers and better citizens? Do higher test scores mean academic standards are rising? Right across the world, parents and educators are coming to the conclusion that the answer to all of the above is no.

Let's not get carried away. The truth is that formal education has had a mixed press for centuries. Shakespeare wrote about the little boy "creeping like a snail unwillingly to school." There is also a long history of dismissing the very idea of sitting in a classroom as absurd and even harmful. Mark Twain quipped that "I have never let my schooling interfere with my education." For generations, critics have attacked schools for failing to teach children properly, for putting ideology before learning, for letting standards slip. Has there ever been a time when teachers did not complain about their working conditions?

Yet today something is clearly awry. Even as spending on education balloons, schools across the world are failing to turn out enough children who are well informed, articulate, creative, disciplined, ethical, and hungry for learning. Instead of being the latest in a long line of carping Cassandras, critics like Marilee Jones have hit the nail on the head.

Consider the facts. Cheating appears to be on the rise in academia, especially among pupils at the top, where the pressure to compete is most fierce. Nearly three-quarters of Canadian undergraduates recently admitted to serious acts of cheating on written work while in high school. At Monta Vista, a hard-driving high school in California, the number of students who confessed in a secret poll to cheating on quizzes, tests, and final exams doubled between 1996 and 2006. Across the world, the academic chicanery runs the gamut from parents who help too much with take-home assignments to pupils who plagiarize work from the Net or send text messages during exams. And the cheating continues after school, too. In 2007, officials revealed that 5 percent of applicants to Oxford and Cambridge had embellished their application forms with material taken from the Web. Explaining why they wanted to study chemistry, 234 applicants cited word for word the same example, "burning a hole in my pajamas at age eight," as a formative experience. Once inside the Ivory Tower, students continue to look for shortcuts to the top. Scores of Web sites now offer assignments written to order by A students, with prices ranging from a few hundred dollars for an essay to $10,000 for a whole dissertation. On top of all the plagiarism, the growing use of drugs such as ProVigil and Adderall as "study aids" makes a mockery of a level playing field in the classroom. The World Chess Federation has tested competitors for Ritalin. Will children soon have to supply urine samples on the way into the examination hall?

Claire Cafaro, a counselor at a high school in Ridgewood, an affluent town in New Jersey, has seen the competitive frenzy throw ethics out the window. "In the past, if a child was caught cheating, we would call the parents, and they would be grateful and want to know how to combat the problem together," she says. "Now they may ask if we have DNA proof of the cheating, or what exactly our security procedures are, or they tell us to talk to their lawyer."

When the classroom becomes a winner-take-all battlefield, friendships can suffer. In a 2007 UNICEF report on the state of childhood across the industrial world, researchers asked eleven-, thirteen-, and fifteen-year-olds whether they felt "lonely" and whether their peers were "kind and helpful." Is it a coincidence that countries that place a heavy emphasis on academic competition and testing, such as Britain, Japan, and the United States, posted some of the worst scores?

A win-at-any-cost academic culture takes a toll on children of every caliber. Competition can be a useful spur to studying, but it starts to backfire when the bar is raised so high that only perfect test scores will do. The gnawing feeling of never being good enough is captured in the recent lament from one able student at Monta Vista: "I remember the days. . . . when it didn't take sleeping four hours to show my parents that I was in fact putting in an honest effort in my work. I remember the days when it didn't take straight As or getting in some amazing honors program at some xyz elite university to make them proud of me." Meanwhile, pupils who cannot or will not do what it takes to be an A student may lose heart altogether. "Sometimes I feel like I'm failing life," says another California teen. "I'm up till 3 a.m. doing homework that I almost never get full credit on, I'm playing a sport that I'm not going to get a position in, and I seem to be losing touch with all my friends. Is it all downhill from here? That's what I fear most." That desperation plays out most vividly in the Far East, which has seen an explosion in the number of children dropping out of school or committing suicide. In high-pressure Hong Kong, nearly one in three teens has had suicidal thoughts. Across Asia, alienated kids are turning to bullying and crime. Faced with reports that up to 5 percent of its children now belong to violent gangs, the government of South Korea, a nation that once prided itself on the deference and discipline of its young, set up a special task force to tackle the problem in 2005.

At the same time, the argument that more testing and toil is the best way to shape young minds for life in the twenty-first century is starting to fray at the edges. Remember that King's College report suggesting that the cognitive development of British children is slowed by spending too little time messing around outdoors? Well, other researchers think part of the blame may also lie with our obsession with academic cramming and exam results. "By stressing only the basics—reading and writing—and testing like crazy you reduce the level of cognitive stimulation," says Philip Adey, professor of education at King's College. "Children have the facts but they are not thinking very well."

The examcentric approach can certainly warp priorities in the classroom, encouraging teachers to teach to the test rather than promoting real learning, imagination, and problem solving. A century and a half ago, England tried paying teachers according to how well their pupils answered questions asked by visiting inspectors. Schools, in response, put more energy into rote learning and began encouraging weaker pupils to play hooky on inspection days. Today, with so much kudos and cash riding on test scores, educators around the world have been caught doing the same or worse. A fourth-grade teacher in Spokane, Washington, recently gave her pupils answers to the mathematics portion of a state exam in advance and allowed some to swap answers during the test itself. Investigators reported that, in the section where students were asked to show their work, one had written, "My techre [*sic*] told me." In England, the headmaster of a primary

school was caught helping pupils cheat on science and math
SATs. Japan was recently rocked by the revelation that hundreds
of its schools allowed pupils to skip entire courses to allot more
time to studying for the country's notoriously competitive university entrance exams.

And then there is the basic drawback of exams: the one thing
they measure better than anything else is how good a child is at
taking exams. Is this really what we need in the New Economy?
In the future, the biggest rewards will go not to the yes-men who
know how to serve up an oven-ready answer but to the creatives,
the nimble-minded innovators who can think across disciplines,
delve into a problem for the sheer hell of it, and relish the challenge of learning throughout their lives. These are the people
who will come up with the next Google, invent an alternative
fuel, or devise a plan to slay poverty in Africa. The problem is
that relentless pressure and scrutiny can make children less creative: rather than take chances or push the boundaries, they play
safe, opting for the answer that earns the gold star and the pat on
the back at home. One couple I know have been asked by their
seventeen-year-old son not to talk to him about any literature,
history, or art that is not on the syllabus at his private school in
London. "He's worried it will get in the way for his exams," says
his father. "Part of me admires his focus, but it's also pretty de-
pressing that education has become so tunnel-vision." Mindless
cramming also leaves less time to develop the Emotional Intelligence Quotient (EQ)—the ability to manage relationships. In
the modern workplace, where networking and innovating in
large teams are crucial, EQ is at least as important as IQ.

We have already seen how eschewing testing and competition
in favor of collaboration and child-centered learning pays dividends at preschool. The same is true in the later years. A major

study published in 2006 examined a large sample of children who entered a lottery to attend a Montessori school in Milwaukee, comparing the winners, who won a place, with the losers, who attended a mainstream school. The fact that all had chosen to enter the lottery meant that they came from homes with similar parental aspirations.

By the age of twelve, the two groups in the study were more or less on a par in math and reading, and their spelling, punctuation, and grammar scores were similar, too. But when it came to writing essays, the Montessori children were way ahead, their written work markedly more creative and their sentences more complex. The Montessori kids also handled social conflict better and felt more respected and supported at their school. "When you teach to the test, you end up with children who can pass tests," says a Montessori teacher in Toronto. "When you forget the test and teach the child, you end up with a whole person."

Too much academic measuring can also suck the joy out of learning. Scores of studies have shown that the more people are encouraged to chase results and rewards—an A+ on the report card, say—the less interest they take in the task itself. In international tests, East Asian students score near the top in math and science, yet rank near the bottom for enjoyment of those subjects. Might this explain why relatively few go into research after graduation, and why famous East Asian scientists and mathematicians are so thin on the ground? Or why a country like Japan has produced so few Nobel Prize winners in any field? Following a test-heavy literacy drive, English ten-year-olds rose to third in international reading scores but were near the bottom for enjoyment of reading outside school. We seem to have forgotten the lesson of Plato: the key to education is "to get children to want to know what they have to know."

To see how attitudes to education are shifting, and to find out what makes for a successful school system, I set off on a world tour. My first port of call is Finland. This country of five million people on the northern fringe of Europe seems to have achieved educational nirvana. In the Programme for International Student Assessment (PISA) test scores, Finnish pupils routinely come first or second in every category: math, literacy, and science. Finland has one of the highest per capita rates of graduation from university in the world and also boasts a dynamic economy bursting with creative high-tech companies like Nokia. In that 2007 UNICEF report, Finnish children came in as the third happiest among developed nations.

All of this has made Finland another mecca for educational observers. Every year, over 1,500 foreign delegates from some fifty countries come to unlock the secrets of the "Finnish miracle." And there are some lessons to draw. One is that there is a robust alternative to the start-them-early, drive-them-hard approach. In stark contrast to their peers in many other countries, Finnish children do not enter formal school until the calendar year in which they turn seven. Their early childhood is spent at home or in nurseries where play is king. When they finally do reach school, they enjoy short days, long vacations, and plenty of music, art, and sports.

Finland also keeps competition to a minimum. It tracks the performance of individual schools but does not publish the findings. Unless parents ask for it, students are not graded until they are thirteen years old; instead they get written report cards from their teachers and do a lot of Reggio-style self-evaluation from an early age. Finland has no advance placement or streaming programs, keeping children of all abilities together until high school. Homework is also light by international standards. Finland is that rare place: a Kumon-free zone. Private tutoring is virtually nonexistent, because even the most ambitious Finnish parents expect the school system to carry the load. "Sending my children to a tutor would be like buying a brand-new house and then having to pay for a new roof every year," says one high-flying Helsinki dad. "Anyway, it's better for children to get away from academics outside school, to have time to rest or play, to just be children."

Another lesson from Finland is that everyone benefits when the teaching profession is held in high esteem. Competition for teacher training is fierce here, and those who make the cut study for five years before qualifying. Most Finnish parents have faith that the country's teachers will do well by their children. Finland has also avoided the temptation to impose a rigid curriculum across the country. Its schools have plenty of scope to determine what their pupils study within very broad national guidelines. One of the conclusions drawn by PISA is that the best schools, public or private, usually have wide authority over their curriculum and budget.

Perhaps most striking of all, testing is a low priority in Finland. Apart from final exams at the end of high school, Finnish kids face no standardized tests. Teachers use quizzes, and individual schools use tests to track their pupils' progress, but the idea of cramming for SATs is as alien to Finland as a heat wave in winter. This presents a delicious irony: the nation that puts the least stress on competition and testing, that shows the least appetite for cram schools and private tutoring, routinely tops the world in PISA's competitive exams.

Domisch Rainer, a German education expert who has lived in Finland for nearly thirty years, thinks this paradox is the result of the Finnish system's putting the needs of children ahead of the

desires of target-happy parents and bureaucrats. "Kids here are
not seen as buckets that you fill up with five or ten or fifteen lessons a week and then measure with test after test," he says. "You
cannot force a child to grow up faster just to fit your system or
your timetable or your ego; you have to find out how children
learn best. Many countries have forgotten this."

To see this philosophy in action, I head north of Helsinki to
Vantaa, the fourth largest city in Finland. My destination is Viertola, a school for seven- to thirteen-year-olds. The neighborhood
is home to a mix of professionals and service workers from the
nearby airport, as well as a sprinkling of immigrants from Eastern
Europe and Africa.

The principal, Pekka Kaasinen, greets me in a red short-sleeved
shirt and sandals over black socks. Trim and genial, with a clump
of keys slung around his neck, he reminds me of an old gym
teacher of mine. We walk into the brick building, past rows of
neatly stacked footwear. To create a relaxed atmosphere, Finnish
children remove their shoes at school, just as they do at home.

Kaasinen is appalled by the academic rat race that grips so
many countries. He believes the first job of a school is to nurture
a passion for learning rather than for acing exams. "Competition
is good for some, but not for others, so it is better not to have too
much of it," he says. "Our teachers know what the kids can and
can't do anyway, so exams don't add a lot." Kaasinen thinks that
separating children by ability demoralizes the less able and the
late bloomers. In Viertola, teachers give extra help to the weaker
students and extra work to the academic thoroughbreds within
the same classroom. That keeps every pupil engaged, which in
turn stops parents or staff reaching for the medicine cabinet. Of
the 470 students in Viertola, only two are on Ritalin. "We get
good results across the board because we take care of everyone,"

says Kaasinen. "The key is for kids of all abilities to be in the same class together—that is society, after all." OECD studies bear this out: more students do well in countries that eschew academic streaming.

After our chat, I sit in on an English class for thirteen-year-olds. It takes place in a very traditional classroom—desks arranged in rows, a blackboard at the front, a window looking out onto the playground. On one wall hangs a series of haikus that the children wrote the previous week to practice English vocabulary. One reads: "A Horse, hungry heavy, hears helps hits, heavily happily, an Animal." The atmosphere is an agreeable blend of discipline and digression: while the teacher is clearly in control, she does not talk down to the pupils. There are no textbooks in sight because today the children will read aloud and discuss their short essays on "my favorite place." The conversation is in a mixture of Finnish and English. One girl describes the "tangled undergrowth" near her family's summer cottage. A boy talks about the place in his mind where "everything is quiet and open" and where "my best ideas come from."

Afterward, I interview some of the pupils in an empty classroom. Patrick, a thirteen-year-old with searching eyes and floppy brown hair, has recently watched a documentary about childhood around the world. He is shocked by the pressure that kids face in other countries. "It made me feel that we are very lucky in Finland because we do not have to worry all the time about exams and marks," he says. "Instead of competing with each other, we can compete with ourselves, which is the best way to learn things."

Jari, his classmate, agrees. "If school is too much like a race, then you get tired and enjoy it less," he says. "I know I learn things best when I am enjoying myself."

Finnish education is not without critics. Some say it demands too much of weaker pupils and too little of stronger ones, that it could do more to foster creativity and problem solving, that Finnish teachers are too fond of the old chalk-and-talk method of instruction. Strangely, given their hunger for technology, the Finns have also been slow to wire up their classrooms.

Even stranger, Finland's very successful schools are starting to face the same parental pressure that warps education in other countries. The older teachers at Viertola notice the change. Today's parents, they say, are more pushy, questioning grades, demanding special treatment for their children, lobbying for more assessment, more homework, and extra language tuition. Some are calling for the state to follow Britain's lead and rank individual schools publicly. The staff at Viertola worry for the future. "Our education system here in Finland is not without flaws, but it is very strong," says one teacher. "We have to have faith in what works instead of trying to make it better by copying the mistakes of other countries."

At the moment, though, Finland remains more leader than follower. Some of the guiding principles of its education system—less testing, less competitive pressure, less toil—are making inroads around the world. The demanding International Baccalaureate program, which caters to more than half a million students in 124 countries, has trimmed its workload in recent years. Wales has scrapped standardized exams for seven-year-olds and made them optional for eleven- and fourteen-year-olds. By 2009, English teenagers will be taking a third fewer exams in their final two years of school. In the United States, despite officialdom's faith in standardized testing, private schools and universities are putting less weight on exam scores when selecting pupils.

Even nations that were once a byword for "exam hell" are losing faith in tests as the sole measure of a child's worth. Parents from South Korea to China are sending their children to study in Western countries, where the academic pressure is less intense. Change is afoot at home, too. Secondary schools in Singapore are now selecting pupils more for their individual aptitudes than for their performance in standardized exams. Officials in the affluent city-state talk of moving from an exam meritocracy to a talent meritocracy. "If we stick only with the national exams as a means of [measuring children] . . . it is transparent and simple, but it will tend to narrow our definition of talent, and it will tend to narrow our definition of success," says Tharman Shanmugaratnam, the country's education minister. "A certain fuzziness . . . comes when you move from a system that is about efficiency to a system that is about choice. And I think that fuzziness is good; it blurs the identity, blurs the definition, no one is about a label, no one is about which stream he is in. He or she is about a set of talents that need to be nurtured." Good-bye Managed Child, hello children.

Japan is even farther down the road to reform, and its experience highlights the benefits and pitfalls of taking a more relaxed approach to education. The country has been trying to ease the academic load for years, but the great leap forward came with the *yutori kyoiku* (pressure-free education) revolution of 2002. This cut school hours by nearly a third, including the abolition of Saturday classes, and reduced the course material covered. It also introduced a general studies class designed to teach children to use knowledge from across the disciplines to tackle problems. The aim was clear: to give Japanese children the time and space to grow up well rounded and hungry for learning.

In practice, though, *yutori* has had a bumpy ride. Ending Saturday schooling went down badly with many Japanese parents who had neither the time nor the inclination to look after their children for an extra day of the week. Critics warned that academic standards would fall, a fear that seemed to be confirmed when Japan's international ranking in reading and science slipped. To compensate, many parents moved their children into private schools. Others bumped up the hours their kids spent in the local *juku,* or cram school. Thanks partly to pressure from anxious parents, many state schools have unilaterally lengthened teaching hours. A similar backlash greeted South Korea's decision to abolish Saturday classes in 2003.

But *yutori* also has an upside. Studies by Japan's Ministry of Education suggest that reducing textbook-based study and competition in the classroom has fostered a desire to learn beyond just studying for exams. Many Japanese parents say that the *yutori* regime has helped their children think more critically and engage more deeply with their school material. Some Japanese youngsters do have more free time to rest, hang out, or spend time with their families. There are also signs that *yutori* has boosted academic performance. In recent aptitude tests, Japanese children from fifth through ninth grade scored higher across all twenty-three subjects (apart from seventh-grade social studies and math).

Where Japan goes from here is hard to say. In 2007, the then prime minister, Shinzo Abe, proposed increasing classroom hours by 10 percent, saying Japanese children needed to work harder. But in the same breath he acknowledged the need to limit the toil and the competitive heat in schools. His bet hedging points up the tension felt by parents and politicians around the world: knowing instinctively that children have limits but feeling that there is no option but to push them harder and harder.

Whether Japan finds the right balance remains to be seen, but in the meantime the *yutori* spirit is blowing across East Asia, with other countries looking for ways to ease pressure in the classroom. South Korea has loosened up its education system to foster creativity, encourage a wider range of learning, and reduce the emphasis on test scores for college entry. Across East Asia, private academies are springing up to offer pressure-free education.

Even some of the region's most achievement-conscious schools are taking a leaf out of the *yutori* book. Consider the mighty Minjok Leadership Academy, a boot camp for South Korea's aspiring masters of the universe. Clad in the classic *hanbok* garments, pupils must speak only English from 7 a.m. to 6:30 p.m., learn traditional instruments, and master tae kwon do or archery. But even into this Confucian stronghold, the headmaster, Lee Don-Hee, a former Korean minister of education, has brought a little light, introducing unsupervised exams and a student council. He has also cast the admissions net far wider. Why? "Because I wanted to find talented youths, not geniuses who had been created by their parents," he says. Lee uses the sort of *yutori* rhetoric that was heresy not so long ago in Korea: "The school tries its best to help students enjoy learning . . . and not to have them study under pressure."

Minjok pupils welcome the change. Dong-sun Park, a gangly seventeen-year-old who hopes one day to be the Korean Richard Branson, believes that academic pressure is a double-edged sword. "Some pressure is good, but if you are always learning under a lot of pressure, then that is not true learning," he says. "You can only do your best when you feel you are working for yourself rather than for the teachers or your parents."

That sentiment animates the conference in Palo Alto where I met Marilee Jones. It is hosted by a group whose name needs no explanation: Stressed Out Students (SOS). A number of schools

in this part of California have worked with SOS to ease the
burden on children, with reforms ranging from cutting homework and testing less to rescheduling exams to remove the need
to study over the holidays. After the conference, I head off to visit
a school that has taken a more radical step.

Saratoga is the kind of town that gives California its reputation as the land of milk and honey. Large houses, many with
swimming pools in the backyard, line the leafy streets. Saratoga
High is a one-story building arranged around a courtyard with
blue metal picnic tables nestling in the shade of imposing California redwoods. The parking lot outside is jammed with shiny
new Mercedes, Audis, and 4x4s. Yet this is not some finishing
school for lazy, rich kids. Saratoga High has a track record as an
academic pressure cooker, notching up some of the best SAT
scores in the United States and sending almost every pupil to
university, many of them in the Ivy League. The school's most
famous alumnus, Steven Spielberg, a gifted filmmaker but a less
than stellar student, described his years here as "hell on Earth."

That was in the 1960s, but by the 1990s the pressure was
starting to take a toll on more than just the daydreaming mavericks. Pupils were coming down with stress-induced illnesses or
turning to medication just to get through the school day. Exam
marks remained high, but something deeper, something harder
to measure, was being lost in the race to be an alpha student.
"Call it a lack of spark or creativity or joy," says one teacher. "You
could see it in the kids' faces."

To ease the pressure, Saratoga adopted the controversial block
schedule in the 2005–6 academic year. That means that instead of
slicing the day into fifty-minute periods, pupils now attend
classes lasting ninety-five minutes. With fewer classes crammed
into the average day, a morning break has also been introduced.

The aim was to slow down the pace a little, to open up time for the children to catch their breath and delve more deeply into the course material.

Though schools across North America have embraced the block schedule, it has many critics. Some say it leaves too little time to cover course material or that it leads to discontinuity because teachers no longer see their classes every day. Several studies have shown that the block schedule fails to boost academic results. But there are schools that do benefit from it, and Saratoga is one of them.

Most of the teachers here welcome the new regime. Jenny Garcia, who teaches physics and chemistry, thinks both staff and students are more relaxed and therefore more productive. "As teachers, we have more time to grade papers, and the kids have more time to unwind during the day, to get their heads in the game," she says. "I find I spend a lot less time ramping them up because we spend less time 'starting class' and more time learning than on the traditional schedule."

On the humanities side, teachers detect a richer, more creative approach to coursework. "Because the pace is less boom-boom-boom, the quality of class discussions is absolutely up," says Jason Friend, an English teacher. "Instead of just touching the surface, we get deeper into things, and the kids clearly enjoy it more."

With more time per class, Kim Andzalone, a U.S. history and film teacher, finds it easier to climb off her soapbox and let the children take control. "Our discussions are richer and broader because the kids now have time to digest the material, to ask questions, to internalize the ideas rather than just sit there being lectured at," she says. Andzalone recently staged a mock debate about slavery. The pro-slavery group argued cogently that "wage slaves" in the nineteenth century were worse off than were real slaves on the cotton plantations of the Deep South. "It's amazing what they come up with," she says. "They just need the time to think outside the box."

Surveys show that most students at Saratoga High are pleased with the new regime. Marks remain high, but stress is down. A quarter of the students say they are sleeping more at night. My own straw poll bears this out. During lunch break, Jenny, a twelfth-grade student, tells me that the rhythm of her day has changed for the better. "I feel less like a rat running on someone else's treadmill now," she says. "I get more out of school." Her friend Susan agrees. "I'm doing better this year because things are more relaxed," she says.

Richard, a philosopher jock, uses a sports analogy to explain the wisdom of the block timetable. "It's just like football or basketball," he says. "To perform at your maximum level, you need pressure, whether it's from the clock or other people's expectations, but if you're always under pressure, if you're always racing the clock, then you freeze up, you start making mistakes, you don't maximize your potential as a player."

To be sure, Saratoga remains a very competitive school. The block schedule may have taken some of the heat from the daily routine, but the pupils still feel a lot of pressure to bring home top marks and win entry into a prestigious university. No amount of fiddling with the schedule can alter that. John, an eleventh-grade student, puts it this way. "Most of us still feel that expectation to be the best from our parents, or society, or even from ourselves," he says. "For a lot of kids here it's still all about 'how do I get into an Ivy?'"

It is a question that torments ambitious children and parents everywhere because there is no simple answer. In many countries, the university application process is clouded by a bewildering randomness. You can spend seventeen years assembling the perfect résumé and still fail to get into the college of your dreams. Princeton rejected four out of every five class valedictorians who applied in 2006. A year later, a twelfth-grade student in New York e-mailed me this dispatch from the front line in the battle to secure a place in the "right" college: "I think there is WAY too much college hype right now. Kids are going crazy trying to be a part of every club and every activity, and the results this year have shown that there really is no magic formula. Valedictorians are being rejected, while the lazier kids are getting into every school they apply to. The entire thing is a crapshoot. I think people should relax and only do what they truly enjoy. This way they'll develop actual useful skills that they can take with them to college, whether that is an Ivy or not." Across the United States, high-school teachers and guidance counselors report that more students are starting to look beyond the big names to find the universities that fit them best, rather than those that make their parents most proud.

That is not easy, though, because one of the central nostrums of modern parenting is that the pot of gold at the end of the rainbow is winning entry to an elite university. Nothing makes a parent preen more than announcing that Junior will be starting at Oxford or Yale in September. And children pick up on that from early on. A nursery helper in Seattle recently asked the kids in her care to define happiness. One boy put up his hand in a flash. "Getting into Harvard," he shouted. He was four.

But even if famous universities deliver pedigree and bragging rights, are they always worth the effort and money that goes in to applying to and attending them? Maybe not. At brand-name colleges, professors often spend more time researching than teaching.

And classes can be enormous. Many smaller, less prestigious colleges offer a first-rate education. In the 2005 edition of *How College Affects Students*, two professors of higher education, Patrick Terenzini of Penn State and Ernest Pascarella of the University of Iowa, found little evidence that attending an elite university "had any net impact in such areas as learning, cognitive and intellectual development, the majority of psychosocial changes, the development of principled moral reasoning, or shifts in attitudes and values." In other words, by the time a child reaches college age, what university she actually attends makes little difference in how she will come out after graduation.

What about earning power? Surely a degree from a blue-chip university is the ticket to a bulging pay packet and a prestigious job. Well, that may be true in more rigid cultures such as South Korea, but it seems to be increasingly less so elsewhere. Mixing with the movers and shakers of the future at Cambridge or Cornell has its benefits, but in the modern economy, where people change jobs at the drop of a hat and new fields spring up all the time, performance counts for more than do old-boy networks. At last glance only seven CEOs from the top fifty Fortune 500 companies earned their undergraduate degrees at an Ivy League college. Again, what seems to count more is the kind of person you are when you arrive on campus rather than the campus itself. One well-known study by Stacy Dale, a researcher with the Andrew Mellon Foundation, and Alan Krueger, an economist at Princeton, concluded that the chief predictor of higher income in later life was whether a student applied to a prestigious university, not whether he actually attended one. "Essentially, what we found was the fact that you apply to those kinds of elite places means that you are ambitious, and you'll do well in life wherever you go to school," says Dale. Think about that for a moment: if you are ambitious, you'll do well in life "wherever you go to school." That means the main purpose of our education system, and our main aim as parents, should not be to maneuver children into a chart-topping university. It should be to raise imaginative, disciplined, dynamic children with a lust for learning and life.

The obsession with brand-name education may also be misplaced in the years leading up to college. A 2006 study from Melbourne offers relief to parents worried that failure to attend an elite private school will doom their children to a life of Mcjobs. The Australian researchers found that students from comprehensive state schools were more successful in their first year of university than were those from private or selective schools. Studies in Britain and other countries suggest that graduates from the state system also go on to earn better degrees. There are various theories for this. One is that because state schools are less prone to hothousing and micromanaging, their pupils learn the self-discipline and self-motivation that are essential in university and later in the workplace.

To escape the high-pressure, exam-mad approach to education, many parents are yanking their children out of school altogether. Just look at the worldwide trend toward homeschooling. Statistics are patchy, but millions of children in the West are now schooled—or unschooled, as some would say—in the family home. The number of home-educated children in England has tripled since 1999. Parents choose homeschooling for lots of reasons, ranging from religious belief to safety, but many embrace it as a way to escape the tyranny of tests, timetables, and targets.

That was the spur for John and Margaret Burke. Their son, Sean, was bringing home decent marks from his state school in Manchester, England, but they disliked the obsession with exams. So in 2001 Margaret quit her job as a supermarket manager and began homeschooling him. Like most home educators, the Burkes let their son take the lead much of the time. When the train whistling past their local park caught his attention, Margaret and Sean spent a few days investigating the history of engines. This sparked an interest in the Industrial Revolution, which led to a family visit to look at paintings by J.M.W. Turner in a local art gallery. Sean has fond memories of his "school" days. "I remember the excitement of always asking questions and looking for the answers," he says. "I learned that having the freedom to follow your curiosity is a healthy thing."

It was not all plain sailing. In the early days, the Burkes fell victim to one of the paradoxes of homeschooling: a bold step taken in the name of freedom can end up exposing the child to a lot more parental monitoring. "Even though I took Sean out of school to get away from the assessment culture, I found myself constantly assessing him in my mind, because we were always together and the responsibility for his education was now suddenly all on me," says Margaret. Some homeschoolers never quite overcome this, but many, including the Burkes, do. "Eventually, I backed off, and we found the right balance," says Margaret.

Studies have shown that homeschooling produces self-starters who love to learn and handle themselves well socially—just the sort of people to thrive in a university tutorial and later in the New Economy. Sean is now studying business at a leading British university and has just landed a summer job with a biotechnology company. "Being educated at home means that you aren't being measured all the time, so you don't worry about making mistakes or looking silly," he says. "That lets you develop the confidence to take chances and try things out."

Home education offers some useful lessons for all parents. As we have already seen, what children really need from us is time and encouragement. That does not mean running the home like an academic boot camp, with every moment scrutinized for its teaching potential. It does mean lots of conversation and curiosity about the world. Often the simple stuff works best. A family trip to investigate butterflies at the local science museum, say, or talking to elderly neighbors about how life was when they were young. Study after study shows that just chatting with children builds their confidence, vocabulary, and articulateness. A child is more likely to fall in love with reading if he gets a regular bedtime story from Mom or Dad rather than a download from iTeddy.

To most parents, though, finding a good school is always going to be more appealing than schooling at home. This poses a big question: what constitutes a good school? Most of us know one when we see one. In a good school, pupils read for fun, not just for homework; they carry on debating ideas raised in the classroom after the bell rings; they come home bursting to tell their parents what they have learned during the day; they challenge teachers rather than scribble down their every word as gospel. In a good school, children walk into class with alacrity instead of creeping in unwillingly like a snail.

The lesson from around the world is that such qualities cannot be measured by test scores, nor can they be conjured by cranking up the academic workload and competition in the classroom. That does not mean that pressure and testing are all bad. Studies show that children from disadvantaged backgrounds benefit when school gives them the sort of structure and academic push that is often lacking on the home front. And even children from high-achieving, highly scheduled households need order, discipline, and direction. Exams can focus minds in a healthy way, especially in the later years. Even rote learning has a role to play: how else can you master the times tables or irregular verbs in foreign languages? The best schools find a happy medium, marrying mastery of the basics with setting children free.

That is not an easy balance to strike, but more schools are trying. The last stop on my educational tour is the state-funded St. John's School and Community College. Set in the small English town of Marlborough, it caters to 1,500 pupils aged eleven to eighteen from a range of social backgrounds. In 2001, Patrick Hazlewood, the headmaster, decided that an obsession with tests and targets was strangling both students and teachers. So he took the radical step of throwing out the National Curriculum altogether. In its place, pupils now study modules that take a single theme and spread it across all the traditional subjects at the same time. During the Going Places module, for instance, the children might study velocity in Math, the environmental impact of airplanes in Science, and the travel writings of Paul Theroux or Bill Bryson in English. At every step, the aim is to build up what the school refers to as the five "competences": managing information, managing change, relating to people, global citizenship, and learning how to learn. Exams are kept to a minimum.

The most important part of the change at St. John's is that, much as in a Reggio preschool, students lead the way. Teachers make sure the class covers certain key concepts, but otherwise the pupils decide how to explore them, writing their own curriculum as they go. What this adds up to is a revolution that may point the way for other schools in the twenty-first century. Traditional schooling is built on the idea of a pupil who can be taught, inspired, and measured in a way that suits the teacher and the bureaucrats at the Department of Education. St. John's has turned that paradigm on its head. "For us the needs of the students, their learning, comes first," says Hazlewood. "Ultimately our aim is to transform the student from a person taking exams into a lifelong learner." Some teachers found the switch daunting, but most have welcomed it like manna from heaven. "When you see children rediscover the joy of learning, it's an incredible feeling," says Kathy Pollard, who has taught Technology for thirty-seven years, fifteen of them at St. John's. "This is what I got into teaching for in the first place."

The new regime seems to be working. Even though St. John's no longer follows the National Curriculum, its pupils pass the standardized exams with flying colors. Marks are up 10–15 percent across the board. The school debate team recently reached the last six in the British championships, edging out Marlborough College, the celebrated private school on the other side of the hill, along the way. Inspectors describe St. John's as "outstanding" and its pupils as confident learners who work well alone or in teams. Bullying and bad behavior have largely vanished, and the incidence of ADHD is also very low. Families now move here from all over Britain so that their children can attend St. John's, and some 450 schools around the country are now following its lead. In 2007, England announced plans to slim its National Curriculum to give teachers more freedom to tailor learning more closely to their students.

I come to visit St. John's on a gray, drizzly morning in late spring. The school building is a dismal box of postwar brick and concrete, but inside the mood is pure sunshine. There is a buzz that is missing from so many other schools around the world. Rather than creep unwillingly to their lessons, the pupils cluster outside their classrooms, eager to get started. Sometimes they chide the teachers for failing to arrive on time. While waiting to sign in, I overhear three pupils chatting about their last class. "I don't think we will ever stop global warming as long as we have a capitalist economy," declares one. "No, I disagree," says her friend. "Consumer power can actually change things—just look at how Fair Trade products are taking off." The third child nods his head. "Maybe we should get the class to debate this tomorrow," he says.

I join an English lesson for eleven- to twelve-year-olds. With rows of desks facing the front and projects pinned to the walls, the classroom looks very conventional, but the lesson is anything but. The children have just started a module entitled "Forest" and are planning a trip to the nearby woods. Four pupils orchestrate things from the front of the room. The rest are divided into teams each charged with handling one aspect of the planning, such as charting the route to the forest, listing what the class will learn, or drafting the letter explaining the expedition to the parents. The teacher stands to one side, tossing in suggestions from time to time but essentially leaving the kids to run the show.

The team writing the letter to the parents is working on the second draft. Tom sounds like an editor in the making. "This isn't working," he says. "We need to make it more persuasive, more parent-friendly." What does he mean?

"Well, we could start by using bigger words that sound more adult, like 'educational purpose' instead of just 'aim.'" Emma chimes in: "I think we need to give them more details about what we're going to do in the forest." That list already includes identifying birds and plants, measuring tree heights, and staging a scene from *A Midsummer Night's Dream*.

At a desk two rows back, the children planning the route huddle around a map. They use fingers and a ruler to work out the distance, and then calculate the time it will take to walk. Josh notices that the route crosses the busy A4 road and decides to go over to alert the team drafting the parents' letter.

"We need to warn the parents about the A4," he tells them. "Maybe we could get a parent to come along." Tom chews his pencil for a moment. "Do you think we should mention that near the top of the letter or at the end?" he asks. "I think it might work better at the end rather than scaring them off at the beginning." The others agree and start hammering out the wording.

After the class, I chat with a random selection of twelve-year-old pupils. They all talk with such enthusiasm about how much fun it is to come to school and learn that part of me wonders if they have been coached. Yet just a few minutes in their company is proof enough that they really mean it. Those who have transferred to St. John's from other schools are especially delighted to have left behind the endless testing and the cutthroat competition it fostered. "We used to spend months revising for exams," says Ella. "It was so much pressure, and it was horrible and boring."

Joey concedes that some pressure and a little friendly competition can bring out the best in a pupil. "We're putting together Forest Survival Guides as part of our homework for the Forest module, and I'm working really hard on mine because I want it to be the best," he says. "And I'm working hard on mine because I want it to be the best, too," says Ella, with a smile. Even so, competition is not an end in itself at St. John's, not least because so much of the work is done in teams. "At our old school it was so competitive that you did all the revision alone and it was every person for themselves," says Joey. "It's way better here because when you're not always thinking about marks and beating other people you can help each other out, and you can concentrate on learning and exploring what interests you."

Not long ago, the seventh years spent time studying the Ancient Greeks. When this sparked comparisons with the Romans, the teacher invited a pupil from twelfth year to give the class a Latin lesson. Joey was blown away. "I liked it so much that I really want to do Latin when I'm older," he says. "I love learning how to speak it and reading stories about the Romans." He and a few other children plan to set up a Latin club next year.

So what have we learned from our education tour? The first lesson is that there is no one-size-fits-all recipe for the ideal school: You cannot transplant the Finnish education system to Italy or Canada or Korea, because it is an expression of Finnish culture. Schools always vary from country to country and even from community to community. But there are some basic principles that seem to hold true across the board: too much testing, toil, and competition eventually backfires; children learn best when given time and freedom to explore topics that interest them in ways that stretch the imagination; project work that embraces multiple subjects at the same time can deliver richer learning; play and pleasure are an integral part of education; teachers need to be well trained and then trusted to do their job without having to explain and quantify their every move; schools need more power to devise their own curriculum and schedules. In education, as in every other aspect of childhood, we need to step back a little and learn to let things happen rather than try to force them.

At the moment, many parents cannot afford, or even find, a school that ticks these boxes, which is why politicians must start hauling state education into the twenty-first century. To summon the courage and the inspiration, they could do worse than to spend a day with the children at St John's. Perhaps the most uplifting news from this English state school is that the pupils' enthusiasm ripples beyond the classroom. All of them talk fondly to me of homework—how they are offered a choice of assignments that really push the imagination and are given days or even weeks to complete them. Instead of math worksheets, for instance, they might be asked to measure all the rooms in their houses and draw them to scale. Or they might read about the wives of Henry VIII and present their findings in a Tudor tabloid newspaper.

"It's quite good fun because we don't get too much homework, and what we get really makes you think about what you're learning in a new way," says Ed. "It lets you be creative."

Ella agrees. "Homework is more like a hobby here," she says.

I can hardly believe my ears. These are twelve-year-olds singing the praises of homework. Clearly St. John's is doing something right.

SEVEN

Homework:
The Sword of Damocles

I like a teacher who gives you something to take home to think about besides homework.
—Lily Tomlin, comedian

It sounds like a schoolboy fantasy. A math teacher assigns homework over the summer vacation, the class groans, but then one pupil decides to take a stand. He doesn't fight back by slashing the tires on the teacher's car or toilet-papering his house. No, he hires a lawyer and goes to court.

Except this is no fantasy. In 2005, Peer Larson sued his math teacher at Whitnall High School in Greenfield, Wisconsin, for ruining his summer break with three calculus projects. "There's not supposed to be any work when someone is on vacation," explained the then seventeen-year-old. "It should be my time to pursue whatever I like without having the school following me when it's not even the school year." Larson's father, Bruce, backed him all the way. "These students are still children, yet they are subjected to increasing pressure to perform to ever-higher standards in numerous theaters," he said. "Come summer, they need a break."

The Larsons became cult heroes, with journalists clamoring for interviews and children in Greenfield wearing T-shirts bearing photographs of them. The school board was less amused. It denounced the lawsuit as a waste of time and money, insisting that teachers had the right to assign homework whenever they wanted. Eventually, a judge agreed, and the case was thrown out of court.

By filing a lawsuit, the Larsons went too far, yet their crusade touched a chord in the United States and beyond. Why? Because most children, not to mention many parents, know what it's like to feel oppressed by homework. Not everyone attends a school like St. John's. "You feel like you work hard at school, then you come home and work hard there—it's like it never ends," says Elliot Marsh, an eleven-year-old in Palo Alto, California. "I even get nightmares about not finishing my homework."

My son is three years younger, and yet his take-home assignments hang over our family like the sword of Damocles. We cut short family outings so that he can complete them on time. Sometimes he ends up racing to finish his homework over breakfast or late at night. Sometimes there are tears. And it will only get worse. Parents with older children can end up overseeing—or even doing—three or four hours of homework a night. A recent cover story in *Time* magazine captured the mood of weary desperation that reigns in many households around the world. The title: *The Homework Ate My Family—Kids Are Dazed, Parents Are Stressed.*

Such resentment is not new. Homework has been a bone of contention since public schooling took off more than a century ago. Early critics warned that it fostered disobedience by taking children away from church and parents, or that it eroded time for play and disrupted family life. In the 1890s, an American war hero and father of two denounced homework as "the means of nervous exhaustion and agitation, highly prejudicial to body and mind." A few years later, the *Ladies' Home Journal* called it "A National Crime at the Feet of American Parents." The backlash was even more virulent across the Atlantic. In 1911, a pupil strike spread to hundreds of British schools, with children marching in sixty-two towns to demand shorter hours in the classroom and an end to homework.

When academics began to question the educational value of taking schoolwork home, officialdom stepped in. By the early twentieth century, two-thirds of U.S. public urban school districts had either curbed or banned homework altogether. Homework came back into vogue after the Second World War amid fears that Soviet whiz kids were pulling ahead, then waned across the West in the 1960s and 1970s, before rebounding in the mid-1980s, partly driven by fears that hard-toiling Asians were stealing a march. Today, the statistics give an uneven picture. Some surveys suggest that the average homework load for U.S. children has risen by half since the early 1980s. Other studies point to a slight fall. Either way, statistical averages conceal big differences between schools. What seems clear is that in affluent areas, where the culture of competition is most pronounced, homework is up sharply. Another step change is that even the youngest students now get homework. Britain has prescribed one hour a week for five-year-olds since the mid-1990s.

Why the surge? One reason is that politicians see homework as a way to boost academic standards, or at least goose test scores. Many teachers see take-home assignments as proof that they are doing their job well. Parental anxiety is also part of the picture. With one eye on exam results and college admission and another on keeping their children out of trouble and harm outside school, some parents pester teachers to pile on the assignments. Homework has become both a status symbol and a safety valve in many high-achieving homes. We tout the nightly load as proof that our children's schools mean business. And with the classroom out of reach, homework gives the twenty-first-century parent a chance to take control, overseeing assignments from start to finish, and even treating them as our own. That third-grade art project looks like the work of a graphic designer because it is (Mom has her own company). In some well-to-do neighborhoods in North America, homework arrives at the school after the children do.

Greta Metzger often tidies up, or finishes off, the assignments her ten-year-old son brings home from his school in Munich, Germany. "I know he can do it, so sometimes I'll just correct his spelling and complete the last few sums for him," she says. "I've actually got quite good at copying his handwriting."

But even as we toil over our children's mathematics worksheets, or sacrifice Sunday to help them finish that five-page book report, a nagging question tugs at the back of the mind: is this really worth it?

Once again, the short answer is that no one knows for sure. Research into the effect of homework on academic performance has turned up mixed results. One study of six thousand American students found that those who started doing an extra thirty minutes of math homework each night at the age of eleven were well ahead of their peers by the time they hit fifteen or sixteen. On the other hand, when two Penn State professors compared math and science marks of children in fourth, eighth, and twelfth grade in fifty countries, they found the opposite effect. Their conclusion: "It almost seems as though the more homework a nation's teachers assign the worse the nation's students do."

When it comes to younger children, the case for homework seems most shaky. International studies suggest that it has little or no effect on academic performance for under-elevens. "Younger children tend to absorb information much more easily at six or seven, whereas older children need to work at learning, so homework is only really useful later on," says Peter Tymms, director of the Curriculum, Evaluation and Management Centre at Durham University.

Some would abolish homework altogether. They argue that weighing down children with assignments that turn the home into a war zone can backfire by putting them off school. They also point to studies showing that playing sports, gardening, or even performing household chores may help children more than hitting the books every afternoon and evening. Remember the charge that logging long hours in front of electronic screens is helping to fuel the global surge in myopia? Well, some put part of the blame on spending too much time indoors hunched over textbooks and not enough time running around outside in the sunlight. One study of fourteen- to eighteen-year-old boys in Israel found that those taught in schools that put a heavy emphasis on reading religious texts had myopia rates of 80 percent, compared to 30 percent in the state schools.

Even the most fervent advocates of homework now agree that it is subject to the law of diminishing returns. Many recommend a daily maximum of ten minutes per grade level. That means no more than forty minutes per night for a child in fourth grade (ages eight to nine) and two hours for a high-school student—far less than many pupils in ambitious schools bring home nowadays.

Experts are also rethinking what kind of homework is most effective. Most recommend shelving the busy work—the math worksheets and spelling lists that are easy to mark—in favor of projects that encourage children to think deeply and stretch their imaginations. That might mean devising a math quiz to test fellow pupils, studying ways to cut carbon emissions in the family home, or designing a poster about a pet or favorite toy.

Are the warnings from experts making waves in the real world? You bet they are. Spurred by mounting complaints from frazzled children and parents, and reassured by the growing body of evidence marshaled in books such as *The Homework Myth: Why Our Kids Get Too Much of a Bad Thing,* schools around the world are starting to reduce and reinvent homework. Many U.S. school districts are once again drawing up guidelines for limiting the assignments that can be sent home. To give students more leisure time with parents and friends, a number of schools in south Australia have banned homework outright. The Central Board of Secondary Education in India has done the same for first and second grades. Some primary schools in Britain have replaced sums and spelling worksheets with family activities such as museum trips or baking bread. Across Asia, elite schools have been reducing homework or banning it altogether. At the Yayuncun Number 2 Kindergarten in Beijing, staff fend off parental pressure to load up the children with after-school assignments. "Sometimes, we have to lecture the parents about what's appropriate for their kids," says Feng Shulan, the principal. "I tell parents it's also important for them to simply spend time with their kids. I tell them it's important for the kids to be happy."

To find out what all of this means for children, I set off to investigate a few schools on the front line of the homework war. The first is the Chinese International School (CIS) in Hong Kong, which caters to 1,406 pupils aged four to eighteen. Teachers here used to shovel on the homework. To the high-achieving

Chinese and expatriate parents who pay the fees, a satchel bulging with books was a reassuring sight. Five years ago, though, it became clear that many of the children were overloaded, toiling over assignments till past midnight and then coming to class tired and inattentive. So the school revamped its homework policy, imposing strict limits on the number of hours allowed per subject. The change was aimed at older pupils, but the ethos has also trickled down into the primary years. For many children, the take-home workload has fallen by 30 percent.

The school also discourages private tutoring, unless the child has a real problem keeping up. At parent-teacher evenings, staff stress the need for children to have time away from the books. "We wanted to counteract the widespread belief that by working longer and harder on academics you'll always achieve better results," says Daniel Walker, the deputy head teacher. "When it comes to homework, there are limits to what makes sense for children, because they need balance in their lives."

Not all the parents agree. Some still lobby for more homework or shuttle their children straight from the school gate to the nearest tutoring clinic. But a cultural shift has taken place within the school. Recently, the year 11 class did what would once have been unthinkable: they complained that the homework burden had crept up again. "They were right—it had got out of hand—so we cut back," says Walker. "We don't want kids overburdened and staying up into the early hours of the morning to finish their schoolwork."

The less-is-more regime has paid off. CIS is now among the top-ranked international schools in Hong Kong for exam results and university acceptance. The children also seem more relaxed, more willing to make room in their schedules for activities that do not involve leaning over a desk. A bulletin board near the main office lists a rich array of extracurricular pursuits: tae kwon do, tennis, sailing, gym, indoor soccer, cooking, table tennis, track, a literary society. "I love that when I'm playing squash my friends in other schools are still doing homework," says David Wei, a fifteen-year-old with a goofy grin. "Especially since my marks are good, too."

At morning recess, the CIS courtyard is an anthill of activity, with boys chasing soccer balls around and girls skipping or playing tag. Voices and laughter echo up through the open staircases on the side of the school building. Walker looks down on the scene and smiles. "There's more joie de vivre here now, and certainly more than you find in the high-pressure schools where they pile on the homework," he says. He feels his pupils have also become more open-minded, more willing to break free from parental expectations and choose their own career paths.

The curb on homework has even made CIS a bit of a role model. Schools from mainland China are coming to investigate. Many Hong Kong parents, both Western and Chinese, now choose CIS for its emphasis on giving children time and space to breathe outside the classroom. The school's waiting list is longer than ever. "On every level, the results speak for themselves," says Walker.

Other schools have found different ways to tame the homework problem. Cargilfield is a prestigious private academy for children aged three to thirteen, set in the rolling woodland outside Edinburgh, Scotland. In 2004, the school made headlines by banning set homework. The idea was to free the children (as well as their parents) from the chore of plodding through assignments that often contributed little to their learning—and to give them more time to relax and have fun.

Cargilfield is no slackers' paradise—the school day can extend to 6 p.m., and teachers are on hand to offer extra help in the lead-up to exams. Banning homework was meant to encourage the children to take control of their own private study outside classroom hours. But the bottom line is that the workload is down, and the payoff is similar to that at CIS in Hong Kong. Exam marks in math and the sciences have risen as much as 20 percent since formal homework was abolished. The children also have more time to unwind. Enrollment in after-school clubs, such as chess, soccer, and kayaking, has surged. "It's very much to do with children enjoying themselves when they are young and not turning their day into one long chore," says John Elder, the Cargilfield headmaster. "We are here to enjoy ourselves, and we never have the chance again to relive our youth."

Both CIS and Cargilfield are posh private schools. Does cutting homework pay the same dividends in the public sector? To find out, I drop in at Vernon Barford, my old junior high school in Edmonton, Canada. When I was here in the early 1980s, homework was never a talking point. We had assignments to do at home but spent most of our time outside school playing sports or messing around. By 2006, however, Vernon Barford had reached homework gridlock. Every morning a parade of children, among them straight-A students, filed through the principal's office en route to a detention for failing to finish the latest diorama or Bristol board. And every day parents were phoning to complain about the workload. "We'd all been under this illusion that lots of homework creates good study habits for the future," says Judy Hoeksema, a longtime math teacher at Vernon Barford. "But eventually we realized it wasn't making much difference."

In the summer of 2006, the staff got together to find a solution. To break the habit of giving homework for the sake of it, they drew up a list of questions to ask before handing out any assignment: Will this boost learning and fire the imagination? Is it a reasonable amount? How much homework are my colleagues giving today? Teachers also undertook to give children a choice of assignments, with pupils even encouraged to come up with questions for the class to tackle.

The net result was that the average homework load fell by half, with ninth-grade students now getting forty-five minutes a day, grades seven and eight, thirty minutes. Parents are free to ask for more but none have, even though some grumble on the quiet that there is not enough now. Teachers welcome the new regime, because they have more time to prepare for lessons and come up with creative take-home assignments. Average marks are up 4 percent, a large jump given how well the school was already scoring. "I didn't think the marks could go up any more, but they did," says Stephen Lynch, the principal. But the change goes much deeper than higher marks. The atmosphere at the school has shifted. Relations among pupils, staff, and parents are less strained. The children also seem more engaged.

Mike Hudson, an eighth-grade pupil, is pleased that the workload is down. "I don't have so many fights with my mom about getting homework done," he says. He puts the extra free time into skateboarding with his friends. "It's a better balance now between school and the rest of my life," he says. "I also sleep in more on the weekends."

Other pupils welcome the move away from box-ticking assignments to projects that get the creative juices flowing. Morgan Belsek, fourteen, talks fondly of making a comic book based on the Russian Revolution for her ninth-grade Social Studies class. "To condense it down like that you really had to know your stuff," she says. "When you go over what you've learned in a deeper way like that, it bookmarks it in your mind so that later you think, 'Yeah, I remember I used that piece of knowledge this way in my project, and now I can use it another way to answer this question.'"

What are the lessons to be drawn here? The first is that homework is not all bad, especially after the elementary years. As Stephen Lynch, the principal of Vernon Barford, says: "Sometimes true understanding happens when you're working at home alone with your thoughts." But there are also limits. Homework works best when it is assigned in reasonable amounts to avoid crowding out time for rest, play, and socializing. It also needs a clear purpose beyond keeping kids busy and making teachers and parents feel good about themselves. At home, parents have to learn to ease off; that means offering guidance when asked, not volunteering answers and correcting every mistake.

Beyond the academic reasons for keeping homework on a tight rein lies the deeper question of what childhood is for. If we want it to be a time of play, freedom, and wonder, then piling on the homework is not the way to go about it. What are your happiest memories of childhood? I'll bet they don't involve slogging through pages of fractions and spelling lists. Mine are of long afternoons playing road hockey with friends in our driveway, and leaving the garage doors covered in a permanent Jackson Pollock of tennis-ball marks. Or war games in the backyard with elastic-band guns made from scraps of wood and bent coat hangers. Or playing Maze Craze, a battle game that we invented using Lego and marbles. Many of the boys with whom I shared those afternoons are still friends today. None of us can remember a single homework assignment.

Of course, when it comes to filling children's spare time with academic toil, homework is only part of the equation. The other is private tutoring, which since the 1990s has swelled into a booming global industry. When I was growing up in Canada in the 1970s and early 1980s, very few children had tutors. Those who did usually had problems at school and kept it quiet. Today, a quarter of Canadian children get some private tutoring, and surveys point to similar levels in many Western countries. In Manhattan, crack SAT tutors charge up to $1,000 an hour—and that's only if you make it to the top of the waiting list. Private consultants offer to groom children for U.S. college application from the age of eleven. One company charges $21,000 in return for securing a place at Harvard or Yale. In East Asia, tutoring is even more widespread. South Korean parents spend the equivalent of half the state budget for education on private tuition. Elite tutors in Hong Kong are household names with their own billboard and bus ads. One recently appeared in a TV commercial dressed in a traditional Chinese heroic costume. Launched by a Japanese father in the 1950s, Kumon has grown into a multinational corporation serving four million children around the world. You can even sign up for tutoring using a Web cam over the Internet. And just as other industries have outsourced to low-income economies, many of those cyber-tutors are sitting at computer terminals in India.

Unlike homework, the tutoring boom is driven mainly by parents. Some want to make up for the shortcomings of the school system, but others are just trying to nudge their children ahead of the pack. And once enough people are hiring tutors, the social pressure to follow suit can be irresistible. Janice Aurini, a Canadian expert in education businesses, argues that tutoring has been added to the ever-expanding job description of the modern parent. "It's part of the repertoire of what a good parent does now: you sign them up for piano, tennis, and soccer, and you sign them up with a tutor," she says. "Of course, the assumption that underlies all of this is that children can't be left to their own devices anymore."

Clearly a bit of professional help on the side can be a godsend for students struggling with school. But does that mean it's good for everyone? As with homework, the picture is mixed. A growing body of research suggests that tutoring is also subject to the law of diminishing returns. A 2005 study in Singapore concluded that many children from high-achieving families are now overloaded, and that "contrary to national perceptions . . . having a private tutor may be counter-productive." A similar study in South Korea found that studying the school curriculum in advance with private tutors did not boost marks at all. Its authors suggested that having a passion for learning is a more reliable indicator of academic success than is having a tutor. And common sense tells us that one way to extinguish that passion is to spend most of your spare time in a crammer.

On my way to meet the parents and children of the Forest School in Taiwan, I shared an elevator with a group of nine-year-olds on their way to an evening session at a private cram school in Taipei. They all gazed at the floor in silence, suppressing yawns, backs bent under the weight of book-stuffed knapsacks. One girl leaned against the elevator wall and closed her eyes. When the door opened, she jolted awake. Like prisoners walking to the gallows, the children bowed their heads and shuffled single file into the crammer. Talk about "creeping like a snail unwillingly."

Of course, other studies suggest—and many parents know from experience—that tutoring can help children do better on some exams. That is not surprising, given that tutors are usually judged by how many points they can add to a child's test score. As we have already seen, though, making exam performance the only measure of success can crowd out more valuable kinds of learning. The Kumon system, for instance, is largely based on rote learning with worksheets. In Taiwan, official efforts to foster broader thinking in mathematics have been hampered by private tutors teaching children to use tricks and shortcuts to come up with the right answers.

This brings us back to an earlier question: what is the point of education? If it is to deliver the highest possible exam scores, then tutoring clearly has a role to play. But if it is to encourage children to be self-starters with richly varied lives and a thirst for learning, to help them light their own academic fire, then maybe not. Tutoring can rob kids of the challenge—and the joy—of mastering a new piece of knowledge on their own. It can also mask weaknesses in the school system and create an uneven playing field among pupils.

Nevertheless, rolling back the tutoring juggernaut will not be easy. Official efforts to curb the practice in countries like Taiwan and South Korea have been thwarted by parental resistance. It is unrealistic to expect parents to renounce private tutoring when so many schools offer a substandard education and exam scores remain so important.

Yet relief might be on the way. As we start to put less stock in exams, tutoring may come to seem less essential. Like CIS in Hong Kong, more schools now discourage tutoring except in emergencies. A friend of mine attended a meeting with teachers from private secondary schools in London the other day, and all of them pleaded with the parents to keep tutoring to a minimum or shun it altogether. "It is our job to teach your children," they said. "Give your kids a break at the end of the day."

In some homes, that message is starting to sink in. Gloria Neasden hired a tutor to help her daughter, Abigail, with algebra in junior high school in San Francisco. But once she cracked it, the coaching stopped. A teacher herself, Neasden feels that tutoring can become a crutch for children. She regards it as a last resort—and a sign that the school, not the pupil, is failing to do its duty.

"There is something wrong with the education system, and probably with society in general, if our children have to spend all this time outside school hitting the books," she says. "There are only so many hours in the day, and children need some downtime."

The trouble, of course, is that in our busy, highly scheduled culture, downtime goes against the grain. If children aren't hitting the books, then the temptation is to sign them up for an extracurricular activity, or two, or three. . . .

EIGHT

Extracurricular Activities: Ready, Set, Relax!

"Oh dear! Oh dear! I shall be late!"
—*White Rabbit*
in Alice's Adventures in Wonderland

Ridgewood is the sort of place that comes to mind when people talk about the American dream. Nestled in the woodlands of northern New Jersey, this quiet, verdant town of 25,000 souls breathes affluence and well-being. The locals work hard at high-powered jobs in Manhattan, but they enjoy the fruits of their labor. Large, handsome houses sit on spacious lots dotted with swing sets and trampolines. Luxury sedans and shiny SUVs glide along wide streets lined with oak, dogwood, and maple trees. A local bumper sticker proclaims, "Ridgewood rocks!"

Move in a little closer, though, and this happy portrait starts to fray round the edges. At the school gates, around the tables in the local diner, and in the supermarket parking lot, you hear the people of Ridgewood voicing the same complaint: we may live inside a twenty-first-century Garden of Eden, but we are too damn busy to enjoy it.

Many families here are scheduled up to the eyeballs. Caught between work and home, parents struggle to find time for friends, romance, or even a decent night's sleep. Their children are in the same boat, filling the hours not already occupied by schoolwork with organized extracurricular activities. Some ten-year-olds in Ridgewood are so busy they carry Palm Pilots to keep track of their appointments. Eating dinner or doing homework in the car while traveling to swimming or the riding club is common here. One local mother e-mails an updated family schedule to her husband and two sons every evening. Another keeps her timetable pinned to the front door and the underside of the sun visor in her people carrier. With so many schedules to mesh, with so much going on, even getting toddlers together for a playdate can be a logistical nightmare. One of my favorite *New Yorker* cartoons was penned with places like Ridgewood in mind. It depicts two little girls waiting for the school bus, each holding a personal planner. One tells the other, "Okay, I'll move ballet back an hour, reschedule gymnastics, and cancel piano. . . . You shift your violin lessons to Thursday and skip soccer practice. . . . That gives us from 3:15 p.m. to 3:45 p.m. on Wednesday the 16th to play."

Unlike other towns, though, Ridgewood has taken a stand against overstuffed schedules. What started with a few moms grumbling over coffee at the kitchen table has blossomed into a mini-movement. In 2002, Ridgewood pioneered an annual event called Ready, Set, Relax! The idea is that one day a year this alpha town takes a breather: teachers assign no homework, extracurricular activities are canceled, and parents make a point of coming home early from the office. The aim is to cast off the tyranny of the timetable; to let children rest, play, or just daydream; and to give families time together that is not built around driving to the next volleyball practice or band rehearsal.

Hundreds of households put down their planners to take part in Ready, Set, Relax! and the event has inspired towns across North America, not all of them as well heeled as Ridgewood, to follow suit. To help out frazzled families, the school board in Sidney, New York, a blue-collar hamlet 130 miles northwest of here, no longer schedules any extracurricular activities or meetings after 4:30 p.m. on Wednesdays. In 2007, Amos, a small forest and mining town in northwestern Québec, held its first activity-free day based on the Ridgewood model. Marcia Marra, a mother of three who helped set up Ready, Set, Relax! in tandem with a local mental health agency, hopes the tide is turning. "People are starting to see that when their lives and their children's lives are scheduled to the hilt, everyone suffers," she says. "Structured activities can be great for kids, but things are just out of control now."

This is not a new panic. Warnings about children being overscheduled, racing from one enriching activity to the next, first surfaced in the early twentieth century. Dorothy Canfield Fisher, a popular novelist-cum-parenting-guru, warned in 1914 that American parents were stripping childhood of its "blessed spontaneity" by placing "a constricting pressure upon the children to use even the chinks and fragments of their time to acquire accomplishments which seem to us profitable." In 1931, Ruth Frankel, a pioneering cancer specialist in Canada, described how "the modern child, with his days set into a patterned program, goes docilely from one prescribed class to another, takes up art and music and French and dancing . . . until there is hardly a minute left." Her fear was that overscheduled children would grow so jaded that they would turn "desperately to the corner movie in an effort to escape ennui."

That same worry has reached fever pitch over the last generation. Books with titles like *The Hurried Child* and *The Overscheduled Child* have carved out shelf space in the library of modern
parenting. Even the kids' section has tackled the topic. In *The
Berenstain Bears and Too Much Pressure*, the famous ursine family
goes into stress meltdown because Sister and Brother Bear are
enrolled in too many after-school activities. No doubt part of this
angst springs from the general panic about childhood. But it also
seems that many children, particularly in middle-class families,
are more scheduled than ever before. A much-quoted study by
the University of Michigan's Institute for Social Research found
that, between the late 1970s and 1997, American children lost
twelve hours a week of free time. Most of that was filled with
sports and other pursuits organized by adults. Today, the average
applicant to the Massachusetts Institute of Technology lists
twelve extracurricular activities on his CV. Though comparative
studies suggest that U.S. children are among the most highly
scheduled in the world, other countries have moved in the same
direction.

Why are so many children so busy today? One reason is the
rise of the working mother. When moms stayed home, it was
easier just to let the kids play around the house. But as women
entered the workplace and the extended family dissolved, someone else had to pick up the slack on the childcare front. Extracurricular activities fit the bill perfectly, promising not only
supervision but also enrichment. Yet putting children on a tight
schedule is not always a response to the child-care gap. Many
stay-at-home moms also sign their children up for endless activities. Part of this is self-defense: when every other kid in the
neighborhood is booked solid, who is going to indulge in free
play with your unscheduled child? In our atomized, bowling-

alone society, organized activities are also a good way—sometimes the only way—to meet other parents. Nor does it help that many extracurricular activities are designed like a slippery slope: you sign up your four-year-old daughter for a weekly dance lesson, and then, before you know it, she has a class every other night and is traveling across the country to compete. Rather than rock the boat, though, we persuade ourselves that lots of scheduled activities are just what children need and want, even when they tell us otherwise. The other day I watched a mother drag her three-year-old daughter from a nursery near our house. The child was weeping. "I don't want to go to ballet," she howled. "I want to go home and play."

The extracurricular treadmill also seems like a good way to keep children out of trouble. After all, you can't smoke pot or lose your virginity when you're at lacrosse practice or in dance class. The fear of what the young might get up to if left to their own devices goes back a long way. The *Office of Christian Parents,* a Puritan manual published in 1616, warned that children with too much time on their hands ran the risk of becoming "idle . . . vile and abject persons, liars, thieves, evil beasts, slow bellies and good for nothing." During the Victorian era, defenders of child labor argued that long hours in the factories kept kids out of mischief. In the risk-averse, childcentric twenty-first century, when the urge to protect children from everything, including the modern sin of wasting time, is stronger than ever, a busy schedule makes perfect sense.

Of course, the extracurricular boom is not only fueled by anxious adults. Much of the push for supercharged schedules comes from the children themselves. The young want to be active, they want to be with their friends, they want to be like everyone else—and in our make-every-second-count culture that means being busy. When Matt Kowalski, an only child in Chicago, turned eleven, he began to resent his parents' refusal to enroll him in more than one extracurricular activity at a time. With all his friends shuttling from one club to the next, he felt left out. So he cajoled his parents into putting him on the extracurricular treadmill. Now, at fourteen, he spends more than twenty hours a week playing on three organized sports teams and acting in a drama club. "I like all the activities that I do, but sometimes I feel like I'm so busy I barely have time to sleep," he says. "I can't even blame my parents, because it's my fault that I'm overloaded."

No one is saying that extracurricular activities are bad. On the contrary, they are an integral part of a rich and happy childhood. Many kids, particularly in lower-income families, would actually benefit from more structured activities. Plenty of children, especially teenagers, thrive on a busy schedule. But just as other trappings of modern childhood, from homework to technology, are subject to the law of diminishing returns, there is a danger of overscheduling the young. When it comes to extracurricular activities, many children are getting too much of a good thing.

Or are they? Some academics argue that the overscheduled, stressed-out child is a media myth. A 2006 study on the impact of after-school sessions by the United States–based Society for Research in Child Development went off like a grenade in child-rearing circles. The researchers examined data from 2,123 American children aged five to eighteen and concluded that supercharged schedules are rare. Even more controversially, they concluded that the busiest children score high marks in school, get on well with their parents, and are less prone to dabbling in alcohol, smoking, or drugs. The media drew a stark conclusion. A headline in the *Boston Globe* declared, "The More Activities the Better."

On closer inspection, though, the study says no such thing. The lead researcher, Joseph Mahoney, an assistant psychology professor at Yale, is more circumspect than that. "This is not meant to suggest that kids involved in these activities should be pushed to do more," he explained. "This is not to argue that family time isn't important, that downtime isn't important."

And there are reasons to take his findings with a pinch of salt. As a staunch advocate of after-school programs, Mahoney has warned that too much talk of overscheduled children could give politicians the excuse they need to cut funding for such programs. Critics point out that his study was based on data gathered by people working on other research projects, that he ignored the hours spent schlepping to and from activities, and that he glossed over inconvenient bits of data suggesting that a heavy load of extracurricular activities erodes family time and boosts underage drinking. Mahoney and his team never asked children if their schedules made them tired or stressed.

At the same time, other evidence is mounting that many children are too busy. In a U.S. study published by KidsHealth.org just a few weeks before the Mahoney report, 41 percent of respondents aged nine to thirteen said they feel stressed most or all of the time because they have too much to do. Nearly 80 percent wished they had more free time. A 2006 report by the American Academy of Pediatrics warned that hurried, overscheduled children run the risk of stress-related illnesses.

Perhaps most important of all, the Mahoney report flies in the face of the experience of parents, children, teachers, and doctors around the world. In many homes the kids' busy schedules have turned family life into a never-ending race against the clock.

When U.S. cities introduced cameras to photograph drivers running red lights, the main culprits turned out to be not boy racers in souped-up roadsters but soccer moms chauffeuring children to their next appointment.

While researching her book *Unequal Childhoods: Class, Race, and Family Life,* Annette Lareau found that hyper-scheduled children from affluent families were more tired, more bored, and less likely to initiate play on their own than were less scheduled peers from low-income families. Wayne Yankus, a pediatrician in Ridgewood since the early 1980s, reckons that 65 percent of his patients are now victims of overscheduling. He says the symptoms include headaches, sleep disorders, gastric problems caused by stress or by eating too late at night, and fatigue. "Fifteen years ago it was unusual to see a tired ten-year-old," says Yankus. "Now it's common." Recently he hired a therapist to spend one day a week in his office to talk to families about the need to prune their planners.

Another drawback of overscheduling is that children, like adults, are left with no time for reflection. More urgent matters, such as "where are my shin pads, we're going to be late for soccer!" come first. When everything is scheduled, you never learn how to come up with your own ideas or make your own entertainment. Lori Sampson sees this in her own family in Ridgewood. She kept her daughter, Megan, busy from early on, shipping her from organized activity to scheduled playdate and back again. By the time her son, Michael, was born three years later, however, she was too exhausted to do the same, and so he grew up with much more free time. Today the two children, aged fourteen and eleven, are like chalk and cheese. "Megan will come to our room in the evening now and ask if she should read a book, whereas Michael will just go to his room and read," says

Sampson. "She is always looking to us for ideas and guidance on how to use her time, while he just gets on with it."

When free time is limited, achievements in structured activities—sports trophies, dance medals, music scholarships—can become the main route to winning approval. One Ridgewood teen says that she feels like a "walking résumé." "I always feel like I need to list off all the things that I do before people will respect me." This means that many kids end up enrolling in extracurricular activities simply to impress Mom and Dad. Or to burnish their résumés. "A lot of my friends do things like sports or clubs or volunteer work not because they're interested in them but because they know it looks good on a college application form," says another Ridgewood teen.

The extracurricular merry-go-round can also ensnare the family in a vicious cycle. Parents resent children for taking up so much time and costing so much money—Britons spend £12 billion a year on their children's hobbies, half of which are abandoned within five weeks—while children resent their parents' resentment. Activities overload also squeezes out time for the unscheduled, simple stuff that brings families together—relaxed conversation, cuddling, shared meals, or just hanging out together in companionable silence. Lareau also found that siblings fight more often in hyper-scheduled families. Yankus sees this disconnect in many Ridgewood households. "When the snow comes and the activities get canceled, everyone is horrified because they're suddenly stuck at home and have to deal with each other," he says. "They don't know how to get along without a schedule."

Ridgewood does not shut down completely on Ready, Set, Relax! day. Some residents regard the event as silly or patronizing. Sporting matches arranged with neighboring districts are not canceled, and the homework ban is not always as strictly enforced as it could be, especially in high school. Yet the town does feel different on the big day. With fewer soccer moms running red lights, the traffic is less frantic. People are more likely to stop and chat than exchange a brief nod before pointing to their watch and rushing off to the next appointment. To many families, Ready, Set, Relax! has been an epiphany. More than a third of those who took part in 2006 trimmed their schedules afterward.

Consider the Givens. The three children used to be enrolled in so many after-school activities that there was barely time to eat, sleep, or talk. Even though she felt overwhelmed and often found herself jogging round the supermarket to save a few seconds, Jenny, the mother, somehow felt that it was her duty to keep the family maxed out on extracurricular pursuits. "Every activity that comes up you want your kids to try, and you fear that you are failing them if they are not busy every second," she says. "You want the best for them, but always at the back of your mind, even if you don't admit it, you have the fantasy that they might turn out to be brilliant at something, that by signing them up for an activity you might uncover some latent genius."

I tell her about my suspicion that my son could be the next Picasso, and she laughs. "You see, that's how it starts, with one little thought like that," she says. "Next thing you know you're signing the kids up for every activity going."

In the Given household, that translated into an eye-watering barrage of art classes, Spanish lessons, soccer, lacrosse, softball, volleyball, basketball, baseball, tennis, scouts, and book clubs. Every weekend, the parents would split up to ferry the children to their various activities. At home, time and tempers were short. Ready, Set, Relax! came as a wake-up call. On the first night, the Givens made Mexican food and chocolate-chip cookies together.

Then they got down Cadoo, a board game that had been sitting unopened on the shelf since Christmas. The evening rolled along in a riot of laughter and cuddles. "It was an amazing revelation for all of us," says Jenny. "It was just such a relief not to be rushing off to the next thing on the to-do list."

After the Ready, Set, Relax! night, the Givens cut back, keeping only activities the children are passionate about. Today Kathryn, sixteen, does an art class, Spanish lessons, and a book club. Chris, fourteen, plays on basketball and baseball teams while Rosie, twelve, concentrates on soccer, tennis, and lacrosse. The whole family is more relaxed, and the children are all doing better at school since the cutback. "Let's play Cadoo" is now Given code for "let's hang out together." "We're all a lot calmer and closer now," says Jenny. "We eat meals together most nights and just talk more to each other."

Other Ridgewood families tell similar tales of escape from Hyper-Scheduling Hell. One mother finally screwed up the courage to pull her dance-obsessed thirteen-year-old daughter from a studio that frowned on anyone who missed a session, even for family events. Her daughter's reaction: "Why didn't you make me leave sooner?" The Carson family decided to limit the children to two or three extracurricular activities at a time instead of five or six. Eleven-year-old Kim now plays tennis and volleyball and acts in a drama club. "It's enough," she says. "My life is way better now that I have some time to just chill out. It's especially nice not spending every weekend in the car going to stuff."

Ready, Set, Relax! inspired the Tindall family to change their approach to summer holidays. With both parents working, organized activities for the two children, aged nine and eleven, are essential. But after several exhausting summers of extracurricular overload, the Tindalls changed tack. They enrolled the children in camps that do not schedule every moment of the day, and they left evenings and weekends open for resting, seeing friends, and family time. Eleven-year-old Jeff loves it. "Last summer was awesome," he says. "I did lots of cool stuff and I never got bored, but I wasn't too busy either."

The spirit of Ready, Set, Relax! has rippled out into other initiatives in Ridgewood. Every Wednesday, weather permitting, about eighty children aged four to seven are now let loose in the playground of the local primary school. This is Free Play Day and parents are confined to the sidelines. Left to their own devices, the children skip, play hide-and-seek and tag, make up stories, throw balls around, sing, and wrestle. The noise is exhilarating, the child equivalent of a Wall of Sound. To many parents it is a revelation. "It never occurred to me to do this, to just let them play like this," says one mother. "You always feel like you have to be organizing something for them, but actually you don't."

There is, of course, something absurd—even a little tragic—about having to schedule unscheduled time, yet given the world we live in, that is probably the first step for many families. And clearly the Ready, Set, Relax! movement reflects a wider rethink. In Asia, Kim Dae-jung, the former president of South Korea and winner of a Nobel Peace Prize, has talked of the need to "free young people from extracurricular activities." Elite universities are sending a similar message. The revamp of the Massachusetts Institute of Technology's application form—less emphasis on the number of extracurricular activities, more on what stokes a candidate's passion—is already paying dividends. Marilee Jones reckons the freshman class of 2007–8 contained seventy students who would have been passed over before. "A thousand kids are taken in every a year, so that's not huge, but it's a start," she said. "It sends a signal that MIT wants human beings, not human doings."

Harvard also urges incoming freshmen to check their over-scheduling ways at the door. Posted on the university Web site, an open letter by Harry Lewis, a former dean of the undergraduate school, warns students that they will get more out of college, and indeed life, if they do less and concentrate on the things that really fire their passion: "[You] are more likely to sustain the intense effort needed to accomplish first-rate work in one area if you allow yourself some leisure time, some recreation, some time for solitude, rather than packing your schedule with so many activities that you have no time to think about why you are doing what you are doing." Lewis also takes aim at the notion that everything young people do must have a measurable payoff or contribute toward crafting the perfect résumé. "You may balance your life better if you participate in some activities purely for fun, rather than to achieve a leadership role that you hope might be a distinctive credential for postgraduate employment. The human relationships you form in unstructured time with your room-mates and friends may have a stronger influence on your later life than the content of some of the courses you are taking." The title of the letter sounds like a direct challenge to the culture of hyper-scheduling. It is called: *Slow Down: Getting More Out of Harvard by Doing Less.*

Around the world, families are heeding the call. For the Kesslers in Berlin, Germany, the turning point came when the two children—Max, seven, and Maya, nine—began fighting constantly. Their mother, Hanna, decided that their busy extracurricular schedule—violin, piano, soccer, tennis, fencing, volleyball, tae kwon do, badminton, and English tutoring—was driving a wedge between them. "When I was growing up, I had lots of free time with my siblings and we got along well, and still do," she says. "When I looked at our family schedule I realized Max and Maya had almost no free time together as brother and sister because one or the other was always rushing off to some activity."

She decided to pare back the load to three extracurricular activities per child. The children do not miss the clubs they ditched, and sibling harmony seems to have broken out in the Kessler household. "We get along better now," says Maya. "We have a lot of fun together." Max rolls his eyes, Maya glares at him, and for a moment it feels like the old hostilities might resume. But then the two children dissolve into laughter. Hanna beams. "I would never go back to being busy all the time," she says.

Haunted by their own memories of extracurricular overload, other parents are resisting the urge to rush their children into structured activities too soon. David Woo, a financial analyst in Singapore, is still scarred by the piano and violin lessons foisted on him by his parents. He had talent and passed exams in both instruments to a high level, but always felt that music was a chore that kept him from playing with his toys or friends. His packed schedule of lessons, practice, and concerts hung over the family like a dark cloud. After he left home, Woo did not touch a piano or a violin for over twenty years. "The music is so beautiful, and yet for me the joy of playing was taken away because it was all so hyper-organized," he says. "I wanted to avoid that with my own children." Woo now has a daughter named Nancy. When she was very young, he played lots of classical music on the stereo at home and took her to musical events, but he refused to enroll her in lessons until she showed an interest. When she did, he put a piano in the living room and found a teacher who stressed enjoying the music more than toiling long hours to pass exams as quickly as possible. Three years later, Nancy, now ten, loves to spend her spare time messing around on the keyboard and plays little bits of Beethoven to her parents at breakfast. The pleasure she takes from the piano has even inspired Woo to start tickling the ivories again. "Nancy loves playing and practicing, and I think that's because she came to it in her own time and is not overloaded with it," he says. "It's also nice that as a family our lives don't have to revolve around her piano schedule."

What if her relatively late start means that Nancy is a prodigy manqué? Woo is not worried about that. He knows that true genius will always shine through in the end. Leonard Bernstein, for instance, started playing the piano at ten. "If Nancy turns out to be a brilliant musician, then that's great," says Woo. "If not, then at least she will reach adulthood with a genuine passion for playing and enjoying music."

Most families that ease the extracurricular load end up spending more time eating together. In a hurry-up, hyper-scheduled culture, where dining *al desko,* in front of the TV or computer, in the street, or in the car is commonplace, the family meal often falls by the wayside. One study found that a fifth of British families never eat together. The irony is that many of the benefits extracurricular activities, including homework, purport to deliver may actually by achieved through the simple act of breaking bread *en famille.* Studies in many countries show that children who have regular family meals are more likely to do well at school, enjoy good mental health, and eat nutritious food; they are also less likely to engage in underage sex or use drugs and alcohol. A Harvard study concluded that family meals promote language development even more than does family story reading. Another survey found that the only common denominator among National Merit Scholars in the United States, regardless of race or social class, was having a regular family dinner. Of course, we're talking here about meals where both parents and children ask questions, discuss ideas at length, and tell anecdotes rather than just watch TV and grunt "pass the salt."

Why does a proper family meal pay such handsome dividends? When it comes to diet, the answer is obvious. A nine-year-old boy is more likely to finish his greens, or to eat any vegetables at all, in front of his mom and dad than when he is dining alone at the computer in his bedroom. Sitting around the dinner table, taking part in conversation, also teaches children that they are loved and cherished for who they are, rather than for what they do. They learn to talk, listen, reason, and compromise—all those essential ingredients of a high EQ. Of course, no one is saying that family meals are always a bed of roses. Sometimes they are sheer hell. Gathering tired toddlers, sullen teenagers, and stressed parents around the table can be a recipe for open warfare. But then, dealing with conflict is part of life, too.

Despite its drawbacks, the family meal is coming back into favor. Launched in 2004, *Fixing Dinner,* a TV program that shows how to cook and eat together in the evening, pulls in millions of viewers in Canada, the United States, and Australia. A 2005 report by consumer research group Mintel showed an increase in the number of British families dining together. Inspired by initiatives with names like Putting Family First and National Family Night, many Americans are doing the same. For the Bochenski family in Minneapolis, pledging to have dinner together at least four nights a week went hand in hand with cutting down on extracurricular pursuits. The three teenage children gave up one activity each and are now sleeping more and doing better at school. The Bochenskis are also getting along better as a family. "The evening meal is when we reconnect by just talking and being together," says fifteen-year-old Angela. "It's a relief not to be doing things all the time."

Some accuse families like the Bochenskis of embracing communal dining and lighter schedules for the wrong reasons, for booking in downtime and family time not for their own sake but because research suggests that it might improve test scores. There may be some truth in this. No doubt some families are just trying to slow-down-with-the-Joneses, but surely that is better than an extracurricular overdose. And often families that start out de-scheduling for the wrong reasons end up carrying on for the right ones. "Whatever your original motivation is, pretty soon you realize that the most precious benefit from cutting back on extracurriculars is just having more time as a family and as individuals," says Simon Bochenski, Angela's father. "Time for the parents to be with each other is important, too."

Extracurricular overload can certainly take a heavy toll on Mom and Dad. When all of family life revolves around the children, when parents have no time on their own, then the relationship upon which the family is built can fall apart, which is bad news for everyone. Complaints about children intruding on adult time are as old as the hills. Anyone who has endured a meal with parents who only have eyes and ears for their own kids will sympathize with James Boswell's grumpy report of an eighteenth-century dinner party ruined by a couple of babies: "They played and prattled and suffered nobody to be heard but themselves. . . . Langton and his wife with a triumphant insensibility kissed their children and listened to nothing with pleasure but what they said." Such scenes are commonplace today. We've all sat at tables with infants and toddlers and struggled to exchange more than a few words with the other parents. Thanks to the extracurricular treadmill, though, children now hijack adult time long after infancy. You hear parents complaining everywhere that their time together as a couple and for seeing adult friends is sacrificed on the altar of their children's packed schedules.

Just ask Benjamin and Sally Rogers, who run a catering company in Brooklyn, New York. In the early years of parenting, they hired babysitters and went out together regularly, but that fell by the wayside as their two children's schedules grew heavier. Once a week became once a fortnight and then once a month. Michael, now twelve, and Jackie, now fourteen, were enrolled in four or five extracurricular activities each. "One day I looked at my PDA and realized Ben and I hadn't gone anywhere on our own together as a couple for over a year," says Sally. "Apart from parent-teacher nights, of course, but that doesn't count." This took a toll. The Rogers began to drift apart and argue. "Our whole lives were lived through the kids, and they were becoming the only thing we had in common," says Benjamin. "It was draining the life from our marriage." When friends in similar circumstances filed for divorce, the Rogers decided to take action.

On the first day of the school summer vacation, the whole family sat round the kitchen table and agreed that their schedule had become too childcentric and that it was time to clear some space for Mom and Dad. Michael dropped hockey—"I didn't like it that much anyway," he admits—and Jackie switched to a volleyball team that travels less. That freed up enough time for the senior Rogers to be guaranteed at least one evening a week to go out alone.

The couple is now getting along much better. "We were doing so much to give them the best childhood possible that it was actually killing our marriage," says Sally. "Giving up some activities isn't such a big deal when you consider that the alternative was divorce." The children welcome the change, too. "Mom and Dad are a lot less cranky, and you can tell they're happier to-gether," says Jackie. "It's great now that the whole family is less busy."

Michael agrees, but his spin on the joys of slimming the ex-tracurricular burden is a little more selfish. "You know what the best part about being less busy is?" he says, grabbing his iPod and heading for his bedroom. "Getting more sleep."

Of course, cutting back is just part of restoring sanity to children's extracurricular hours. Another is to rethink how the activities are run. In this hyper-competitive age, soaring expecta-tions have turned everything from piano to pottery into a battle for supremacy. One mother recently confided to me that she lies in bed at night plotting ways for her son to earn the most badges in his Boy Scouts troop.

And then there are sports—the most popular extracurricular activity of all, and the one that stokes the competitive fires like no other.

NINE

Sports: Play Ball

*What really counts is the kid and the ball, the ball and
the kid.*

—*Chico Buarque, singer-writer*

Christophe Fauviau really wanted his children to do well at
tennis. The former helicopter pilot bought the finest equipment
for his son and daughter, paid for private coaching, and attended
every match they played. As the pair climbed up the youth tennis
rankings in France, he followed them round the European cir-
cuit. After a while, though, his dedication turned into something
more sinister. Unbeknown to his children, Fauviau began spiking
their opponents' water bottles with Temesta, an anti-anxiety drug
that causes drowsiness. This went on for nearly three years, with
at least twenty rivals succumbing to fatigue and blurred vision.
Eventually, the scam came to light after one victim crashed his
car and died on the way home from a match against Fauviau's
son. In 2006, the tennis dad from hell was sentenced to eight
years in prison.

The case made headlines around the world, and sparked plenty
of editorial soul-searching. The fall of Fauviau was presented as a

cautionary tale, a warning to parents everywhere about the hazards of getting too wrapped up in their children's sports. "This case holds up a mirror to the modern parent who turns every aspect of his child's existence into a matter of life or death," intoned one French commentator. "We are all in danger of doing as Fauviau did."

That may be going a little far, but it is true that adults are more involved in children's sports—logistically and emotionally—than ever before. Organized youth sports started in schools in the nineteenth century and took off after the Second World War. In many countries, joining a local recreational team, often coached by a parent, became a rite of passage for the baby boomer generation. Nevertheless, children continued to play sports informally in their free time, not least because they used to have lots of free time. On an empty field or street, they would agree to the rules, choose the teams, and referee the game—no uniforms, no benching weaker players, no tactics boards, no adults telling anyone what to do. I spent most of my childhood playing hockey, football, soccer, basketball, and tennis without a grown-up in sight. Everything changed when a new generation of adults brought the same old cycle of rising expectations to bear on youth sports. As schools switched their focus from athletics to academics, youth teams went private—and into the hands of people like Fauviau.

And just look at the effect. In many countries, children now play sports like miniature professionals, with structured leagues, personal statistics, specialist coaching, and a win-at-all-costs ethos. Toddlers barely out of diapers are drilled in sports clinics, while children as young as four travel across the country to take on other four-year-olds. Many teams now play year-round, making their seasons longer than in the professional leagues. To whip their children's teams into shape, parents headhunt expensive coaches and hire personal trainers. According to one survey, U.S. parents now fork out more than $4 billion a year on sports training for their kids.

This is not all bad news. Organized sports can be wonderful for children, keeping them away from the Xbox and other temptations, giving them exercise, and teaching valuable lessons about teamwork, discipline, and the ups and downs of winning and losing. Private coaching can hone throwing, catching, swinging, and other skills. The problem is that many coaches and parents get carried away. How to rein in out-of-control adults is now a constant theme at the annual International Youth Sports Congress.

Around the world you find mothers and fathers trying to browbeat coaches into altering team selection, tactics, and training to suit their own children. Even college sports programs field calls from irate parents demanding to know why their son is playing soccer on the wing rather than in central midfield, or why their daughter is not yet captain of the volleyball team. "Every time my secretary tells me there's a parent on the phone, my heart sinks," says a coach at one U.S. university. "I just know they're going to give me hell for failing to recognize that their child is the next Michael Jordan."

Many parents are a menace on the sidelines. Schools complain of sports days ruined by mothers and fathers screaming at their children to go faster in the egg-and-spoon and sack races. All over the world, you see parents berating their kids for dropping the ball, missing a shot, or botching a pass. The occasional taunts I heard while refereeing soccer in the 1980s have morphed into a veritable Greek chorus of vitriol—or worse.

To call attention to the problem, Douglas Abrams, a law professor at the University of Missouri and longtime youth ice hockey coach, sends out a daily e-mail bulletin with newspaper and magazine articles chronicling the ugliest examples of adult misbehavior around the world. Here is a sample of recent stories: police are called to an under-sixteens rugby match in the English village of Churchdown when more than twenty parents start brawling after the final whistle; a mother is banned for life from attending youth basketball games in North Carolina after she jumps on an official and scratches his face and neck; a father pulls a gun on a football coach in Philadelphia because he feels his six-year-old son is not getting enough playing time. Such is the threat from overzealous parents that some youth league referees now take mobile phones onto the field to call for help if attacked, while others demand security to escort them away from games. The abuse from the crowd is now so bad in Edinburgh, Scotland, that youth soccer leagues can no longer find enough referees to officiate games.

Why does this happen? Perhaps because sports get the competitive juices pumping even more than do academics and other extracurricular activities. Or maybe some parents are desperate for their children to win athletic scholarships to offset spiraling college fees. One underlying reason, though, is that too many of us now live through our children's sporting exploits. It is no longer enough for a child to enjoy playing the game: she must be a star athlete who wins trophies and appears in the local newspaper. During the Fauviau trial, the prosecutor described the defendant as "an adult who turned his children into objects of his own fantasies of success." Fauviau himself told the court, "I felt like I was being permanently judged on how well my kids performed." Diane Wiese-Bjornstal, a sports psychology professor at the University of Minnesota, thinks many parents have come to expect their children to have the perfect sporting experience. "There is an entitlement mentality," she says. "Many parents treat their children as commodities and investments. They feel it is owed to them—playing time, scholarships, and status. It's competitive parenting lived out through our kids." In other words, youth sport is no longer about the children. It's about the adults.

And just as in every other corner of childhood, from schooling to toys, when the grown-ups come first, children lose out. Desperate to be the star athlete or to live up to their parents' expectations, or both, many kids are risking their health by taking performance-enhancing drugs. One study found that the number of U.S. high-school students using anabolic steroids has tripled since 1993. Children as young as eleven have been caught popping pills to boost their strength, speed, or endurance. That winning-is-everything ethos also seeps back into the classroom. The most recent study by the United States–based Josephson Institute of Ethics found a growing willingness among young athletes to cheat in school. The conclusion was that nowadays "for most kids, sports promotes rather than discourages cheating."

The sports overload is also causing serious injury to rising numbers of children. Kids as young as eight are turning up in doctors' offices with damaged growth plates in their shoulders and stress fractures in their backs. Or consider the case of Budhia Singh, who became the world's youngest marathoner when he began competing in races at the age of three. His exploits made headlines around the world, and he appeared in several TV commercials. He was even dubbed "the Indian Forrest Gump." But the early start soon caught up with him. In 2006, Singh was urged to stop running after doctors found that he was undernourished, anemic, and suffering from high blood pressure and cardiological stress.

Just as pushing academics too soon can backfire, so, too, can overdosing on a single sport from an early age. Throughout his golfing career, Severiano Ballesteros was plagued by back trouble caused by training too hard after an injury in his youth. Still, parents hear experts explain that it takes ten thousand hours of practice to master a sport and think, the sooner my child racks up those hours, the better. Coaches also push for early specialization because it can give a competitive advantage, especially in sports like gymnastics and ice skating. The problem is that children are better served in the long run by starting out as all-rounders, by testing their bodies in a range of ways before later concentrating on one sport. Most sports scientists discourage specialization before age thirteen. "Narrowing the variety of physical activities before an athletic foundation has been laid can risk a child's long-term development and suffocate the real potential later on," says Tommi Paavola, director of junior conditioning programs at the Elite Athletic Performance Institute in Ramsey, New Jersey. "Too often, we try to create players without creating athletes first."

Early specialization also crowds out the late bloomers. We all know the roll call of child prodigies, from Tiger Woods to the Williams sisters, steered to the top of the sporting pyramid by dedicated, self-sacrificing, even obsessive parents. But what really makes these prodigies-turned-superstars stand out is that they are the exception to the rule. For every Michelle Wie there are hundreds of other hothoused child athletes who burn out or lose interest along the way. And there are those, like tennis ace-turned-shoplifter Jennifer Capriati, who make it to the top only to self-destruct. What's more, Woods, the patron saint of sporting prodigies, was not fast-tracked as much as people assume. He played one U.S. PGA Tour event at sixteen, three at seventeen and eighteen, four at nineteen, and three at twenty, before turning pro at twenty-one. His father, Earl, made a point of not rushing his development: "I had one rule: never put him in over his head. Why subject him to that?"

The simple truth is that precocious sporting talent is no guarantee of future prowess. I know this from personal experience. I was an early walker, toddling in my eighth month and dribbling a ball a few weeks later. My father thought he had sired the new Pelé, yet I turned out to be no more than an average soccer player. The truth is that children develop at different rates, and puberty can change everything. The clumsy kid who always gets picked last in the playground at primary blossoms into a star quarterback in high school, while the nine-year-old soccer prodigy can barely keep up at fifteen. Many famous athletes have hit their stride, or found their calling, long after today's youth leagues have given up recruiting new talent. Jack Nicklaus first ventured onto a golf course in high school. Theo Walcott, the boy wonder at Arsenal, only took up competitive soccer at the age of eleven. Michael Jordan was famously cut from his high-school team; a few years—as well as inches and pounds—later he was arguably the best basketball player the world has ever seen.

Lena Nyberg, the children's ombudsman in Sweden, recently ran into the same problem with her own son. He dabbled in various sports growing up but at twelve decided to focus on soccer. The only problem was that all the clubs in Stockholm told him he was too old. "Society has a completely wrong view of how to handle childhood if you have to start a sport at five years of age and specialize by ten," says Nyberg.

Bob Bigelow, author of *Just Let the Kids Play* and himself a former NBA player, worries that many potential athletes are being frozen out by our obsession with ranking children as early as possible. Bigelow himself was still an awkward beanpole at the age of fourteen. "I would never have made it as a professional basketball player nowadays because my skills would be evaluated and found wanting by parents who think they understand the sport but don't," he says. "How many future stars are now being cut in elementary school by accountants, lawyers, butchers, bakers, and candlestick makers?"

Once the selection is out of the way, adults often make playing itself too competitive. Studies of pickup sports show that children's priority is to keep the game going and the teams fair. In organized leagues, adults are more inclined to stack the teams and give extra playing time to star players. To many parents, the score—like exam results in school—becomes more important than the game itself. No wonder some youth coaches treat their players like indentured servants. One recently cut a high-school girl from a lacrosse team in New York for attending a church retreat. An obsession with individual statistics can also take the fun out of sport. Sally Cheng, fourteen, plays competitive badminton in Beijing, China. Her father attends all her matches, delivers a sermon on the flaws in her game on the way home, and pins up her scores on the refrigerator at home. "If I have a bad game it bothers me all week, because I see it every morning at breakfast right there on the fridge door," says Sally. "Even though it's obvious I am not a world-class talent, my dad is just obsessed with me going to the Olympics one day."

Like exam marks in the classroom, setting too much store by statistics can warp priorities in sports. A hockey coach in Calgary, Canada, tells of how the best playmaker on his team of ten-year-olds suddenly stopped passing in the offensive zone. After he stripped the puck from a teammate to score himself, the coach finally asked why. The boy explained that his dad "now adds five dollars to my allowance for every goal I get."

This is not to say that keeping score or statistics is always a bad thing. Competition can be thrilling for children and spur them on to play better; it can also teach them about winning and losing. But when the final result becomes all-important, when the first question after the game is always "Did you win?" other things get crowded out. Too much competition forces children to play to their strengths rather than work on their weaknesses. League schedules are packed with so many competitive games now that there is little time left for learning the basics. Convinced that what is good for the pros is good for our children, we set them loose on adult-sized fields, courts, and rinks, where they spend less time touching the ball or puck and more time dashing around trying to impress us. "What does the routine of elite athletes aged nineteen to thirty-four have to do with coaching eight-year-olds?" says Bigelow. "It's like trying to teach algebra to kids in primary school—there are a whole lot of levels of math to get through before they're ready. It's the same in sports. You have to break them in slowly, treat them like children rather than mini-pros."

Just as it does in the classroom, the constant pressure to win, to rack up world-beating numbers, can hamper creativity. In children's play there is no such thing as a mistake, only different ways of trying things out, but once grown-ups get involved there is a right and wrong way. Children are less likely to attempt a Ronaldo step-over on the soccer field, a Sidney Crosby behind-the-back pass on the hockey rink, or a Vince Carter under-the-leg layup on the basketball court when there is a coach or parent pointing at the scoreboard and hollering about not taking unnecessary risks. Buck Showalter, a former manager of the New York Yankees, believes that children in Central America play baseball with more freedom and flair than their highly coached American peers. Scouts in other sports notice a similar trend. John Cartwright has spent years working in youth soccer development in England. A former professional player himself, he thinks the kids coming up through the ranks now are less skillful because they are overcoached and spend too little time just kicking the ball around outside with their friends. "When we were growing up, we didn't need a proper pitch, goalposts, kit, people to coach us," he says. "We threw down coats, played chaotic football in our street shoes, sharpening ball control and decision making. All the greats will have known that experience: Stanley Matthews on the streets of Stoke, Pelé growing up on the dusty roads of a railway junction in Brazil, Maradona in a deprived area of Buenos Aires. In Britain, street football has long since disappeared. In its place we have a system that simply doesn't work well enough."

Of course, most children will never grow up to be professional athletes. The best we can hope to give them is a lifelong passion for sport. But the opposite is happening. Studies in the United States show that 70 percent of children who play youth sports quit by age thirteen, with many more dropping out by the time they turn fifteen. In surveys, kids blame exhaustion, burnout, and the pressure-cooker atmosphere created by coaches and parents for taking the joy out of sports.

Even elite players perform best when they are having fun. The starting point for sporting success, for winning trophies and breaking records, for lifting spectators from their seats is the simple, childlike thrill of the game. Just look at Brazilian soccer. Though most of the country's stars are now groomed in private clubs from an early age, winning games takes a backseat to learning the game, and many kids do not start playing eleven-versus-eleven matches with full-size nets until they are twelve. They also spend long hours honing their skills and practicing tricks in the street or on the beach, far away from coaches and parents. Some of that boyish adventure comes with them onto the pitch in real games. Chico Buarque, the Brazilian songwriter, summed up the power and the glory of children playing unencumbered by adult rules, routines, and rants: "What really counts is the kid and the ball, the ball and the kid."

Behind all this lies the greatest sadness of all. In our headlong dash to raise little star athletes, we are killing off the art of playing sports for the sheer hell of it: take away the structure, the statistics, the league standings, and we no longer see the point. Not long ago, two teams of seven-year-olds arrived at a field in Cleveland, Ohio, for a soccer game. All the ingredients were in place for a Saturday afternoon kickabout: freshly mown grass, blue skies, and a crowd of kids dressed up and raring to go. The only problem was that the referees failed to turn up. What did the parents do? They piled their children back into the cars and drove off.

Is it possible to make adults back off a little and give youth sports back to children? The answer is yes. Around the world, leagues, parents, star athletes, and politicians are finding ways to give priority to the kid and the ball. Cal Ripken Jr., an American baseball legend, is leading a crusade to change the culture of youth sports, telling anyone who will listen that "everybody needs to remember it's about the kids, not the grown-ups." He advises parents that the first question they should always ask themselves after the game is: "Did my child enjoy himself?" In a similar vein, youth leagues across North America are setting up codes of conduct and asking moms and dads to sign pledges or attend workshops on good behavior. Many towns now hold "silent Saturdays" and "silent Sundays," when parents and coaches are forbidden to raise their voices above a whisper. Under the "silent sideline" system in Australia, spectators at children's rugby games can only shout words of encouragement. In 2007, a new British action group called Give Us Back Our Game launched a campaign to reclaim youth soccer from overbearing coaches and parents. One of its proposals is to hold four-a-side games that children referee themselves. In Lancashire, England, many under-twelves already play soccer on smaller pitches without the offside rule. The net effect is less bitching from the sidelines and more time on the ball for the kids. Youth leagues are also starting to tackle the mounting problem of burnout. In 2007, Little League Baseball International imposed a limit on the number of pitches that children can throw.

Even hard-core sports parents are learning to relax. Vicente Ramos, a lawyer in Barcelona, Spain, used to patrol the sidelines whenever his eleven-year-old son, Miguel, played soccer. Most of the time he was shouting: Run into the box! Pass the ball! Cover that man! Track back! He would then dissect the match in the car on the way home, giving his son marks out of ten. One day, Miguel, who is strong, quick, and blessed with a mean left foot, announced that he wanted to quit soccer. "I was shocked," says Ramos. "There was a lot of shouting and arguing and crying, and eventually it came out that he was fed up with me always being on his back."

Ramos decided to ease off. He still stands on the sidelines but now keeps his comments to a minimum. On the drive home from games, he no longer grades Miguel's performance, and sometimes the two talk about things other than soccer. Ramos is surprised and relieved to find that his own mood for the week is no longer colored by his son's fortunes on the field. Even more important, Miguel has rediscovered his love for soccer and feels he is a better player. "Now I just think about the game and what

I am going to do with the ball instead of worrying about what my dad is going to shout next," he says. "It's a big relief."

Across the Atlantic, another parent is turning that same thinking into a public crusade. Danny Bernstein lives in Scarsdale, New York, an affluent suburb an hour's train ride north of Manhattan. Many of the residents here work in high-powered jobs, and they bring home the same winner-takes-all spirit that reigns in the office. Giving children a competitive edge is top of the agenda in many homes. The day I arrive, a local magazine, *Westchester Family*, has a cover story entitled *Parenting in the Age of Anxiety*.

Bernstein is tall, lean, and looks younger than his forty years. Like many natural athletes, he has a coiled energy that suggests he might suddenly leap in the air or break into a sprint. Now a father of two, he still plays recreational soccer and basketball in his spare time. Bernstein noticed, however, that the children of Scarsdale no longer play sports the way he and his friends did a generation ago. There are few informal soccer games in the backyard or on the school fields, and the driveway basketball nets are in pristine condition from disuse. Most children are enrolled in organized sports run by zealous parents. To redress the balance, Bernstein quit his job running the family apparel business and set up a company called Backyard Sports. Its aim: to bring back the simple magic of the kid and the ball.

Bernstein is no fool, though. He sees the irony of an adult creating a company that aims to free children from adults. "I know it's a paradox, but we've reached a stage where we have to organize freedom for kids," he says. "It is possible to realize the values of free play, and for the kids to learn from each other, within a supervised and structured environment. And maybe once they see how much fun they have here, they'll start playing in their own backyards again." He also understands that however much modern parents talk about the importance of fun, they want a lot more from youth sports. "Unfortunately, you still have to sell it to them as a means to an end," says Bernstein. "As well as the fun, we have to tell parents that we'll also teach their children confidence and ball skills and that they will learn about tactics, team-building, and competition. Things that can help them be successful in the outside world."

To see how this "organized freedom" works, I drop in on one of his Sunday morning basketball clinics. The venue is not a backyard at all, but a school gymnasium. The walls are plastered with photographs of sports stars: David Beckham, Michelle Kwan, Serena Williams, Brett Favre. A sign hanging by the door says, "If you had fun, you won!" Despite Bernstein's desire to rescue children from parental meddling, several moms and dads stay to watch from the stage at the end of the gymnasium.

The clinic begins with a dozen seven- and eight-year-olds gathering in the middle of the basketball court. "Anyone ever play ball in the backyard? You know, where it's just your friends and there are no grown-ups telling you what to do?" asks Bernstein, kneeling on the floor. Some of the children nod, others look blank. "I want you to imagine this gym is your backyard. We're going to have some fun."

Part of the Backyard ethos is to resist pressure from parents—and from children—to play competitive scrimmages at too early an age. Bernstein focuses on drills instead, encouraging each child to learn at his own pace. The children flick the ball between their fingers, pass it through their legs, then bounce it on the spot. They practice holding the ball and pivoting on one foot, then dribbling and stopping. Rather than expect them to shoot on regulation baskets, Bernstein hangs hula hoops low down on the walls. This is the sort of technique that seems like a waste of time to a parent already imagining his child on an ESPN highlight reel, but the children clearly love it. They take turns doing layups. One boy struggles to score a basket but tries again and again until he gets it right. "You did it!" Bernstein exclaims. The other boys give him high fives. "Way to go, man," says one of the better players. The parents remain quiet as the sound of young laughter fills the gym.

The session culminates in a shooting contest. The children split into two teams and try to score as many shots as possible through the hula hoops hanging from the real baskets. Bernstein adds the two scores together to come up with fourteen baskets. He then challenges the children to beat their "team" total. This time they net seventeen, and a dozen small voices cheer.

At the end of the session, Bernstein asks if anyone wants to show what he has learned. A dozen hands shoot up from children begging to be chosen. Each child demonstrates a move or trick picked up during the ninety-minute clinic. Bernstein then lets the children have some time playing on their own. They run around the gym, dribbling, shooting, and shouting at each other over the sound of a dozen balls thundering on the floor.

On the sidelines, however, not everyone is convinced. One father tells me that while the idea behind Backyard Sports is noble, parents in Scarsdale are just too competitive to embrace it. "They may say sports are all about the kids, but when push comes to shove, when trophies or team selection is on the line, that all goes out the window," he says. "Parents here are way too intense to let their kids play like this without interfering." But others are more sanguine. Michael Philipps, a stockbroker, is here with his daughter. He coaches children's football and lacrosse and is familiar with the pressure to push them into competitive games before they can even catch or throw a ball properly. "This is really refreshing," he says. "The kids are obviously having fun, they're learning, and there's no one pushing for a scrimmage that they won't get anything out of. I've definitely learned some things here that I'll incorporate into my coaching."

Sally Winton agrees. Her son is the boy who eventually mastered the layup. At the end of the clinic, he runs up, face flushed, to ask if he can stay for the next session. "It's really cool," he says, before running back out to join the mayhem. Winton is amazed. "I've never seen him so enthusiastic," she says. "Usually he just wants to go straight home."

Over a hundred families have now signed up their children, aged four to fourteen, for Backyard Sports, which is clearly tapping into a broader trend. Helyn Goldstein has sat on the board of the local sports association in Scarsdale for the last ten years. She is also the mother of three athletic sons aged ten, thirteen, and seventeen. She detects the beginnings of a shift in parental attitudes. "People are starting to say they've had enough of all the travel, and the selection, and the whole whose-kid-is-better-mine-or-yours thing," she says. "They're tired of it all, and the younger parents definitely have less time for all the craziness." Already some sports leagues in the Scarsdale area are starting to put off selection until the children are older.

Even so, crusaders like Bernstein still face an uphill battle. His clinics will mean little unless parents start to give children enough time and space to play sports in the backyard or driveway or park—and that implies a tectonic shift in parental attitudes, family schedules, and the use of technology. The Sunday I visited Scarsdale, the weather was crisp and sunny, yet the public parks and basketball courts stood empty, the children all off doing organized activities elsewhere or cloistered indoors. The biggest challenge facing Bernstein may be persuading parents that putting fun and free play first can actually make their children better players in the long run. "The adult world is all about competition and winning, about ranking and measuring people against each other, but that doesn't work for kids," says Bernstein. "It's going to take time to persuade people that it's when children are having fun with sports that they really develop."

That principle was brought to life by the Humbar Valley Sharks, a youth ice hockey team in Toronto. When Mike McCarron, a lawyer and parent, took over the squad in 2002, he decided to break the mold. Instead of following the norm in youth hockey by giving more ice time to star players, he decreed that every Shark, whatever his ability, would get the same number of minutes. If a power play or a penalty kill came up, and it was your shift, you played. Even when the team was trailing by a goal in the third period, McCarron sent out the same lines in the same order. He also banned personal statistics, to stop everyone, kids and parents, from obsessing about who scored the most points or had the best plus-minus rating. Though certain boys emerged as leaders both on and off the ice, the Sharks had no official captain. The mission statement—that the team comes first, and that having fun and learning the game are more important than winning—was a bracing counterblast to the ultracompetitiveness of many youth sports. "A lot of parents see winning as an end in itself, but for kids winning is important only in terms of setting and reaching your goals," says McCarron. "The priority should be to play and enjoy the game and let the score take care of itself."

The approach paid off. Though not blessed with the biggest or fastest players around, the Sharks melded together as a team so tightly that their camaraderie, positional smarts, and knack for moving the puck as a unit earned plaudits from rival parents. The boys worked hard on their skills in training but also had the freedom in a match to try out a new trick or move, or simply to make a mistake, without fear of being pilloried or benched. Thomas Skrlj, now thirteen, spent two years as a defender on the Sharks and loved every minute of it. "People weren't judging you all the time or worrying about the score, so you could make mistakes and not feel nervous about it," he says. "It completely changed my whole way of playing the game. I learned so much and I became a way better player."

The irony is that by taking a stand against excessive competition, the Sharks ended up posting the sort of record that would thrill even the most competitive hockey dad. Over three years, the team lost only one regular season game. They won more than twenty tournaments, including back-to-back North American championships. Not bad for a team where winning came second.

Would the Sharks parents have been so happy with McCarron's methods if the club had posted a losing record? Hard to say. But it is clear that the players thrived under a regime that gave precedence to the kid and the puck, the puck and the kid.

Like most of his teammates, Skrlj has moved up to play in a higher league—and he misses the Sharks approach.

"It's different now," he says. "Hockey is just more fun when winning isn't everything."

When we take time out to listen, that is the message trickling back to us from every quarter. That competition is fine, but not if it squeezes the fun out of sports. That children want us to share their athletic ups and downs without taking over. That sports, in its purest form, is always about the kid and the ball.

As all those who have ever watched their own children chasing a ball around a field know, embracing that message, and resisting the urge to morph into a screaming maniac on the sidelines, take a lot of discipline. The problem, of course, is that these days discipline is in short supply.

TEN

Discipline:
Just Say No?

If you have never been hated by your child you have never been a parent.

—Bette Davis, actress

Not long after my return from the sports fields of Scarsdale, I come face-to-face with a different kind of anxiety about children. The scene is a community center in a well-to-do corner of London. Posters about vaccinations and children's art courses hang on the walls. An ancient coffee machine gurgles sleepily in the corner. Six mothers in their thirties and forties have come here to attend a parenting workshop. All are career women, and most have experience telling other people what to do in the workplace. The theme this afternoon is how to say no to your child.

In the style of an Alcoholics Anonymous meeting, the women take turns sharing recent setbacks. "The other day I let my son take his Game Boy to school even though I really, really didn't want him to," says the first mother. "I just couldn't face having a fight about it at the school gate in front of everyone else."

The others nod with a mixture of sympathy and recognition. Another woman, who is pregnant, chimes in. "My husband and I have basically given up on getting our five-year-old to go to bed in the evening," she says. "He falls asleep downstairs with us long after we're dying to be rid of him."

Welcome to the central paradox of modern childhood. On the one hand, many of us schedule, push, polish, and protect our children to the limit of our budget and ability. But then when it comes to imposing discipline, to setting limits, to saying no to this whim or that desire, we go a bit wobbly.

June Walker has witnessed this shift over the last generation at her family therapy practice in Sydney, Australia: "I see a lot of cases now where educated, professional parents don't know how to say no to the children, and you see seven-year-olds pretty much running the household."

Like every other worry about the state of modern childhood, this complaint is not new. Earlier generations also fretted that kids were getting away with murder. "Our earth is degenerate in these latter days. . . . Children no longer obey their parents; and the end of the world is evidently approaching." So ran the inscription on an Assyrian clay tablet from 2800 B.C. In the 1530s, Conrad Sam issued a similar lament in Ulm, Germany: "Children today are badly raised," he said. "Not only do parents permit them their every selfish wish, but they even show them the way to it." Child-rearing experts spent much of the twentieth century warning that parents were losing their nerve.

Over the last generation, however, that prophecy has come to pass. Newspaper advice columns around the world are stuffed with letters from readers unable or unwilling to discipline their children. Television schedules are clogged with programs like *Nanny 911* that show out-of-control brats terrorizing their parents. For the first time in human history, children really do seem to have the upper hand in many homes.

Does that mean children's behavior is worse today than in the past? Hard to say, but there are troubling signs. One major study found that fifteen-year-old Britons are more than twice as likely to lie, steal, or disobey figures of authority than they were in 1974. In a 2004 Public Agenda report, nearly 80 percent of U.S. teachers said students had warned them that their parents could sue if they were disciplined too severely or their rights were violated. In 2006, Kidscape, a British charity, blamed permissive parents for creating a new playground scourge: the middle-class bully. "They come from homes where they are so indulged that they go to school and behave like little gods who think that everything just revolves around them and that other children should be as in awe of them as their families are," says Michele Elliott, the charity's director. "They expect all the teachers and other kids to kowtow to them. If they don't, they start to bully the other children." In Japan, a word for bullying, *ijime,* entered the vernacular in the 1980s.

How did we get here? One factor is the modern habit of putting our children on a pedestal. Rule number one seems to be to tell them, as often as possible, just how perfect they are. You're so clever, we gush. You're beautiful. You're wonderful. You can be anything you want to be. At nursery schools children sing "Frère Jacques" with the lyrics switched to "I am special. I am special. Look at me. Look at me." Every doodle ends up on the fridge door, every sports trophy on the mantelpiece, every academic achievement in the Christmas brag letter. Look at the trend for celebrating the minutiae of children's lives in elaborate scrapbooks, or for hiring professionals to shoot and edit family videos. The aim is to create a perfect portrait of childhood, a sunny, airbrushed homage with all the bumpy, messy bits cut out.

As a father, I can understand this impulse. We all want to remember the good stuff. And we all want our children to be happy and to feel good about themselves. Many of us have absorbed the idea that high self-esteem is the springboard to success—that if a child grows up believing herself to be a star, then she eventually will be.

But is that really true? A recent review of over 15,000 studies concluded that high self-esteem does not boost grades or career prospects, nor does it cut alcohol use or curb violent behavior. Obviously, self-confidence is an asset, but children who are overpraised can end up more worried about maintaining their image and more inclined to undermine their peers to do so, as well as more likely to look to parents and teachers for approval. Instead of making things happen, they sit around anxiously waiting for the world to fit their vision of how it should be. When everything you do is praised to the heavens, you may also start to believe your own press—that setbacks are not a part of your life, that everybody loves you, that you are so uniquely fabulous that the world owes you everything. Such narcissism may help on *American Idol*—though even there it can backfire—but it doesn't wash in the real world. Human resource managers complain that many recent graduates struggle to be punctual and respectful of others or to work in teams. They expect rich rewards without putting in the work to earn them and will move on if they are not made to feel special enough. This may be fine when the economy is buoyant, but what happens when a downturn hits?

A growing body of evidence suggests that putting a child on a pedestal makes it harder for him to take risks, to experiment, to stick with a difficult task, to make mistakes and learn from them—because anything that smacks of failure would disappoint his parents and therefore tarnish his credentials as an alpha child. In 2006, Monta Vista, a competitive high school in California, began publishing a monthly newsletter where pupils could vent their feelings anonymously. Tellingly, the theme of the first issue was "Anxiety and Fear." Many of the contributions pointed to the paralytic effect of always being told that you are perfect and the world is your oyster. Here is a typical lament from one pupil: "I'm scared of failing. People have always told me that I can do anything in the world and I can accomplish anything I set my mind to. This idea, although wonderful, terrifies me. My brother is one of those people who has all the 'potential' in the world, but he doesn't use it. I think this is because he thinks it is better to pretend he doesn't care than to try and possibly fail. This has effectively rubbed off onto me and my own outlook. I find myself always questioning my capabilities, and giving up before it gets too hard because I am scared about what people will think if I do not succeed. I am scared of how people will react if I do not live up to their expectations. I do not want to embarrass myself in my failure. . . . I am discovering that as I continue on this somewhat downward spiral, it is getting easier and easier to just let go and give up. I am scared that I will ultimately just stop trying completely and fail miserably." And here is another pupil: "I'm sure you'll agree that no one wants to fail. But what if this sort of fear went to a whole new level? To the point where you're so afraid to even try just because there's the possibility that you might fail. Being such a disappointment to everyone that wants you to be more. . . . Maybe if I slack off, maybe I can use that as my excuse for my failure."

The research strongly suggests that praising a child only for her ability ("You are so intelligent") can backfire in the long run. When the going gets tough, she is more likely to give up, believing that her innate talent has reached its limits and can carry her no further. But a child that has been praised more for her effort ("You stuck with that so well") has a variable to change when the chips are down: she can work harder.

Another downside of putting a child on a pedestal is that it makes it harder to say no. If our wunderkind is a paragon of talent and virtue, if his happiness is paramount, then where do we get off standing in the way?

Nor does it help that our Peter Pan culture has eroded the very idea of adult authority. Growing old—and by extension growing up—is now deeply uncool. As families have grown less authoritarian and the whole culture more indulgent, imposing limits on our children has become anathema to hip moms and dads in touch with their inner child. As a member of the live-and-let-live generation, I feel a little uneasy just typing a word like *discipline*. What does it mean? When is it called for? What about freedom and fun?

Even when we crave obedience from our children, other things stop us cracking the whip. We may be too tired from our own hectic lives to summon the energy. I see this in my own family. Bedtime in our house is often a Sisyphean struggle. My wife and I start off by announcing, with a pleading edge in our voices: "It's time to put the lights out and go to bed." The children shout down the stairs: "Ten more minutes!" We sigh and call back, "Okay, ten more minutes." Ten minutes later the same cycle starts up again.

Many of us prefer to cut our children some slack because we feel guilty for not spending enough time with them, for the pressure we put on them to be successful, for the constant meddling and monitoring they endure in so much of their lives. We also want to develop a closer relationship with them than we had with our own parents. We want family life to be smooth and harmonious—and nothing spoils a Kodak moment more than a parent's saying, "No, you can't do that" or "You're grounded."

"We use kids like Prozac," says Dan Kindlon, a child psychologist at Harvard University and author of *Too Much of a Good Thing: Raising Children of Character in an Indulgent Age.* "People don't necessarily feel great about their spouse or their job but the kids are the bright spot in their day. They don't want to muck up that one moment by getting yelled at. They don't want to hurt. They don't want to feel bad. They want to get satisfaction from their kids. They're so precious to us—maybe more than to any generation previously. What gets thrown out the window is limits. It's a lot easier to pick their towel up off the floor than to get them away from the PlayStation to do it."

Rob Parsons, author of *Teenagers: What Every Parent Has to Know,* agrees. "The problem is not that we don't love our children enough, but that we love them too much," he says. "We want everything for them—the extra tutors, the holidays, the custom-made ski boots that won't rub. Instead of saying, 'Go get a Saturday job if you want to go clubbing,' you see parents hand over the money—and then ask their teenagers if they can go clubbing with them. That may appear cute, but it is not good. As parents, you have got to be prepared to take the unpopularity hit."

That reluctance to exercise authority is mirrored outside the family, too. The notion that adults should play a part in protecting and shaping all the children within their community—that, as the African proverb goes, "it takes a village to raise a child"— now seems out of step with the times. In our me-first culture, it's every parent for himself. We refrain from scolding someone else's child for dropping litter or scratching his initials on a bus shelter, because he might swear at us or pull a knife. Or his parents could turn on us.

The new balance of power between children and adults is not all bad. Taking the authoritarianism out of family life has brought parents closer to their children in wonderful ways. It has also freed adults from the stuffy stereotypes of yesteryear. Hurray for that. But the pendulum has swung too far. Children can only really be children when adults are adults. That is not a plea to bring back the Victorian matriarch or the nerdy 1950s dad. It just means exercising adult authority once in a while.

The first thing to remember is that almost every child expert agrees that the young thrive on rules and boundaries. "Children need limits on their behavior because they feel better and more secure when they live within a certain structure," says Laurence Steinberg, a professor of psychology at Temple University and author of *The Ten Basic Principles of Good Parenting*. "As adults, we don't like it when other people tell us what we can and can't do. To children, it doesn't feel that way." Pushing against limits teaches a child about her own strengths and weaknesses and equips her for life in a world built on rules and compromise. Without boundaries, children never learn to cope with disappointment or defer gratification.

Yet change is in the air. Discipline is making a comeback. Books like *Silver Spoon Kids* and *No—Why Kids of All Ages Need to Hear It and Ways Parents Can Say It* are rolling off the printing presses around the world. An expanding smorgasbord of TV shows, workshops, and Web sites offers advice on how to say no. Discipline is so much a part of the *Supernanny* phenomenon that its star, Jo Frost, meets the family of the week dressed like a stern matron.

Many parents are putting the advice into practice. Usually that means less time chumming around trying to be their child's best friend, and more time laying down the law. Even Madonna, the patron saint of bad behavior, boasts of imposing limits on her own children. In a recent issue of *Harpers & Queen,* she came out as a "disciplinarian" who enforces strict rules on chores, home-work, and keeping bedrooms tidy. "My daughter has a problem picking things up in her room, so if you leave your clothes on the floor, they're gone when you come home," she said. "Lola has to earn all her clothes back by being tidy, making her bed, hanging up her clothes."

A similar crackdown is under way in noncelebrity homes. The Marshalls decided it was time to start saying no when their twelve-year-old son, Dylan, took a call on his mobile phone during a family funeral in Cleveland, Ohio. "We had just given up trying to stop him using his cell all the time, but when I saw him yakking to a friend during the service I just snapped," says his mother, Kathy, a nurse. "I thought, 'This has gone way too far and we need to start drawing some lines here.'" So she and her husband drafted a set of rules for Dylan: turning off his mobile phone, TV, and computer when asked, taking out the garbage once a week, and putting all his dirty clothes down the laundry chute instead of dumping them on the floor around the house. If he failed to play ball, his parents would stop paying his mobile phone bill. There was plenty of grumbling and muttering about the injustice of it all, but that faded away after a few weeks. Dylan is playing by the rules now, and the family is getting along much better than before. "We have ups and downs and argu-ments, but that's life, isn't it?" says Kathy. "I feel a lot better now that I'm not bending over backwards to do whatever Dylan wants."

In Edinburgh, Scotland, the Clapton family went through a similar shift with Alice and Morag, their seven-year-old twins. "They definitely used to call the tune," says mother Maggie. With busy careers, she and her husband did not want arguments to spoil family time. "I admit it," says Maggie. "We buckled, we took the easy option, we wimped out, because we wanted harmony." Though both parents felt sheepish about ducking the discipline question, and despite disapproving noises from the grandparents, they relished the absence of family strife. The wake-up call came when the head of Alice and Morag's primary school complained that the girls were being rude to teachers and bullying their peers. "I was shocked," says Maggie. "I began to get visions of the girls turning into those spoiled brats you see on *Supernanny.*" The Claptons decided to change tack. Instead of caving in to the twins' every wish, they now make a point of saying no several times a day. The girls are no longer allowed to watch TV on demand and have to clean their room before bedtime. Nor are they allowed to dictate every family outing. Three months later, both girls are behaving better at school, and the parents have regained their self-respect. "We call it the 'Power of No,'" quips Maggie. "When you're raising children in an instant gratification society, the most valuable lesson you can teach them is restraint and respect for others, and the only way to do that is for the children to be children and the grown-ups to be grown-ups."

Like every other aspect of child rearing, discipline is not a one-size-fits-all recipe. The principle that children need limits is universal, but where and how a family chooses to draw lines will vary, because every child and every parent is different. Yet there are some guidelines. The first is to forget trying to be an unwaveringly consistent and fair dispenser of justice and discipline.

Mistakes and a little inconsistency are inevitable and will not damage your children for life.

Most experts recommend that when disciplining kids you should always explain your motives. But that does not mean it's the end of the world to lay down the law sometimes with a curt "Because I say so!" Nor is it a catastrophe to lose your temper occasionally. Parenting gurus who declare that you must always remain unruffled and calm when dealing with children are living on another planet. Parents are human, and that means we blow our lids, too. And anyway, seeing Mom and Dad blow a valve teaches children that other people have feelings and limits.

By the same token, we also need to resist the temptation to open the medicine chest at the first sign of waywardness. Using drugs to manage children is not new. In eighteenth-century Britain, parents pacified unruly infants using opium-based solutions with names like Mother's Helper, Infant's Quietness, and Soothing Syrup. In 1799, a British doctor warned that thousands of babies were being killed by nurses "forever pouring Godfrey's Cordial down their little throats, which is a strong opiate and in the end as fatal as arsenic. This they pretend they do to quiet the child—thus indeed many are forever quieted."

Today's soothing syrups are designed to help children of all ages sit still and concentrate. Around 10 percent of twelve-year-old boys in the United States are now on Ritalin or some other drug to combat attention deficit/hyperactivity disorder. Prescriptions are up tenfold in Britain over the last decade. Worldwide, the use of ADHD drugs such as Ritalin, Attenta, and Focalin has tripled since the early 1990s.

Why the spike in hyperactivity? Many doctors think that ADHD is a genetic-neurological condition that has always affected between 3 and 5 percent of the population and that we are just better at detecting it today. An early description of the symptoms can be found in *The Story of Fidgety Philip*, a poem written by Heinrich Hoffman in 1845:

> *He won't sit still;*
> *He wriggles and giggles . . .*
> *See the naughty restless child,*
> *Growing still more rude and wild.*

Many children credit drugs like Ritalin with helping them to lead more normal lives. Yet there is a rival view. Skeptics question whether ADHD really is a neurological condition at all or whether drugs should ever be used to treat the symptoms associated with it. Many practitioners have had success curing hyperactivity with therapy and parenting classes, or by altering the child's diet and exercise routine.

Either way, there is a consensus that many children are being diagnosed with ADHD for the wrong reasons. This is part of a broader cultural shift. These days, rather than change the environment we live in, we prefer to rewire our brains to fit the environment. Shyness, anger, sadness, and other "undesirable" emotions or traits are increasingly seen not as a natural part of the human condition but as diseases, symptoms of an imbalance in the chemistry of the brain, problems to be fixed with drugs. This is particularly so with children, where soaring expectations have narrowed the definition of what is normal and acceptable. How else to explain parents' sending their toddlers to psychotherapists to be "cured" of tantrums? "We are not prepared to live with variation as we did in the past," says Professor David Healy, director of North Wales Department of Psychological Medicine. "We want kids to conform to ideals based often on parental insecurities and ambitions."

Perhaps that explains why Ritalin is so prevalent in high-achieving schools. Tranquilizing uppity pupils can seem like an attractive option to teachers lumbered with large classes and desperate to boost test scores. Doctors report mounting pressure from parents to put their children on medication that might help them behave or perform better. For some, ADHD can be an excuse for an underachieving child: "It's not his (or our) fault he's floundering in school; it's a neurochemical imbalance." And there are other advantages to blaming a faulty brain for a tendency to daydream or act up in the back row of the classroom. In some countries, schools receive extra funding for every child diagnosed with ADHD, while the affected children receive free tutoring and the right to take exams under easier conditions. Ritalin has also gained a reputation as a "smart" drug, with high-school and college students using it to stay focused during all-night study sessions.

The allure of the medicine cabinet is easy to understand. What parent has not fantasized about inventing a get-ready-for-school-in-the-morning-faster pill or a go-to-sleep-for-twelve-hours-right-now tablet? I know I have. The danger is that we are now playing Russian roulette with our children's minds. Some research suggests that Ritalin reduces creativity, spontaneity, and the ability to take calculated risks. And a question mark still hangs over the possible side effects of drugs that fiddle with the brain's chemistry. Already some children have suffered hallucinations and even heart attacks after taking Ritalin. Another fear is that putting small children on brain drugs might set a pattern for addiction in later life. Both Courtney Love and Kurt Cobain were on Ritalin as children, and both talked of carrying the "happy pill" mentality into adulthood. "When you're a kid and you get this drug that makes you feel that feeling, where else are you going to turn when you're an adult?" Love told one inter-viewer. "It was euphoric when you were a child—isn't that memory going to stick with you?"

Some parents whose children go on behavior-altering drugs are deciding that the price is too high. That is what happened to the Shaw family in London. Their son, Richard, was diagnosed with ADHD and eventually put on Concerta after his twelfth birthday. The drug cured his hyperactivity, but it also killed off his appetite and gave him insomnia. Richard went from being a bundle of energy to spending whole afternoons playing on the Xbox in a zombie-like state. His mother, Victoria, was appalled. "Suddenly we had this boy who was perfectly well behaved, who did everything we said, but it was like he had been lobotomized," she says. "You looked into his eyes, and you felt his soul had been taken away."

Victoria took Richard off Concerta and put him on tablets of omega-3 fish oil instead. He still has moments of overexuberance, but his hyperactivity is largely under control now. "The worst of it is gone, but because he's not a zombie anymore he resists and there is conflict," says Victoria. "But that's what normal family life is about, isn't it?" More important, her son is back to being himself. "We have our boy back now," she says.

Richard agrees. "I argue with my mom and dad about what I'm allowed to do, but I'm cool with that," he says. "At least I feel like myself now."

Perhaps the broader lesson is that there is no magic formula for keeping children in check, nor should there be. Just think about it for a second: is there anything more spooky than a child who behaves impeccably all the time? Or a family that never fights? Chafing against authority is part of growing up—we all know that instinctively—and conflict is a feature of family life. It may not be pleasant when children sulk, slam doors, or hiss, "I hate you," but it's part of the parenting deal.

Once we accept that children need limits, the next step is for each of us to decide where those limits lie, to find the balance between discipline and indulgence that suits our family best. One caveat to bear in mind is that there are no shortcuts when it comes to exercising adult authority. Good behavior, like exam results or sports trophies, should not be an end in itself. Sometimes we need to dig deeper. That means making the effort to find out why a child is misbehaving in the first place—is she unhappy or worried or frightened?—rather than just sending her off to sit on the Naughty Step or handing her a pill. And we can only do that when we spend less time managing our children and more time talking and listening to them.

The trouble, of course, is that the slow, messy, unglamorous business of building relationships is at odds with the consumer culture of instant gratification.

ELEVEN

Consumerism: Pester Power and the Walking, Talking ATM

The one who dies with the most toys wins.
—popular bumper sticker

It is Saturday afternoon and the largest mall in my corner of London is thronged with shoppers. Many seem to be enjoying the "Fantastic Day Out!" promised in the brochure. Couples wander arm in arm, sipping lattes. Young women sit gossiping and giggling on the benches, shoals of shopping bags pooled around their feet. It looks like a tableau of consumer bliss—until you notice that open warfare is raging within the families.

Among the potted plants and water features, many parents are fighting a rearguard action against Pester Power. One child drags a despairing mother into a shop to look at the latest Play-Station console. Another throws a tantrum when Dad refuses to buy a bracelet from a jewelry kiosk. A well-dressed woman is locked in a tussle outside a toy shop. Her son, who looks about six years old, is pulling her toward a display of Bionicles. Her mouth curls into a rictus that suggests she is close to the end of her tether.

"Stop asking for things," she hisses. "You've just had a whole load of presents for your birthday."

"But I want a Bionicle, too," the boy wails.

This is a scenario known to almost every parent on earth, but today I am hoping to avoid it. My five-year-old daughter and I have come to buy tights, so there's no need to go anywhere near a toy display. Yet as soon as we enter the children's clothing shop, the battle is on. "Jingle Bells" is playing on the sound system, triggering a Pavlovian response. "That's a Christmas song—we'll be getting our presents soon," says my daughter. "Can I have . . ."

My heart sinks. I've only just finished shelling out for Halloween and already Christmas is on the radar. Isn't it a little early to begin the Yuletide onslaught? I look at my phone to check the date. It's November 9.

We live in a consumerist world. Brands and logos are worn like tribal colors, the siren call of advertising turns every desire into a need, and you are what you own. Shopping is touted as the panacea for every ill. When the economy sags, politicians urge us to spend money to boost GDP. When spirits droop, it's time for a little retail therapy. When a relationship stumbles, we buy chocolates or flowers. We even pay personal shoppers to help us shop better. No longer a means to an end, shopping has become an end in itself. A recent Nielsen survey of forty-two countries found that three-quarters of consumers shop purely for fun.

Along the way, consumption has become a central feature of modern childhood. That is not to say that children did not lust after stuff before now. In the early fifteenth century, a cardinal named Giovanni Dominici observed that the young of Florence were in thrall to "little wooden horses, attractive cymbals, imitation birds, gilded drums and a thousand different kinds of toys." Yet today some children grow up amid an affluence never seen before in human history. What would Dominici have made of Christmas morning in a twenty-first-century household?

Consumption began to carve out a larger place in childhood in the seventeenth century, with clothes, books, toys, and games designed specially for children pouring onto the market in Europe. Not by coincidence, complaints about Pester Power multiplied soon after. Here is Locke writing in 1693: "And I have known a young Child so distracted with the number, and Variety of his Play-games, that he tired his Maid every day to look them over; and was so accustomed to abundance, that he never thought he had enough, but was always asking, What more? What more? What new Thing shall I have?" Sound like anyone you know?

Even Locke could not have foreseen how commercialized childhood would become today. In the early twentieth century, advertisers began targeting the young directly, with prepubescent stars, such as Shirley Temple, Judy Garland, and Mickey Rooney, endorsing children's clothing brands or launching their own lines. Experts hailed shopping as a way for children to develop their personalities and tastes. In 1931, the *New York Times* opined that "the little boy who puts all his pennies in his metal bank no longer is ranked . . . as the shining financial example for childhood."

After the Second World War, as television began pumping ads for toys and cereal into the home, the first child consumer crazes erupted. The humble hula hoop sold in the hundreds of millions around the world after bursting on the scene in 1958. Boredom came to be seen as a blight on childhood, spending money on toys and activities as the cure. The money spent on marketing to children in the United States is 150 times what it was in the early 1980s. Other countries have seen a similar jump.

Like anthropologists studying a remote tribe in the Amazon, marketers stalk children in their natural habitat—playgrounds, parks, malls, classrooms, even their bedrooms. The aim is to get inside young minds so as to devise ad campaigns that will seduce them. Michael Brody, chairman of the television and media committee of the American Academy of Child and Adolescent Psychiatry, likens this corporate helicoptering to the grooming carried out by sexual predators: "Just like pedophiles, marketers have become child experts."

As a result, advertising now touches almost every corner of children's lives. Schools clear wall space for posters of the latest movie releases, invite corporate sponsorship for sports days and drama productions, and accept free field trips to visit companies like Domino's Pizza. In schools across the United States, nearly eight million pupils watch twelve-minute current affairs programs (including two minutes of ads) supplied by Channel One. Even the traditional ride to school has been pimped. In 2006, a company named Bus Radio began broadcasting music, news, and ads on some eight hundred yellow school buses in twelve U.S. cities.

Not even the curriculum is safe anymore. In the 1920s, toothbrush makers, cocoa manufacturers, and other companies established a foothold in the American classroom by sending staff to give talks and later by supplying "educational" films, all with the same underlying message: buy our product! Today that infiltration goes much deeper. Some U.S. schools use literacy materials supplied by Pizza Hut, Kmart, and other companies that are riddled with corporate messages. A Revlon-sponsored "learning module" explains the nuances of good and bad hair days and asks pupils to list three must-have products they would take to a desert island.

Beyond the classroom, consumerism has crept into corners of children's lives that once seemed untouchable. Even the humble sleepover is now an advertising opportunity, with companies such as Girls Intelligence Agency sponsoring slumber parties where tweens sample new products and fill in questionnaires. Toys R Us runs its own in-store summer camps for children as young as three. Cheerios publishes a counting book that invites toddlers to put its little cereal rings into slots on the page. McDonald's workers visit the children's wards of hospitals in Britain to hand out toys and balloons, as well as leaflets promoting their food. Put all this together, and many children now see an estimated forty thousand ads a year.

What's more, the tone of advertising has shifted. Marketers tap into the Peter Pan zeitgeist by denigrating adults, portraying them as killjoys who stand between children and Fun. The subtext is that Pester Power is a force for good.

The net effect is that children are now full-fledged consumers who know their brands, expect their shopping whims to be satisfied, and have a say in big family spending decisions, ranging from where to go on vacation to what sofa to buy. In the United States, kids under fourteen influence up to $700 billion of spending every year, including two-thirds of all car purchases. No wonder children's TV channels like Disney-ABC and Nickelodeon carry commercials for minivans and Caribbean holiday resorts, or that Hummer and other automakers offer branded coloring pages and "advergames" on their Web sites. Family groups across the industrial world warn that children as young as ten now qualify as shopaholics.

Why have we let this happen? It's pretty clear that business targets the young to boost profits and that schools open their doors to corporate messages because they need the cash. But the reasons that parents surrender to consumerism are more complex and contradictory. Part of it is showing off. From Prada booties to the iPod Nano, what our offspring own has become, even more than before, a way to strut our own status, wealth, and taste. Another part is just going with the flow: when everyone else's children consume, why shouldn't ours do the same? Peer pressure comes into play, too. We all know that feeling of being out with other families when the call goes up for an ice cream or a Coke. Once one parent caves in, all the others find it a lot harder to hold their ground. Then there is the desire to give our children the best of everything and to make them happy: if shopping puts a smile on our faces, then why deny the same pleasure to our kids? Many of us also feel guilty for not spending enough time with our children or for the pressures that they face—and so we buy them things to make up for it.

Reluctant to say no, we would rather reach for the wallet than risk upsetting our children or causing a scene. I have a lot of experience of caving in to Pester Power myself. In our family, the phrase "special treat" is now uttered with a hint of irony—treats being dispensed so often that they long ago ceased to qualify as either "special" or "treats." Perhaps modern parents are also haunted by the memory of being denied consumer goods as children. I still resent my parents for refusing to buy me a BMX bicycle—one of those with the fake shock absorbers and the long, black cushioned seat—when I was nine. When I mentioned this to a colleague, he confessed to harboring a grudge against his parents for denying him a Raleigh Chopper bike at the same age. He even found a Web site where men discuss how to come to terms with their Chopper-less childhoods. Maybe we prefer to say yes because we don't want our children to remember us as Scrooge twenty years from now.

Of course, not all consumption is bad. Children, like adults, can derive a lot of harmless pleasure from material goods. Many of the boys at my son's primary school collect Dr. Who cards. Every morning in the school yard, they huddle together to trade them. They have evolved a complex system of rules for determining the relative value of each card: two Daleks for the Imperial Guard Group, three Cybermen for one Werewolf. The swapping and collecting are part of the fun. I remember doing the same with hockey cards a generation ago.

We should therefore be skeptical of warnings that the consumer culture has killed off childhood. But that does not mean swallowing the line that advertising is harmless and every child should shop till he drops. Like toys that do too much, untrammeled consumption can narrow children's experience of the world around them. When author Frank Cottrell Boyce recently asked a group of primary-school pupils in London what they would do if given a large sum of money, all of them rattled off a list of designer goods they would buy. None talked about building a spaceship or anything else that smacked of adventure or imagination. Says Boyce, "All this consumerism is crowding out the capacity to fantasize, to disappear into another world of your own creation."

Studies around the world are linking an immersion in consumer culture to depression, anxiety, eating disorders, low self-esteem, drug abuse, and other problems. In her book *Born to Buy,* Juliet Schor, a professor of sociology at Boston College, conducted a survey of children aged ten to thirteen. Her data showed clearly that "less involvement in consumer cultures leads to healthier kids and more involvement leads kids' psychological well-being to deteriorate." Other research suggests that children feel status anxiety more acutely than do adults. Published in 2006, *Shopping Generation,* a landmark survey by Britain's National Consumer Council, found that young Britons feel overloaded with marketing messages and half of them wish their parents earned more money so they could buy more things.

I recently witnessed my daughter going into consumer meltdown in a grocery store. We had come to buy drinks to take to the park on a warm day and were standing in front of a giant freezer stocked with more than thirty different juices and sodas. My daughter looked up at this wall of choice and froze. Her eyes darted across the shelves, moving from one garishly colored label to the next, then back again. Most of the bottles and cartons bore pictures of Shrek or other characters that she knows well. I urged her to choose, but she stood rooted to the spot, sucking her thumb and looking more and more perplexed. Eventually, she began to cry. "I don't know which one I want, I just know I want one," she sobbed, hot tears in her eyes.

Giving a child "the best of everything" robs her of the chance to learn how to make the best of what she has. This applies to every aspect of childhood, from education to sports, but especially to navigating the consumer culture. Later in life, the overindulged child can grow into a financially incontinent adult who spends first and asks questions later. Eighteen- to twenty-nine-year-olds now account for one-fifth of bankruptcies in England and Wales. Higher student loans and property prices don't help, but "Generation Broke" seems to be on an eternal spending spree. Take Cheryl Tawiah, a twenty-four-year-old packaging consultant who grew up in a middle-class home in Tampa, Florida. She left college with very little debt and walked straight into a $55,000-a-year job in Charlotte, North Carolina. Three years later, she is $18,000 in the red. "My generation doesn't do delayed gratification," she says. "If we see something we want, we buy it, even if we don't really have the money." Tawiah seems bewildered and slightly amused by her own inability to put away the plastic. "Does that mean I'm, like, spoiled?" she says.

In this "because I'm worth it" culture, putting the consumer genie back in the bottle will not be easy. Yet a backlash is brewing. Jerry O'Hanlon has spent nearly twenty years making ads for children at various New York agencies. After his son was born in 2005, he began mingling with other parents and instantly felt a social chill. "When you tell folks what you do for a living, you can see them thinking, 'This is the evil guy who makes my kid pester me for junk food and toys,'" he says. "There's a lot more anger out there today about the whole idea of marketing products to children than when I started in the business." Now the victim of his own son's pestering, O'Hanlon has decided to take a stand. He is looking for a job that only involves advertising products to adults.

In a similar vein, some psychologists have started denouncing colleagues who use their expertise to help companies market to children. Raffi the singer and other child-friendly celebrities have added their voice to the chorus. Schools around the world now run seminars on how families can combat Pester Power. When one primary school held a forum in a shopping mall in Hong Kong, dozens of parents unconnected with the school turned up. Everywhere, groups like Commercial Alert organize marches, boycotts, and letter-writing campaigns against companies that target children. Under pressure from parents, politicians, and other campaigners, many schools in the United States have kicked Channel One out of the classroom, slashing the company's revenue by more than half from its peak in the mid-1990s.

The junk food industry is the most popular target. Schools around the world are removing food and drink vending machines, or at least toning down the advertising that goes along with them. In 2006, Latvia became the first European country to impose a ban on the sale and marketing of junk food in all its public schools. A few months later, Britain banned junk food ads during TV shows aimed at under-sixteens.

Will this go farther? In many countries, consumer groups are pushing for a ban on all or most advertising to children. Sweden and Norway already forbid ads on television for children under twelve, the province of Québec for those under thirteen. Other countries, including Greece, the Flemish part of Belgium, and New Zealand, have also imposed restrictions. How much effect this has is open to debate. One problem is that TV is just one of many platforms for advertising, along with the Internet, mobile phones, and even computer games. Another is that kids no longer confine their viewing to children's TV. In Britain, the show most watched by under-sixteens is *Coronation Street,* a gritty soap opera aimed at adults.

Nevertheless, as the public mood shifts, companies are finding it trickier to market to children. For Christmas 2006, Wal-Mart launched a Web site where two elves urged kids to click YES when a toy appeared on the screen. "If you show us what you want on your wish list, we'll send it straight off to your parents," promised the elf with the faux-cockney accent. Consumer groups attacked the site for promoting Pester Power, and even readers of *Advertising Age,* the in-house bible for the ad industry, had misgivings, with more than half agreeing that Wal-Mart had gone "too far."

Even at the London Toy Fair, I find companies beating the anticonsumerist drum. A family firm called Charlie Crow is here to display costumes that deliberately avoid tie-ins with TV characters or the latest movie. There are maids, soldiers, lions, sheep, kings, and queens but no Spiderman or Batman. There is a princess but no Princess Leia, a witch but no Hermione Granger. Marketing director Sue Crowder tells me that the aim is to curb the consumerism in childhood. "You walk around this fair and it sometimes feels like the child is the least important part of the process, that it's all about selling rather than playing," she says. Charlie Crow costumes break the mold by staying generic. "When everything is merchandised or branded, it's harder for children to be themselves," says Crowder. "We want to give them costumes that don't impose a formula, so that the story and the character are up to them—that's when their imagination really runs wild." Four years into production, Charlie Crow costumes are selling briskly in Britain and abroad, snapped up by schools keen to encourage historical role-playing and by parents tired of branded costumes that lead to endless demands for more accessories ("I need the wand *and* the broom to go with my Harry Potter robes!").

It may seem like a paradox for a company to cast itself as a champion of anticonsumerism, but that is the world we live in. Consumption is a part of life. When it comes to children, the challenge is not to stop it altogether but to impose limits.

In the end, much of that will depend on parents finding the strength to say no—and perhaps we are starting to learn how to do it. Sophie Lambert, a public relations consultant in Paris, used to buy her two young daughters anything they asked for. She basked in their gratitude until one day she overheard them making up stories with their dolls. One character said to the other, "I don't want a cuddle; I want you to buy me a present.

Buying me something means you love me." Lambert froze. "It was like getting an electric shock," she says. "I suddenly realized that I was teaching them that material things were more important than love." Lambert put away the credit card and began getting down on the floor to play with her daughters. She now buys presents only occasionally and feels that her relationship with the girls is much richer. "We shop less and talk more," she says. "They also play more deeply with the toys they have because they're not always thinking about the next purchase."

What children really need and want from us is the thing we often find hardest to give: our time and attention, with no conditions attached. When they don't get it, they go for the money. Malcolm Page learned that lesson when his seven-year-old son, Noah, brought home a school project called "Why I Love My Parents." On the first page was a long list of things his mother did, which included making him laugh, cooking nice things to eat, and cuddling him when he got hurt. On the dad page, Noah had simply scrawled: "He buys me things." Page, a financial analyst in London, felt a horrible stab of recognition when he read it. "I'd always wanted to have a closer relationship with Noah than I had with my own father, but somehow I never found enough time or energy to make that happen," he says. "I guess I saw the presents as a peace offering, or as a way to ease my conscience about not being a better father." Page decided there was only one way to break the cycle: to spend less money on Noah and more time with him.

He started dropping him off at school one day a week, taking him to the park on weekends, and coming home more often to read bedtime stories in the evenings. He also cut back on the presents. Six months later, their relationship has changed. "Before, whenever the two of us were alone, he was always at me about buying him this or that, but that's pretty much gone now," says Page. "The last time we went to the park he spent the whole time talking about what it would be like to live on the moon—how you would eat, walk to school, play football, even go to the loo. It was hilarious and amazing. And it was such a relief not to have the 'what are we going to buy next?' question hovering between us the whole time."

Melinda Ball, a single mother in New York, took a more formal route to reining in her shopaholic teenage daughter, Hannah. She dubbed breakfast an official "pester-free zone." The rules: no asking for money, no talking about consumer goods, but anything else goes. Sometimes mother and daughter sit over their muesli in moody silence, but often they chat about school, their friends, or Hannah's plans to be an architect when she grows up.

"It's nice not being treated like a walking ATM, so it's a relief that Hannah is starting to be a little less obsessive about getting me to buy her things, even away from breakfast," says Ball. "I'm actually thinking about making dinner pester-free as well."

In the fight against the consumerization of childhood, the birthday party has emerged as a key battlefront. The very idea of celebrating a child's birth date is a modern one. In the early Middle Ages, the church denounced birthday parties as pagan and tried to stamp them out. The ritual gradually spread in the modern era, and by the nineteenth century middle-class families were marking their children's birthdays by gathering a few relatives together in the home. After the Second World War, the parties grew more elaborate, with trips with friends to the swimming pool or some other destination. More recently, party budgets have ballooned, with the superrich ostentatiously raising the bar. David Brooks, chief executive of a bulletproof vest manufacturer, made headlines in 2006 for allegedly blowing $10 million on his daughter's thirteenth birthday party. A dream team of pop stars, including Tom Petty, Stevie Nicks, and 50 Cent, entertained three hundred girls at the Rainbow Room in New York. Guests went home with party bags containing digital cameras and iPods. Supersizing the birthday party has even become a form of entertainment in itself, thanks to *My Super Sweet 16,* an MTV reality show that depicts spoiled teenagers planning parties and balls of breathtaking extravagance. Though many watch the program to sneer at the excess, others clearly treat it as a source of ideas.

Even ordinary parents feel the pressure to make every birthday party more spectacular, more lavish, more memorable than the last. Think petting zoos in the backyard, limousine service for five-year-olds, and themed cakes worthy of a society ball. As with so many other features of modern childhood, the "perfect" birthday party is often more about the adults than it is about the children. One U.S. Web site runs a monthly contest that rewards parents who come up with the "best party ideas." A 2006 survey found that in the run-up to the big day British parents are three times more likely than their children to suffer from headaches, upset stomachs, and other symptoms of stress. The survey also found that while two-thirds of adults think their child wants to invite the whole class to a hired venue with professional entertainment, 59 percent of children would actually prefer to have a few friends over for a bit of fun at home. One London mother recently attended a birthday party where eight four-year-olds visited a fire station, made Play Doh sculptures, assembled and ate their own pizzas, and watched a show by a professional puppeteer—all in the space of two hours. The birthday boy actually fell asleep during the puppet routine. "It was such a blur that I don't think the kids really registered what was going on," says the mother. "I'm not sure if they even realized they were there to celebrate someone's birthday."

Sometimes the scramble to host the Best Party Ever can be downright dangerous. In 2006, a family in Coral Gables, Florida, hired a company to bring a coterie of wild animals to entertain the guests at their seven-year-old's birthday celebration. When the trainer released the cougar from its cage, the cat clamped its jaws around the head of a four-year-old girl, severing part of her ear and lacerating her eyelids and cheeks.

Exhausted and appalled by the one-upmanship, many parents are starting to scale down the birthday party. Susan Sawchuk in San Francisco decided to go back to basics when her son Jack turned five. He had been to some very lavish parties, including one that involved a private tour of an aquarium and a professional fire-eater. He had come back with party bags stuffed with everything from Giants baseball tickets to an MP3 player. "It was the MP3 player that did it," says Sawchuk. "I just thought, this is getting out of control. These kids aren't even in school yet—what do they need an MP3 player for?"

So she took a stand. On his fifth birthday, she invited six of Jack's closest friends to spend a couple of hours at their house. The children played all the games that professional entertainers look down on and that many parents assume are no longer enough to keep modern children happy, including hide-and-seek, pin-the-tail-on-the-donkey, and Kim's game. Sawchuk also set up a treasure hunt, where the treasure was the right to the first slice of birthday cake. During the final thirty minutes, the children played musical statues to a Beatles CD. None of the boys complained that the party bags contained only a coloring book and a lollipop, and everyone went home in high spirits. Several months later, Jack remembers the day with a big smile. "It was the best party ever," he says. "I played a lot with my friends."

Sawchuk felt the chill of disapproval from parents who favor bigger budgets, but plans are to do the same next year. "You just have to ignore the peer pressure, which mostly comes from other parents," she says. "And the only way to do that is to remind yourself over and over again that birthday parties are for the children; they're not for the grown-ups."

To make it easier to resist the arms race for the "perfect" party, parents are banding together to sign their own nonproliferation treaties. Some are fixing spending limits on gifts and party bags, or eliminating them altogether. Others are agreeing on guest quotas. Campaign groups are even starting to appear.

Bill Doherty is a professor of family studies at the University of Minnesota. I first met him at a conference in Chicago, where he talked about the pitfalls of overscheduling children. In 2007, he turned his attention to the scourge of the supersize party by helping launch a grassroots parent group called Birthdays Without Pressure in St. Paul, Minnesota. A genial figure with an easy sense of humor, Doherty is no puritanical killjoy. He just wants to dampen down the frenzy surrounding children's birthday parties—and to root that change in a broader challenge to the culture of soaring expectations.

"I want to give parents permission not to apologize for having a family-only party or for inviting a few friends and having a few simple games. And I want these parents to feel that they are part of a larger social change," says Doherty. "We're not trying to create new rules about birthday parties—there is nothing inherently wrong with gift bags or entertainers or inviting the whole second-grade class. The point is that there is no such thing as a perfect party, either large or small. You just need to ask yourself if you are planning from your own values or from community pressure to oversize."

One way to ease the peer pressure is to make birthday parties "children only." That takes away the need to impress other parents with the caliber of your food, entertainment, handling of small children, even the tidiness of your home. We've done our fair share of parties in puppet theatres and soccer clinics, but the one I remember most fondly was my daughter's fifth. The parents dropped off their children at our house and then left. We kept it very simple, with a treasure hunt, musical chairs, and pass-the-parcel. The girls had a ball—and so did we.

Of course, unchecked consumerism does more than just spoil children. It also forces them to grow up faster, a phenomenon described in marketing-speak as KAGOY ("kids are getting older younger"). But is this really a good thing? Should we be encouraging children to confront adult hang-ups, vices, and fears at younger ages? My own childhood was marred by a family expedition to see *Invasion of the Body Snatchers,* a science-fiction-cum-horror movie about aliens taking over the world by manufacturing replicas of people. Despite the 14+ rating and my being only eleven, my father somehow managed to get us in. Images from the movie haunted me for years afterward, especially the final scene, where the Donald Sutherland character points at the heroine and unleashes that bloodcurdling, unearthly howl that the aliens use to identify a human. Until I was fourteen, I went to bed every night buried under a pile of cushions, or I'd sneak into my brother's room to sleep with him.

We are not the first generation to fret about the young being exposed to adult material too soon. Though our ancestors were less concerned about children being terrified by noises in the night, they did worry that they might be corrupted. Plato warned that the works of dramatic poets would pollute the minds of the young. In the first century A.D., a rhetorician named Quintilian upbraided his fellow Romans for encouraging children to join in the lewd antics enjoyed by the grown-ups: "We rejoice if they say something over-free, and words which we should not tolerate from the lips even of an Alexandrian page are greeted with laughter and a kiss. . . . They hear us use such words, they see our mistresses and minions; every dinner party is loud with foul songs, and things are presented to their eyes of which we should blush to speak." In 1528, William Tyndale, who produced the first widely distributed English translation of the Bible, denounced England's clergy for permitting the young to read "Robin Hood and Bevis of Hampton, Hercules, Hector, and Troylus, with a thousand histories and fables of love and wantons and of ribaldry, as filthy as the heart can think, to corrupt the minds of youth withal."

After the Romantics enshrined the idea of childhood innocence, that fear of corruption grew steadily stronger. Critics warned that reading comics would overstimulate the young and lead them into crime and debauchery. Others fretted that children would be morally tainted by working in the factories of the Industrial Revolution, spurring some bosses to hire nuns or matrons to set minds at ease. Like every other fear about childhood, the fear of corruption intensified through the twentieth century, widening to include everything from rock music to *Happy Days*.

This brings us to one of the most curious paradoxes of modern childhood: today, even as we fret about their loss of innocence, we allow, even encourage, children to dip their toes into the adult pool earlier and earlier. One reason for this is our urge to get closer to our kids, to cement that "best friend" status. After all, nothing bonds two people like a shared hobby. Just listen to mothers rave about getting facials and pedicures with their nine-year-old daughters. I began reading Tintin books to our son very early on because I wanted us to share my love for the stories. I was delighted when he began playing make-believe games featuring Captain Haddock and Professor Calculus. I was less happy when he started talking about heroin smugglers in the playground.

Eager to build a customer base for the future, companies groom the young with "starter" products. Witness the boom in spas offering beauty treatments and makeovers for under-tens. Or the way the gambling industry is making casino hotels more child-friendly, even introducing slot machines with Pink Panther themes. Kidsbeer, a popular nonalcoholic drink in the prepubescent market in Japan, looks like beer, comes in brown glass bottles, and is promoted with slogans like "Perfect for those evenings when you want to be a bit like an adult." One of the company's commercials shows a boy crying about failing a math test, and then weeping with delight after downing a Kidsbeer.

And then there is the sex thing. Through most of history, and across cultures, the young tended to dress as smaller versions of their parents. The son of a laborer wore workmen's clothes, the daughter of a society family lacy finery. In paintings, aristocratic girls as young as six posed in low-cut tops and with alluring hairdos in the hope of catching the eye of a distant monarch. From the eighteenth century, however, as the notion of childhood innocence took hold, such images began to jar. In 1785, the poet William Cowper lamented that girls were dressing above their age: "E'en misses, at whose age their mothers wore the backstring and the bib, assume the dress of womanhood."

Today, we've turned back the clock to the pre-Enlightenment era, with people of all ages dressing the same. The difference now is that children are being ushered into an adult culture that grows raunchier by the day. Good-bye backstring and bib. Hello Little

Miss Naughty padded bras. On children's TV, the staid presenters of yesteryear have been replaced by Shakira wannabes sporting cheeky tattoos and bare midriffs. Barbie, whose anatomically impossible figure and glamorous wardrobe made her the original feminist bête noire, has been eclipsed by the uber-sexy, sneering Bratz dolls. You can even buy a onesie emblazoned with the slogan "Jr. Pimp Squad."

When it comes to ramping up the sex quotient in childhood, girls are on the sharp end. Retailers such as La Senza Girl, Limited Too, and Abercrombie and Fitch sell fishnet stockings, padded bralettes, and saucy message panties in micro sizes. Stationers carry pink pencil cases, notepads, geometry sets, and other classroom gear bearing the Playboy bunny logo. Even if we don't buy our little girls T-shirts declaring, "So many young boys, so little time," they still seem to pick up the sexual vibe by osmosis. I was stunned the other night when my five-year-old daughter started gyrating in the bath while singing the jingle from that Renault ad: "Shaking that ass, shaking that ass."

Am I being uptight? Is all this raunch just a bit of harmless fun or postmodern irony? Maybe up to a point, but it also feels as if a line has been crossed. As we have already seen, blurring the boundary between adulthood and childhood can have a cramping effect on the young, cutting down the space where they can be children. Girls have always dressed up to play mom, nurse, or glamour-puss as a way to have fun or explore and experiment with female identities. But that was play, which a child could turn on or off. The current vogue for embracing the trappings of womanhood seems less playful, more about adopting an attitude or buying into a way of life. So our daughters' painted nails are no longer just for fun, they're part of their "look"; that halter top is not a costume, it's a wardrobe accessory.

When it comes to aping grown-ups, children may know the script and how to strike the right poses, but there is little evidence that they understand the emotional and moral complexity of playing adult roles. They are not miniature adults; they are children. When a society both venerates the innocence of childhood and hurls its children into the sexual melting pot of pop culture, the upshot is likely to be confusion, or worse. Perhaps that explains why childhood anxiety is on the rise. Or why children in many countries are becoming sexually active earlier. Or why eating disorders, body dysphoria, and other ailments once associated with adults are now rife among the young. In one recent survey in Australia, over 70 percent of seven- and eight-year-old girls told researchers they wished they were slimmer, with most believing that losing weight would make them more popular. A 2007 study by an American Psychological Association task force concluded that the sexual depiction of girlhood promotes body dissatisfaction, depression, and low self-esteem.

And then there is the most uncomfortable question of all: if we dress our daughters like Lolita, what kind of message does that send to the pedophiles that we are all so worried about?

As these questions climb up the agenda, the raunch culture is coming under siege. Schools across the West have banned outfits that afford a peek of the pupil's thong underwear. In 2007 the British Teachers Union called for an end to the "sexploitation" of children by advertisers and the media. Abercrombie and Fitch famously withdrew its kiddie thong collection after complaints by parents and politicians. Asda, a British supermarket chain, stopped selling black and pink lace lingerie for children following a public outcry. Next, a clothing retailer, dropped the "So many young boys, so little time" T-shirts for the same reason. Other products torpedoed by parental protests include a range of Bratz bras for little girls and a line of Hasbro dolls for six-year-olds that were based on a scantily clad pop group called the Pussycat Dolls.

Children themselves are joining the battle against raunch. In the United States, over 2.5 million teenagers have taken the "virginity pledge," vowing to eschew sex until marriage. Other children are taking aim at eroticized products. Mattel mothballed Lingerie Barbie—"Her enchanting ensemble begins with a delicate black merry widow bustier with pink bow accent. Her matching robe offers alluring cover"—after public protests that included a letter-writing campaign by schoolgirls. In 2005, girls aged eleven to fifteen picketed a London branch of W. H. Smith, a stationery chain that stocks Playboy-themed classroom equipment. "They're using things we need for our education to sell us the idea that we are sex objects," said one thirteen-year-old protestor. "It's disgusting and it makes me angry." W. H. Smith stood its ground, but other British retailers, including Claire's Accessories and John Lewis, later ditched the Playboy stationery.

Making childhood a consumerism-free zone is impossible in a consumer culture. But the time has come to set limits. Not only are the health and happiness of our children at stake but also the future of the planet: mankind simply cannot go on consuming the way it does now. The upside is that more and more people are waking up to that fact.

The best place to begin reining in the consumer culture is with the young. Collectively, that means keeping commercial material out of schools, tightening the restrictions on children's advertising, and toning down the raunch quotient. For parents, it means, once again, striking a balance. Buying things is fine, but most of us know when we are giving in too much to Pester Power. We can feel it in our gut.

Yet saying no is only the start. We also have to deal with the fallout: the cries of "You're the worst mother in the world!" or "If you don't buy me an iPhone, I'll never talk to you again!" Such rancor will surface no matter how much or how little you buy, because consumer lust can never be snuffed out altogether, especially in children—that is the price we pay for living in an age of abundance. But we can begin to tame those cravings. One way is to stop using cash as a substitute for time and attention. Another is to tame our own shopaholism.

Malcolm Page has stopped buying every high-tech gadget that catches his fancy. He hopes his example will help his son, Noah, grow up at least partly inoculated against the virus of materialism. "It's a lesson that all of us, children and adults, need to learn," he says. "That spending time together is more important than spending money."

TWELVE

Safety:
Playing with Fire

To keep oneself safe does not mean to bury oneself.
—*Seneca (4 B.C.–65 A.D.)*

It was on a squally morning in early spring, with the temperature hovering around zero, that Magnus Macleod first learned that fire is hot. Very, very hot. As a member of the Secret Garden nursery group, the three-year-old had spent the day tramping round a forest in eastern Scotland. To beat the chill, the children, helped by their child-minder, built a campfire using twigs, branches, and leaves gathered from the ground. They formed a circle around the flames, warming their toes and fingers and drinking hot lemonade. Then, without warning, Magnus reached into the fire and picked up a glowing ember with his bare hand. His howl echoed through the woods.

What happened next? Well, these days, you would expect all hell to break loose. A lawsuit launched against the Secret Garden. A blizzard of angry questions from the health and safety inspector: Where was the supervising adult when Magnus picked up the ember? Why was there no qualified nurse on hand? Why were three-year-olds anywhere near an open fire? And you can imagine the parents queuing up to yank their children out of the nursery.

In the end, none of the above came to pass. Everyone took Magnus's mishap with the burning ember in stride. Sure, the wound on his right index finger lasted for a fortnight, but he also learned a valuable lesson about the dangers of fire. Now, when he finds a box of matches, he hands it to the nearest adult. And he never touches hot embers. His mother, Kate, not only kept Magnus in the Secret Garden, she also enrolled his younger brother, Freddie.

"Of course, we were a little concerned at first when he got burned, but the main thing is that Magnus is now very sensible about fire—he knows not to get too close to it," she says. "The truth is that there are risks in the world and that children benefit from being exposed to them within reason."

As the first outdoor nursery in Britain, the Secret Garden is a direct challenge to many of the shibboleths of modern childhood. Like other schools using nature as a classroom, it posits a new way for children to learn, play, and socialize. But it also challenges the very modern belief that children need to be handled with extreme care, that the way to rear them is indoors, in places that are rigorously hygienic, accident-proof, climate-controlled, and under constant supervision.

The Secret Garden curriculum is the opposite of all that. Whatever the weather, and in Scotland that can mean subzero temperatures, icy winds whipping in from the North Sea, or never-ending rain, the children spend the whole day outdoors. They pee in the woods without washing their hands. The forest they explore is strewn with poisonous fungi as well as tasty-looking yew berries and foxglove flowers that if eaten can cause vomiting, dizziness, and fluctuations in a child's heart rate. Stroking chickens, lambs, and other livestock means exposure to God knows how many germs. Oh, and let's not forget those open campfires.

Yet despite, or perhaps because of, those perils, the Secret Garden is winning converts. Its founder is Cathy Bache, a brisk middle-aged woman with a penchant for colorful knitwear. Living for a while in Norway inspired her to import the Scandinavian idea of the outdoor nursery. In 2005, she began looking after a handful of children in the woods around her house in Letham, a village in Fife. The Secret Garden recently won a state grant, and Bache now has twenty-four kids on the books and a long waiting list.

"Some parents are a wee bit nervous at first, but when they come along and see how well the children cope, how much fun they have, and how much they learn, they relax," says Bache. "A lot of children nowadays are cooped up indoors like battery hens; they have no freedom, because as a society we have become so uptight about safety. We seem to exist in a constant state of fear."

You can say that again. As we have already seen, much of our thinking about children is shaped by fear—the fear that a shred of their potential will go untapped, that they will fail to shine, that they will be unhappy, lose their innocence, or dislike us, that they will grow up too quickly or too slowly, that they will reflect badly on us as parents.

But in some ways the most visceral fear, the one that taps deepest into our evolutionary hard drive, is the fear that our children are in physical danger. Worrying about the young getting hurt is common across all cultures and times. Even in the prehistoric family, the mother, and probably the father when he was home, kept an eye out to prevent toddlers burning their fingers in the fire as Magnus did. Every society has its bogeymen. In the Middle Ages, Christians in Europe fretted that Jews would murder their children and use their blood to make matzo bread for Passover.

In the modern era, however, worries about the physical welfare of children have exploded, fueled by a growing belief that the young are inherently fragile and the world increasingly dangerous. In the early twentieth century, officialdom began warning that the home was a minefield of germs, electric sockets, hot stoves, and water to drown in. As the car came to dominate the urban landscape, cities built fenced playgrounds and passed laws banning marbles, soccer, play fighting, and other street games. At home, parents set aside rooms where children could play safely indoors.

Each new threat to the young, real or imagined, triggers more panic and a further safety clampdown. Remember the fuss in the early 1980s about psychos handing out poisoned candy and apples containing razor blades on Halloween? Such incidents were so rare as to be almost urban myths, but that did not ease the hysteria. We used to rake through our haul of candy with a fine-toothed comb, searching for any sign of tampering. And the apples went straight in the bin. It was also around this time that parents began accompanying children trick-or-treating.

Over the last decade, however, worries about child safety have reached fever pitch. Just look at the twenty-first-century home, with safety catches on the doors and kitchen cabinets, plastic stoppers in the outlets, and padded bumpers on all the sharp edges. You can even buy a lock for toilet seats. My editor paid an expert $1,500 to "baby-proof" his house. And the fear is even sharper outside the home. Letting a child ride a tricycle without a helmet or play in the park without first dousing her in half a bottle of sunblock is now considered gross abuse. Snowball fights, once a cherished rite of childhood in the winter months, have been banned by schools across northern Europe and North America. At one school in Cumbria, England, pupils wear industrial safety goggles to play conkers, an ancient and hugely popular game that involves battering chestnuts attached to strings. Another English school has replaced traditional ties with clip-ons to reduce the risk of choking. An elementary school in Attleboro, Massachusetts, decided that tag was a health hazard and banned it. Many children now go to school armed with sachets of sanitizer gel designed to zap every germ in sight. Around the world, teachers report that when classes go on field trips some parents now trail along behind in cars to make sure their little one is okay.

The upshot is that the twenty-first-century child is raised in captivity, cooped up indoors and ferried between appointments in the backseat of a car. Many schools in Sweden no longer permit children under eleven to bicycle to and from home by themselves. Two-thirds of British eight- to ten-year-olds have never walked to a shop or park alone, and a third of them have never played outside without a grown-up supervising.

Why the recent surge in fear? One reason may be the trend toward smaller families. As David Anderegg, author of *Worried All the Time: Rediscovering the Joy of Parenthood in an Age of Anxiety,* puts it: "The fewer kids you have, the more precious they become and the more risk-averse you get." The fear may also spring from those busy schedules that keep us apart: the more time families spend together, the easier it becomes for the parents to trust their children's capacity to handle risk. But our cities have changed, too. There is a lot more traffic around these days. And many communities are more anonymous, which means that the streets around our homes are full of strangers rather than neighbors whom we know well and can rely on to look out for our children.

We are also victims of a basic paradox: being more secure can actually make people feel more afraid. Even when traffic is calm and crime rates low, fear remains the default mode. A ripple of unease passes through our house whenever the front door is open: Where are the kids? Are they playing near the road? Is that a car coming? Or a mugger? According to UNICEF, Sweden is now the safest place in the world to grow up, yet Swedish parents and bureaucrats are so paranoid about children coming to harm that one of the country's leading psychiatrists, David Eberhard, published a book entitled *Land of the Safety Junkies* in 2006. "Sweden is a perfect example of how the safer you are, the more anxious you become about even the tiniest risks," he says. "And this is especially true where children are concerned."

It does not help that some people have a vested interest in spotlighting, or even exaggerating, the dangers that children face in daily life. That includes companies that sell child safety products (think UV sunglasses for toddlers), health and safety bureaucracies with budgets to justify, and advocacy groups with a message to sell. It also includes the media. With so many pages and so much airtime to fill, news editors are looking for stories that stand out—and nothing grabs the attention like a report about something horrible happening to a child. Even if pedophile crimes have not risen over the last twenty years, the coverage devoted to them has mushroomed. You can hardly pick up a newspaper or switch on the TV news without catching a lurid report on a child sex crime, complete with heartrending footage of the victim. The blanket coverage has clearly had an effect on me. As a teenager, I did a lot of babysitting. It was an easy way to earn pocket money, and I am still in touch with some of the families I worked for twenty years ago. Today, though, I feel queasy about letting a teenage boy or a male nanny look after my own children. Part of me knows this is unreasonable, unfair, and even a bit hysterical, but another part is paralyzed by the two words that brush aside even the most comforting statistics and act like a trump card for every modern parent: "What if . . ."

Marinated in adult panic, children have clearly absorbed the message that the world is a perilous place and the only way to survive it is to put safety first. A recent British poll asked seven hundred children around the age of ten to identify the most important lesson from their upbringing. The number one answer was: stay safe.

Now, the upside is that all this caution and cosseting probably saves many children from getting into scrapes, or worse, but at what cost? What do we sacrifice when we make a cult of child safety? Well, where do you want to start?

When child safety becomes an obsession, trust evaporates. Every adult suddenly looks like a potential pedophile—the most heinous crime in a culture in thrall to children. Modern dads receive a mixed message: be touchy-feely with your own kids but, when it comes to other people's, keep the touching and feeling to yourself. The other day I was in the playground when a toddler fell off the slide and started bawling. My first instinct was to console him, but I checked myself. What if someone thinks I'm a pervert? So I stood there, mouthing platitudes at a safe distance, until his mother came over. That same paralysis can have appalling consequences. In 2002, a two-year-old girl wandered out of an open door in her nursery in Lower Brailes, a quiet, picturesque village in the Cotswolds region of England. A bricklayer passing in his truck noticed the toddler ambling along the edge of the road and thought about stopping to make sure she was safe. Instead, fearing he might be branded a pedophile, he drove on. A few minutes later, the little girl tumbled into the village pond and drowned. "I kept thinking I should go back," the bricklayer later told investigators. "The reason I didn't was because I thought people might think I was trying to abduct her."

Cloistering children narrows their horizons by cutting them off from the community. You don't get to know the neighbors or the local shopkeepers if you travel everywhere in a car. Oversheltered children may also fail to learn basic street smarts, which may explain why early teens are knocked down by cars more than any other age group.

Psychologists argue that when children are overprotected, when every moment of their day is regimented and supervised, they are more likely to grow up to be anxious and risk-averse. Brain scans lend credence to the well-established observation that around 15 percent of all children are born predisposed to anxiety and shyness. Longer studies now suggest that more than half eventually outgrow that early awkwardness. Why? It seems to come down at least partly to parenting: if parents are encouraging, optimistic, and willing to accept risks in daily life, then the anxious child is more likely to come out of his shell.

Kids who are wrapped in cotton wool may eventually swing to the other extreme, seeking out the turbo-charged thrills of drugs, sex, dangerous driving, or violence. Perhaps that is another reason that rates for substance abuse, self-harm, and anxiety are now highest among children from the kind of affluent families that put a premium on child safety.

As a clinical psychologist in Halifax, Nova Scotia, Michael Ungar has a front-row seat on the fallout from the culture of overprotection. In 2007, he published a book entitled *Too Safe for Their Own Good: How Risk and Responsibility Help Teens Thrive.* "There's a terrible irony here," he says. "By trying so hard to eliminate risk from our children's lives, we end up making them more anxious. We can also make them less safe and less successful in the long run because they don't get all the benefits that come from taking risks." Ungar is referring to research suggesting that fortune favors the bold: those who are confident and willing to take chances are less likely to suffer accidents of any kind.

And what about freedom and adventure? Surely taking risks, flirting with danger, is one of the joys of childhood. Recently, our family stayed a week with friends in a small village in southern Spain. My son and his pal spent every day wandering through the hills, collecting sticks, building little stone forts, and eating oranges straight from the trees. Sometimes they were completely out of sight of the house. Afterward, when I asked what the best part of the holiday had been, my son answered in a flash. "The freedom," he said.

I was stunned. Freedom seemed like such a big concept for a seven-year-old. But it made me realize that my children inhabit a highly circumscribed world. At home, they are not allowed to walk to school, go to a friend's house, or even cross the street without an adult. At my son's age, I was walking and cycling around the neighborhood alone with my friends. Sometimes it seems to me that the nearest my children get to adventure is watching TV shows like *Raven,* where other children compete in "dangerous" events that have been vetted by health and safety officials.

If a surfeit of protection is the problem, then what is the solution? How do we break free from the cycle of fear? The first step is to tune out the background hysteria and take a hard look at the facts.

Fact 1: The world is now a safer place for children than it has ever been. Child deaths by injury have fallen by 50 percent in developed countries over the last thirty years. Between 1970 and 2000, the number of British minors killed in accidents fell from 17.5 for every 100,000 to 4.5. And the trend is the same in other countries.

Fact 2: Our panic about stranger danger does not fit the statistics. Random pedophile attacks are extremely rare; strangers are not the chief threat to our children. A child is far more likely to suffer violence or sexual abuse at the hands of his own parents or relatives.

Fact 3: Keeping children locked up indoors or ferrying them around in the back of the car is not as safe as we think. Thousands of kids suffer accidents inside the home. And in many countries, more children now die as passengers in traffic accidents than as pedestrians. Risk is everywhere; the trick is to find the right balance.

Fact 4: Children are a lot more resilient and robust than we give them credit for. Though the early years are formative, a few knocks along the way are unlikely to scar anyone for life; they might even make them stronger. A recent Danish study found no link between trauma suffered in childhood and the quality of life in adulthood.

Fact 5: Children are often more sensible, competent, and able to manage risk than we imagine. Just look at the way the young cope in the harshest corners of the Third World. Among the Fulani people of West Africa, girls as young as four venture out of the village to fetch firewood and water. Many street children in Brazil survive a slew of perils that would make the average Western parent break out in a cold sweat: malnutrition, gang violence, hostile shopkeepers, sexual predators, corrupt police, and drug dealers. As Samuel Butler, the English novelist, quipped in the nineteenth century: "Young people have a marvellous faculty of either dying or adapting themselves to circumstances."

And look how well children cope with risk in the affluent, uptight West when given half a chance. Remember the Reggio preschool at Prampolini? Visitors are always amazed by the way the children are free to use scissors, tacks, and many other objects that are banned elsewhere as a swallowing or cutting hazard. The head teacher explains that although the more risky items are introduced slowly to the youngest children, the assumption is always that every child can learn to cope, even if they get into a scrape or two along the way. "Dangerous things happen in life, so there is no point trying to eliminate all risks from childhood," she explains. "We explore the dangers of certain objects, and the children learn very quickly how to handle them."

Armed with the facts and alarmed by the sight of their children growing up in a fishbowl, more parents are coming round to the idea that a little bit of risk is an essential ingredient of a happy, healthy childhood. One of the publishing sensations of 2006–7 was a tome whose very title sounds like a call to arms against the stifling culture of overprotection. The *Dangerous Book for Boys* is stuffed with tips on how to enjoy all kinds of high-risk pastimes, from racing go-carts to making a slingshot/catapult to playing conkers (without safety goggles).

The trend toward making playgrounds safer by removing "high-risk" apparatus, such as tall slides and merry-go-rounds, seems to be going in reverse. Under pressure from children and parents seeking greater thrills, officials in Britain are now introducing more adventurous playground equipment, including scramble nets inspired by army assault courses, maypole swings, and hair-raising merry-go-rounds known as Dutch discs. And families love it.

Pressure is also building to get children back on the streets. Cities are imposing traffic calming measures to give more space and protection to pedestrians. At the same time, campaigners are showing that even now many streets are not as dangerous as we think. Once a year, millions of children in forty countries take part in the International Walk to School Day. Of course, parents and teachers are often hovering nearby, or even leading group walks, but for many children the day offers a small taste of freedom. And for some it changes everything. In 2006, Cindy Browning left the Ford Explorer at home in Indianapolis, Indiana, and walked with her ten-year-old son, Max, to his school a kilometer away. Browning was amazed by how safe the route turned out to be, with lights or special road markings at all three intersections. The only other people out and about were local residents heading off to work. Some of them smiled and waved, and Browning even recognized one woman as a secretary at the building where she works as an insurance broker. The upshot: Max now walks to and from school every day, usually with a friend and almost always without a grown-up. "Looking back, I'm really not sure why I thought going on foot was so dangerous," says his mother. Max loves the independence: "It makes me feel less like a baby," he says proudly. "And I have a lot of fun with my friend on the way." The exercise is good for him, too. A British study that monitored 5,500 children born in the early 1990s found that even a small increase in physical activity—and that includes a short walk to school—sharply reduced a child's chances of being overweight.

Another walk-to-school initiative gave Martha Kane the courage to let Ethan, her eleven-year-old son, cycle home after dark from his friend's house in Toronto. The trip involves crossing two busy roads. "I'll admit that the first few times I was sitting by the window until he got home, but then I realized it wasn't such a big deal," she says. "I mean, when I was his age I used to ride my bike all over our neighborhood by myself after dark, and we live in a much better neighborhood now than my family did." Some of Kane's friends have followed her example.

Once you overcome one parental fear, it gets easier to go far-ther. When my son turned eight, we decided it was time to let him walk down to the corner shop. Harry's Newsagent is set on a busy shopping street around the corner from our house, but the journey is less than fifty meters and does not involve crossing any streets. The first couple of times he went we hovered nervously by the gate, but now he makes the trip with the front door closed. I feel a bit silly for having waited so long to let him make the journey: he could easily have managed it a year or more ear-lier. Emboldened by his success, we now allow my daughter free-doms that would have been unthinkable for my son, such as playing in the front yard without supervision.

A few months after Magnus burned his finger, I decide to join the Secret Garden for a day in the outdoors. It is late January and the temperature is around zero Celsius. Six three- and four-year-olds, including Magnus, arrive dressed from head to toe in warm, waterproof clothing. They make a beeline for the chicken coop at the back of Bache's garden. Avian flu is in the news again, yet none of the parents dropping off seems alarmed by the re-ports. Two of the children are feeding pellets to the hens when another discovers a dead sparrow on the ground. "Maybe it's sleeping," says Alexia. "No, he's not dreaming, he's dead," says Duncan. Bache picks up the bird and fans out its soft wing for the children to touch. They then find a place to bury the corpse behind the old dovecote, marking the grave site with rusty nails and shards of broken glass and pottery left behind by the previous owners. I think of tetanus shots, and feel relieved that the children do not cut their fingers.

Then we head off into the woods. Along the way, the children stop to smash the frozen puddles on the lane. Sometimes they tumble into the dirty water underneath. Magnus picks up a chunk of ice from the ground and starts sucking it.

All of this makes the Secret Garden sound like a parent's worst nightmare, a breeding ground for illness, injury, or worse. But it turns out to be just the opposite. Studies in Denmark show that children in outdoor preschools catch 80 percent fewer colds, sore throats, ear infections, and other contagious illnesses than do those cooped up indoors. Studies in Germany have found that outdoor pupils also suffer fewer injuries and are less aggressive. Parents at the Secret Garden bear this out: Bache's twenty-four pupils seem immune to many of the bugs that strike down their friends in mainstream nurseries.

In recent years, allergy rates have soared among children around the world. Scientists are still trying to work out why, but some suspect part of the blame may lie with the highly sanitized environment in which so many kids grow up nowadays. Just look at what happened in Germany. Before unification, allergy rates were much higher in the western part, even though the Communist-run eastern half had much worse pollution and more children living on farms. After the countries reunited, East Germany was cleaned up and urbanized—and allergy rates soared. Other research suggests that the sharp rise in children with type 1 diabetes may also be the result of oversanitized environments. This brings us back to the same old irony of modern childhood: by striving to create for children an ideal environment, in this case a scrupulously hygienic one, we may actually be making them weaker. Every spray from the Febreze bottle, every antibacterial wipe, every hour of outdoor play replaced by an hour of indoor play could be denying them another chance to build up their immune systems. If so, then nurseries like the Secret Garden are just what the doctor ordered.

Nature is a risky place, but children learn quickly how to navigate the dangers. At one point, Magnus leads a group of us up a steep, winding track through a thick bank of bushes, some of them quite thorny. "It's my secret path," he says. Halfway up the hill, he stops to point out a branch hanging across the track at my waist height. Like the doorman at a posh hotel, he holds it back so I can pass unscathed. "If you're older than four you need to watch out for this branch," he tells me. "It can scratch you in the face."

Farther along the path, a three-year-old named Alice picks up a mushroom from the foot of a tree. "It's beautiful," she says. My reflex is to swipe it from her before she swallows it, so I feel pretty silly when her next words are: "But it might be poisonous, so I'll take it to Cathy." She gives the mushroom to Bache, who holds it up to the light and agrees that it is beautiful. "I don't recognize this one, Alice, so we'll just get rid of it," she says, tossing the mushroom into a bush.

Spending time in the Secret Garden clearly makes the children more self-reliant. The other day, four-year-old Eileen Sutherland went for a walk in the woods with her family. She got her foot stuck under a tree trunk and began to cry, looking to her parents for help. Instead of rushing to the rescue, however, they asked her what she would do if something similar happened at the Secret Garden. Eileen laughed, pulled her foot out, and carried on walking. "All we have to do is mention the Secret Garden and it's like she clicks into a different mode," says her mother, Jenny. "She becomes a more able and less fearful child."

In many families, this sets up a virtuous cycle: the more confident the child, the less fearful the parent, and so on. Jenny feels she does a lot less helicoptering and worrying now. "Before the Secret Garden, I think I babied Eileen and made things too easy and too safe," she says. "Now that I see what she is capable of, I try to be more hands-off. If she comes home with her bottom covered in mud, or with some bumps and bruises, well, that's just life."

Another mother, Natalie, tells me that there is strength in numbers. "At the Secret Garden you meet other parents who let their kids take more risks, and that gives you the confidence to do the same," she says. "It helps you challenge your own paranoia about child safety. And it makes you realize that not only is it impossible to create a perfectly safe world for your child, it's also not very good for them."

Nevertheless, the pressure from other parents can be hard to take. Many people complain that fellow moms and dads raise an eyebrow if they allow their children to walk home from school. On a recent winter vacation in Canada, my children went skating on the same outdoor ice rink that I grew up on. A generation ago, few, if any, kids wore helmets; today, they all do, including the most able skaters, with some even sporting full face-cages. On our second day, another father skated up to suggest that my children might suffer a terrible head injury if they fell. My first reaction was to feel ashamed—I'm failing to protect my kids. Then I came to my senses and followed my instincts. My children spent three weeks on the rink without helmets. They fell a lot, and even bumped their heads a couple of times, but neither got hurt. Both learned to skate. Afterward, when I asked my son what he liked best about going to the outdoor ice rink, he said,

"When you get going really fast and you feel the wind in your hair." Believe me, you don't ever feel that with a helmet on.

Back to the Secret Garden. After seven hours of climbing trees, hunting for hibernating ladybirds, and splashing in puddles in freezing temperatures, one thing is clear to me: children are a lot hardier than we adults imagine. As the day draws to a close, the kids all have rosy cheeks, and some have flecks of mud on their faces, but no one has complained once about being cold or wet.

I wish I could say the same for myself. My toes are so cold that I'm relieved when Bache suggests making a fire in a clearing in the woods. True to the Secret Garden ethos, the children take charge, gathering twigs and branches for kindling. Magnus volunteers to light the fire. Bache hands him a Swedish firestarter and a scrap of charred denim. With intense concentration, he scrapes the striker along the small rod of steel, sending sparks of up to 3,000°C arcing into the air. After several tries, one lands on the denim, causing it to ignite. Magnus picks up the material, keeping his fingers well away from the smoldering corner, and places it on the kindling. Within minutes we are all sitting round a roaring fire.

A smile crawls across Magnus's mud-streaked face. "You have to be careful with fire," he tells me, in an almost professorial tone. "But you don't have to be afraid of it." He throws another log on the flames and then whispers, as if to himself: "I'm not afraid of anything."

Leave Those Kids Alone

Not everything that can be counted counts, and not everything that counts can be counted.
—*Einstein*

When Europe developed a taste for prodigies in the eighteenth century, an English writer named Hester Lynch Thrale made it her mission in life to turn her eldest daughter into a superchild. By the age of two and a half, Queeney was already showing signs of having a prodigious memory. She could name the nations, seas, and capital cities of Europe; she knew the solar system, the compass, and the signs of the zodiac; she could recite the days of the week and months of the year, as well as sundry religious texts. By four and a half, little Queeney knew Latin grammar to the fifth declension. With a very familiar blend of boasting and self-pity, her long-suffering mother wrote: "I have never dined out, nor ever paid a visit where I did not carry her, unless I left her in bed; for to the care of servants (except asleep) I have never yet left her an hour."

All this micromanaging ended badly. None of Thrale's children achieved intellectual stardom, and she eventually fell out with them all, especially Queeney, whom she described as "sullen, malicious, perverse, desirous of tormenting me, even by hurting herself." She decided not to bother meting out the same treatment to her youngest daughter, Sophy. "I have really listened to babies learning till I am half stupefied—and all my pains have answered so poorly. I have no heart to battle with Sophy. . . . I will not make her life miserable."

The yearning for an uber-child has always been there, buried deep within the DNA of every parent. What has changed is that many more of us now feel the social pressure, and have the time and money, to try to create one. Thrale's failure is a reminder of how futile and ruinous this quest can be—in any century.

Let's not be too downhearted. As we have already seen, one of the lessons of history is that the state of childhood is seldom as bleak as the doomsayers paint it. Today, there are plenty of wonderful things about being young. Many children have a closer, easier relationship with their parents than at any time in history. The world is full of rich opportunities to learn, travel, and have fun. The Internet offers all the intoxicating adventure of a new frontier.

At the same time, however, much has gone wrong. The physical and mental health of children is suffering. Many are denied the freedom to play outdoors, to chart their own course through life, to see a world in a grain of sand. They grow up terrified of failure and expecting everything on a silver platter. Parenthood is at risk of becoming a rat race of panic, guilt, and disappointment, making us less likely to worry about the welfare of other children, or even to trust them. When was the last time you saw kids playing alone in your street? Or when was the last time you saw a group of unsupervised youths and didn't wince?

Yet there is hope. Another lesson of history is that childhood evolves. The pressure to give our children the best of everything and make them the best at everything is strong, but it is not irre-sistible. No one is holding a gun to our heads and forcing us to rear the next generation with the neurotic zeal of a Hester Thrale. We have it within our power to change, to ease off.

How do we start? The first step is to accept that children have a range of aptitudes and interests—and that there are many paths to adulthood. Life does not end if you don't get into Harvard or Oxford. Not everyone is cut out to work on Wall Street, and not everyone wants to. By definition, only a handful of children will ever grow up to be truly exceptional in any field. If we are going to reinvent childhood in a way that is good for both children and adults, then we must learn to tolerate diversity, doubt, rough edges here and there, even conflict. We have to cherish children for who they are instead of for what we want them to be.

The pendulum is starting to swing back. Inspired by a grow-ing body of evidence and scientific research, schools, coaches, communities, and families everywhere are finding ways to treat children as people instead of as projects—and finding that they grow up happier, healthier, and more able to make their own mark on the world.

Resisting the pressure to micromanage in one sphere often leads to doing the same in another. When Vicente Ramos saw how his son fell back in love with soccer after he stopped scream-ing at him from the sidelines, he started putting less pressure on him at school. Cutting back on extracurricular activities inspired the Carson family to limit the hours their children spend sitting in front of the computer screen. When Malcolm Page stopped behaving like a walking ATM, he found it easier to say no when his son insisted on staying up past his bedtime. When Beatrice Chan began to flourish at her Waldorf school in Hong Kong, her father cleared more time in her schedule for unstructured play.

Seeing her daughter cope with life in the forest at the Secret
Garden nursery persuaded Jenny Sutherland to stop mollycoddling her during the rest of the day. "Once you realize that the
world doesn't end if you don't hover over your child every second
of the day, your whole outlook changes," she says. "Instead of
trying to make everything just right, you back off a bit so that
your child can live her life instead of having you live it for her."

What people like Sutherland are discovering is the joy of a
child who does not meet every adult expectation but carves out a
different, more exciting path by being her own person.

I have a confession to make. At the start of this journey, I
hoped to come out at the other end with a step-by-step recipe for
raising children in the twenty-first century, a complete antidote
to the frenzy of keeping up with the Joneses. But now I realize
that would simply mean replacing one dogma with another.
What I discovered instead is that there is no single formula for
child rearing. Sure, there are some basic principles that hold true
across class and culture: children need to feel safe and loved; they
need our time and attention, with no conditions attached; they
need boundaries and limits; they need space to take risks and
make mistakes; they need to spend time outdoors; they need to
be ranked and measured less; they need healthy food; they need
to aspire to something bigger than owning the next brand-name
gizmo; they need room to be themselves. But after that the details—how many extracurricular activities, how many hours on
the computer, how much homework, how much pocket money,
how much freedom—vary. Because every child and every parent
is different, every family must find the formula that works best
for them. That is not as daunting as it sounds. It can be done if
you shut out the background noise and listen more to your instincts, if you look for your own way to parent instead of striving

to match someone else's. Of course, expert advice can be helpful, but no matter how many parenting manuals you read, how many parenting workshops you attend, or how hard you work at being Mom or Dad of the Year, you will always fall short. And that's okay, too. You don't need to feel guilty if you lose your temper, or get bored playing Barbie, or can't face baking cupcakes this afternoon. Or if you don't eat every meal *en famille* and you sometimes let the kids watch more TV than feels right. Children can handle it.

Half a century ago, an influential English pediatrician called D. W. Winnicott argued that engineering the perfect childhood was impossible and that striving to do so was damaging both to the parent and to the child. Instead, parents should aspire to meet their children's needs most of the time and accept that they will mess up occasionally. Do a "good enough" job, said Winnicott, and most children will grow up fine.

Of course, parenting is just part of the equation. Beyond the family, we need to rethink the rules that govern everything that touches children's lives—school, advertising, toys, sports, technology, traffic. That means accepting some inconvenient truths: that cars should take up less space on our roads, that much of the richest learning cannot be measured, that some things should not be replaced by electronic gadgets, that medication should be the last resort when dealing with awkward behavior, that our collective addiction to consumption has to end.

What all of this adds up to is finding a new definition of childhood. Perhaps what we need now is an amalgam of the Romantic and Lockean philosophies: accepting that childhood is a dress rehearsal for adulthood but not always treating it as such. That means giving children structure and guidance along with some of the freedom they would find in Neverland. It also means planning for the future without losing the magic of the present. Instead of baking a cake with your children because it will teach them about weight, volume, and arithmetic, or canoodling with your baby because it will build his prefrontal cortex, do these things for the sheer joy of it. Leave the developmental payoff to take care of itself.

This definition of childhood puts new demands on adults, and especially parents. Children need us to set an example, make sacrifices, and impose limits. The twenty-first-century parent has to strike a balance between growing up and never growing up.

Like any social change, forging a new form of childhood and adulthood will be driven by millions of small acts of defiance. Whenever anyone chooses to let a child be herself, the cultural scales tilt slightly—and it becomes easier for others to follow suit. It will take time, but the change will be worth it.

My own journey is a work in progress. I am getting better at resisting Pester Power and laying down the law in general. We enforce the lights-out rule at bedtime more these days. We also make sure our children have plenty of free time, and ration how much of it they spend in front of electronic screens.

I still hope my kids will turn out to have a genius for something—that will probably never go away—but at least now that hope does not turn me into a drill sergeant at the first hint of potential. My aim is to encourage my children to stretch their wings but to let them choose the flight path. Instead of squeezing them into my master plan, I'm enjoying finding out who they are as they grow up.

The starting point for this book was the crusade to turn my son into a great artist. He still loves to draw, and his best works still find their way onto the fridge door or above my desk. I am looking at a portrait of Darth Vader as I type these words. But my yen to turn him into the next Michelangelo has dimmed.

The other day something happened that suggested I may be on the road to recovery. We were kicking a soccer ball around in the park when my son announced that his school runs a weekly sketching club. My heart skipped a beat, but I resisted the urge to frog-march him down to the office to sign up. Instead, I answered in a neutral tone.

"That sounds interesting," I said. "Are you thinking of joining?"

"The thing is, it's mostly girls and I don't really want to be the only boy," said my son. "But I am quite interested in having a teacher who knows a lot about art show me how to draw better. I think I might learn some useful things in the club."

"That makes sense," I said, kicking the ball back to him.

We dropped the subject and went back to soccer for a while. On the final play, my son lifted the ball off the ground, volleyed it past me into the goal, and then ran around with his arms in the air as his heroes do on *Match of the Day*. As we gathered up our things to leave, he returned to the question of the sketching club. "Daddy, I know you want me to join," he said. "But I'm the one who has to decide."

I agreed and told him I was happy to wait for him to make up his mind. And I meant it.

My son picked up the ball and promised to draw a picture of himself scoring for England when we got back. I smiled, put my arm round his shoulder, and we headed for home. We talked about soccer the whole way.

Resources

I read many books and articles for my research into childhood. Below are a few of those that stood out. Farther down is a list of useful Web sites. These are a good starting point for helping people explore ways to give children more time and space. I will keep adding to this the list on my own Web page: www. carlhonore.com.

Anderegg, David. *Worried All the Time: Rediscovering the Joy in Parenthood in an Age of Anxiety.* New York: Free Press, 2004.

Cunningham, Hugh. *The Invention of Childhood.* London: BBC Books, 2006.

Elkind, David. *The Hurried Child: Growing Up Too Fast Too Soon.* New York: Perseus, 2001.

Furedi, Frank. *Paranoid Parenting: Why Ignoring the Experts May Be Best for Your Child.* New York: A Cappella Books, 2002.

Hirsh-Pasek, Kathy, and Roberta Michnick Golinkoff. *Einstein Never Used Flash Cards: How Our Children Really Learn—And Why They Need to Play More and Memorize Less.* New York: Rodale Books, 2003.

James, Oliver. *They F*** You Up: How to Survive Family Life.* New York: Marlowe and Company, 2005.

Jardine, Cassandra. *Positive Not Pushy: How to Make the Most of Your Child's Potential.* London: Vermillion, 2005.

Levine, Madeline. *Price of Privilege: How Parental Pressure and Material Advantage Are Creating a Generation of Disconnected and Unhappy Kids.* New York: HarperCollins, 2006.

Linn, Susan. *Consuming Kids: Protecting Our Children from the Onslaught of Marketing & Advertising.* New York: Anchor, 2005.

Manne, Anne. *Motherhood: How Should We Care for Our Children?* Sydney: Allen & Unwin, 2005.

Mead-Ferro, Muffy. *Confessions of a Slacker Mom*. Cambridge: Da Capo Lifelong, 2004.

O'Farrell, John. *May Contain Nuts*. London: Doubleday, 2005.

Palmer, Sue. *Toxic Childhood: How the Modern World Is Damaging Our Children and What We Can Do About It*. London: Orion, 2007.

Pope, Alexander. *Scriblerus*. London: Hesperus Press, 2003.

Pope, Denise. *Doing School: How We Are Creating a Generation of Stressed-Out, Materialistic, and Miseducated Students*. New Haven: Yale University Press, 2003.

Postman, Neil. *The Disappearance of Childhood*. New York: Vintage, 1984.

Robb, Jean and Hilary Letts. *Creating Kids Who Can Concentrate: Proven Strategies for Beating A.D.D. Without Drugs*. London: Hodder and Stoughton, 1997.

Rosenfeld, Alven. *The Over-Scheduled Child: Avoiding the Hyper-Parenting Trap*. Irvine: Griffin Press, 2001.

Schor, Juliet. *Born to Buy: The Commercialized Child and the New Consumer Culture*. New York: Scribner, 2004.

Stearns, Peter. *Anxious Parents: A History of Modern Childrearing in America*. New York: New York University Press, 2003.

Thacker, Lloyd. *College Unranked: Ending the College Admissions Frenzy*. Cambridge: Harvard University Press, 2005.

Zelizer, Viviana. *Pricing the Priceless Child*. New York: Basic Books, 1985.

WEB SITES

General

www.hyperparenting.com

Education

www.montessori.edu
www.zerosei.comune.re.it (Reggio Emilia international site)
www.awsna.org (Association of Waldorf Schools of North America)
www.steinerwaldorf.org.uk
www.stanford.edu/dept/SUSE/sosconference/ (SOS: Stressed-Out Students)
www.nhen.org (home education, US)
www.home-education.org.uk
www.flora.org/homeschool-ca/achbe/index.html (home education, Canada)

www.stjohns.wilts.sch.uk/home.htm (St. John's School and Community College, Marlborough)

www.rsa.org.uk/newcurriculum (curriculum reform in UK)

Extracurriculars

www.froginthehole.com

www.ipaworld.org (International Play Association)

www.ipaargentina.org.ar/laboratorio.php (Toy and Play Laboratory, IPA Argentina)

www.sitrec.kth.se (International Toy Research Center, Stockholm)

Technology

www.childrenssoftware.com (children's technology review)

www.blogging.wikia.com/wiki/Blogger's_Code_of_Conduct

www.lazytown.com

www.mediadietforkids.com/book/book_authors.html

Sports

www.giveusbackourgame.co.uk (Give Us Back Our Game)

www.bobbigelow.com

AbramsD@missouri.edu (daily e-mail updates on youth sports)

www.silkensactivekids.ca/content/Home.asp (Canada)

www.byardsports.com (Danny Bernstein's Backyard Sports)

Consumerism

www.commercialalert.com

www.charliecrow.co.uk

www.birthdayswithoutpressure.org

Safety

www.homezones.org

www.iwalktoschool.org

Notes

INTRODUCTION: MANAGING CHILDHOOD

PUPILLUS IDENTIFIED PUSHY PARENTS IN ANCIENT ROME: Jo Ann Shelton, *As the Romans Did: A Sourcebook in Roman Social History* (New York: Oxford University Press, 1997), p. 19.

DISTANCE FROM FAMILY HOME DOWN NEARLY 90 PERCENT: Frank Furedi, *Paranoid Parenting: Why Ignoring the Experts May Be Best for Your Child* (New York: A Cappella Books, 2002), p. 13.

LOOK MORE TO PARENTS WHEN MAKING CAREER DECISIONS: Erin White, "Employers Court Mom and Dad," *Wall Street Journal*, Classroom Edition, May 2007.

ACL INJURIES: Based on research by Dr. Mininder S. Kocher, spokesperson for the American Academy of Orthopaedic Surgeons and associate director, Division of Sports Medicine, Children's Hospital, Boston, Massachusetts.

A BRITISH TEENAGER TRIES TO COMMIT SUICIDE EVERY TWENTY-EIGHT MINUTES: Based on figures from the European Association for Injury Prevention and Safety Promotion.

400,000 HIKIKOMORI IN JAPAN: Based on research carried out by Okayama University in 2002.

FIFTEEN-YEAR-OLDS IN PSYCHOLOGICAL DISTRESS: Patrick West and Helen Sweeting, "Fifteen, female and stressed: changing patterns of psychological distress over time," *Journal of Child Psychology and Psychiatry*, vol. 44, no. 3 (2003), pp. 399–411.

RITALIN, ATTENTA, FOCALIN PRESCRIPTIONS TRIPLED: Richard M. Scheffler, Stephen P. Hinshaw, Sepideh Modrek, and Peter Levine, "The Global Market for ADHD Medications," *Health Affairs*, vol. 26, no. 2 (March/April 2007), pp. 450–457.

GROWTH HORMONE FOR NORMAL KIDS: Joyce M. Lee, Matthew M. Davis, Sarah J. Clark, Timothy P. Hofer, and Alex R. Kempe, "Estimated Cost-effectiveness of Growth Hormone Therapy for Idiopathic Short Stature," *Archives of Pediatric and Adolescent Medicine*, vol. 160 (March 2006), pp. 263–269.

RISE IN NARCISSISM: Based on the responses by 16,475 college students to the 2006 Narcissistic Personality Inventory survey devised by Jean Twenge, an associate professor of psychology at San Diego State University.

CHILDREN FROM LOWER-INCOME LATINO FAMILIES: Po Bronson and Ashley Merryman, "Baby Einstein vs. Barbie," *Time*, 22 September 2006.

CHAPTER ONE: IT'S THE ADULTS, STUPID

SCHOOL ATTENDANCE IN BRITAIN QUADRUPLED: Michael Sanderson, *Education and Economic Decline in Britain, 1870 to the 1990s* (Cambridge: Cambridge University Press, 1999), p. 5.

WANT TO BE OUR "CHILD'S BEST FRIEND": Based on survey carried out by Synovate in 2004.

CHAPTER TWO: EARLY YEARS: WHEN MILESTONES BECOME MILLSTONES

MONTAIGNE ON INFANT DEATHS: Lawrence Stone, *Family, Sex and Marriage in England, 1500–1800* (London: Penguin Books, 1990), p. 82.

CUT LIGAMENTS IN INFANTS' TONGUES: Lloyd de Mause (ed.), *The History of Childhood* (London: Souvenir Press, 1976), p. 314.

INFANTS GRASP OBJECT PERMANENCE AT TEN WEEKS: Based on research by Su-hua Wang, a psychologist at the University of California, Santa Cruz.

BABIES DISTINGUISH BETWEEN LANGUAGES: Janet Werker and Whitney Weikum, "Visual Language Discrimination in Infancy," *Science*, 25 May 2007, p. 1159.

ENRICHED RATS: Kathy Hirsh-Pasek, Diane Eyer, Roberta Michnick Golinkoff, *Einstein Never Used Flash Cards: How Our Children Really Learn—And Why They Need to Play More and Memorize Less* (New York: Rodale Books, 2003), pp. 27–28.

15,500 CHILDREN: Based on research carried out by the University of London's Centre for Longitudinal Studies at the Institute of Education.

CRAMMING STRESSES BABIES: Jeffrey Kluger and Alice Park, "The Quest for a Super Kid," *Time*, 30 April 2001.

PLAY PEAKS WHEN BRAINS AT MOST ELASTIC: C. H. Janson and C. P. Van Schaik, "Ecological Risk Aversion in Juvenile Primates: Slow and Steady Wins the Race," in M. E. Pereira and L. A. Fairbanks (eds.), *Juvenile Primates: Life History, Development and Behavior* (Chicago: Chicago University Press, 2002), pp. 57–76.

RATS DEPRIVED OF PLAY: Kathy Hirsh-Pasek, Diane Eyer, Roberta Michnick Golinkoff, *Einstein Never Used Flash Cards: How Our Children Really Learn—And Why They Need to Play More and Memorize Less* (New York: Rodale Books, 2003), p. 214.

CHAPTER THREE: PRESCHOOL: PLAY IS A CHILD'S WORK

HOTHOUSED KIDS MORE ANXIOUS, LESS CREATIVE: Kathy Hirsh-Pasek, "Pressure or challenge in preschool? How academic environments impact upon young children," in L. Rescorla, M. Hyson, and K. Hirsh-Pasek (eds.), "Hurried children: Research and policy on early academic learning for preschoolers," in B. Damon (gen. ed.), *New Directions in Developmental Psychology*, vol. 53 (New York: Jossey-Bass, 1991).

DANISH AND FINNISH CHILDREN CONCENTRATE BETTER: Based on a 2003 study by Britain's Office for Standards in Education.

REGGIO SCHOOLS: Reggio Children confirmed that all the facts in my section on Reggio were accurate. Nevertheless, the organization always asks visitors to include the following disclaimer: "The views expressed in this book are those of the author representing his own interpretation of the Reggio Approach to education. The content of this book reflects the point of view and the opinion expressed by the author who had the opportunity to visit several Municipal preschools and the International Center Loris Malaguzzi in Reggio Emilia."

CHAPTER FOUR: TOYS: JUST PUSH PLAY

SCOTT AXCELL QUOTED IN: Amelia Hill, "Educational toys? An old box teaches just as much," *Observer*, 25 September 2005.

1890S WORRIES ABOUT OVERACTIVE TOYS: Bill Brown, "American Childhood and Stephen Crane's Toys," *American Literary History*, vol. 7, no. 3, *Imagining a National Culture* (Autumn, 1995), pp. 443–476.

ITEDDY: Visit www.iteddy.com.

FROG IN THE HOLE: Visit www.froginthehole.com.

CHAPTER FIVE: TECHNOLOGY: REALITY BITES

SEVEN HOURS A DAY IN FRONT OF A SCREEN: Based on the Youth TGI report, copyright BMRB International 1994–2006.

SAME TIME GAZING AT SCREENS AS PLAYING OUTDOORS: Elizabeth Vandewater and Dr. Ellen Wartella, "Zero to Six: Electronic Media in the Lives of Infants, Toddlers and Preschoolers," The Henry J. Kaiser Family Foundation, October 2003.

QUARTER UNDER TWOS HAVE TV IN BEDROOM: Elizabeth Vandewater and Dr. Ellen Wartella, "Zero to Six: Electronic Media in the Lives of Infants, Toddlers and Preschoolers," The Henry J. Kaiser Family Foundation, October 2003.

ELECTRONIC INTERRUPTIONS MAKE IQ FALL TEN POINTS: Based on a Hewlett-Packard study conducted in 2005 by Glenn Wilson, a psychiatrist at the University of London.

MICROSOFT WORKERS LOSE CONCENTRATION FOR FIFTEEN MINUTES: Steve Lohr, "Slow Down, Brave Multitasker, and Don't Read This in Traffic," *New York Times,* 25 March 2007.

EVERY HOUR OF TV INCREASES ADHD: Dimitri A. Christakis, Frederick J. Zimmerman, David L. DiGiuseppe, and Carolyn A. McCarty, "Early Television Exposure and Subsequent Attentional Problems in Children," *Pediatrics,* vol. 113, no. 4 (April 2004), pp. 708–713.

VIOLENT VIDEO GAMES AFFECT FRONTAL LOBE: Helen Phillips, "Mind-altering media," *New Scientist,* 19 April 2007.

MYOPIA EPIDEMIC: Rachel Nowak, "Lifestyle causes myopia, not genes," *New Scientist,* 8 July 2004.

RADIO MADE CHILDREN PSYCHOPATHIC: Peter Stearns, *Anxious Parents: A History of Modern Childrearing in America* (New York: New York University Press, 2003), p. 178.

NO LINK BETWEEN WATCHING TV AND ADHD: Tara Stevens and Miriam Mulsow, "There Is No Meaningful Relationship Between Television Exposure and Symptoms of Attention-Deficit/Hyperactivity Disorder," *Pediatrics,* vol. 117, no. 3 (March 2006), pp. 665–672.

VIDEO GAMES BOOST ABILITY TO DISCERN OBJECTS: C. S. Green and D. Bavelier, "Action-Video-Game Experience Alters the Spatial Resolution of Vision," *Psychological Science,* vol. 18, no. 1 (2007).

COMPUTER GAMES HELP WITH ALZHEIMER'S: Oscar Lopez and others, "A randomized pilot study to assess the efficacy of an interactive, multimedia tool of cognitive stimulation in Alzheimer's disease," *Journal of Neurology, Neurosurgery and Psychiatry,* vol. 77 (October 2006), pp. 1116–1121.

ELEVEN- AND TWELVE-YEAR-OLDS THREE YEARS BEHIND: Based on research published in 2006 by Michael Shayer, professor of applied psychology at

King's College, University of London, and funded by the Economic and Social Research Council (ESRC).

MENNONITE CHILDREN FITTER: Mark Tremblay and others, "Conquering Childhood Inactivity: Is the Answer in the Past?" *Medicine & Science in Sports & Exercise*, vol. 37, no. 7 (July 2005), pp. 1187–1194.

KIDS GET TWO HOURS LESS SLEEP: Based on figures from the United States–based National Sleep Foundation and a 2004 study by the Oxford Child and Adolescent Psychiatry unit.

PRIMARY SCHOOL CHILDREN LOOK FIRST TO TV SCREEN: Based on research conducted by Markus Bindemann, researcher in psychology at the University of Glasgow.

FEWER TEENS HAVE A BEST FRIEND: Based on a YouthTrends study funded by the Nuffield Foundation and published in 2007.

JIMMY WALES AND TIM O'REILLY: The pair announced their Blogger Code of Conduct in 2007.

EXTRA HOUR OF WEEKEND TV RAISES OBESITY RISK 7 PERCENT: R. M. Viner, T. J. Cole, "Television viewing in early childhood predicts adult body mass index," *Journal of Pediatrics,* vol. 147, no. 4 (October 2005).

CRAM 8.5 HOURS' WORTH OF MEDIA INTO 6.5 HOURS: Donald Roberts, Ulla Foehr, and Victoria Rideout, "Generation M: Media in the Lives of 8–18 Year-Olds," The Henry J. Kaiser Family Foundation, March 2005.

RELAXATION FOSTERS RICH, CREATIVE THOUGHT: Guy Claxton, *Hare Brain, Tortoise Mind: Why Intelligence Increases When You Think Less* (London: Fourth Edition, 1997), pp. 76–77.

DIPCHAND NISHAR ON GENERATION ADD: David Kirkpatrick, "Do you answer your cellphone during sex?," *Fortune,* 28 August 2006.

LIVE PUPPET SHOW BEATS VIDEO: Cited in a 2005 research review by Dan Anderson, a University of Massachusetts psychology professor.

STUDYING IN NATURE BOOSTS LEARNING AND DISCIPLINE: Based on a 2002 study by the State Education and Environmental Roundtable, a U.S. organization that examines "environment-based education."

CHAPTER SIX: SCHOOL: TESTING TIMES

CHINESE SPEND THIRD OF INCOME ON EDUCATION: Based on a 2006 survey by the Horizon Research Group.

SERIOUS ACTS OF CHEATING BY CANADIAN UNDERGRADUATES: Based on a 2006 study by Julia Chirstensen Hughes, director of teaching support services at the University of Guelph.

BURNING HOLE IN PAJAMAS: "Student web cheats caught out by 'pyjama inspiration,'" *Evening Standard,* 7 March 2007.

PEERS "KIND AND HELPFUL": Peter Adamson, "Child poverty in perspective: An overview of child well-being in rich countries," Innocenti Report Card 7, UNICEF 2007.

VIOLENT GANGS IN KOREA: Donald Macintyre, "Too Cruel for School—South Korea's youth gangs," *Time,* 25 April 2005.

CHEATING TEACHERS: Brian Grow, "A Spate of Cheating—By Teachers," *Business Week,* 5 July 2004.

MONTESSORI STUDY IN MILWAUKEE: Angeline Lillard and Nicole Else-Quest, "Evaluating Montessori Education," *Science,* vol. 313, no. 5795 (29 September 2006), pp. 1893–94.

CHASING RESULTS REDUCES INTEREST IN TASK: Oliver James, "Mrs Mac's Elementary Lesson," *London Times,* 2 October 2006.

SINGAPORE STRESSES TALENTS BEFORE TESTS: Based on an interview given by Tharman Shanmugaratnam, Singapore's education minister, to Channel NewsAsia in December 2005.

JAPANESE CHILDREN SCORED HIGHER AFTER YUTORI: Based on aptitude tests conducted in 2004 by Japan's Education Ministry.

IVY UNDERGRADUATE DEGREES IN FORTUNE 500: Nancy Gibbs and Nathan Thornburgh, "Who Needs Harvard?," *Time,* 13 August 2006.

CHAPTER SEVEN: HOMEWORK: THE SWORD OF DAMOCLES

1911 PUPIL STRIKE: Harry Hendrick, *Children, Childhood and English Society, 1880–1990* (Cambridge: Cambridge University Press, 1997), p. 75.

6,000 AMERICAN STUDENTS DOING EXTRA MATH HOMEWORK: Based on research by Julian Betts, associate professor of economics at the University of California, San Diego.

EXTRA HOMEWORK HURT ACADEMIC PERFORMANCE: David P. Baker and Gerald K. LeTendre, *National Differences, Global Similarities: World Culture and the Future of Schooling* (Palo Alto: Stanford University Press, 2005).

ISRAELI RELIGIOUS STUDENTS MORE MYOPIC: Rachel Nowak, "Lifestyle causes myopia, not genes," *New Scientist,* 8 July 2004.

Yayuncun number 2 kindergarten in Beijing: Liam Fitzpatrick, "Asia's Overscheduled Kids," *Time,* 20 March 2006.

Tutoring failed to boost marks: Lee, Jong-Tae; Kim, Yang-Boon; and Yoon, Cho-Hee: "The Effects of Pre-Class Tutoring on Student Achievement: Challenges and Implications for Public Education in Korea," *KEDI Journal of Educational Policy,* vol. 1, no.1 (2004), p. 39.

Tutoring counterproductive: Cheo, Roland, and Euston Quah, "Mothers, Maids and Tutors: An Empirical Evaluation of their Effect on Children's Academic Grades in Singapore," *Education Economics,* vol. 13, no. 3 (2005), p. 276.

Tutors hamper Taiwanese math reforms: Mark Bray, "Adverse Effects of Private Supplementary Tutoring," International Institute for Educational Planning, UNESCO, 2003.

CHAPTER EIGHT: EXTRACURRICULAR ACTIVITIES: READY, SET, RELAX!

Dorothy Canfield Fisher: Ann Hulbert, "Ready, Set, Relax! America's Obsession with Telling Its Kids to Stress Less," *Slate,* 18 March 2003.

Ruth Frankel: Peter Stearns, *Anxious Parents: A History of Modern Childrearing in America* (New York: New York University Press, 2003), p. 168.

U.S. children among most highly scheduled: Based on a 2007 comparative study by Isabelle Gingras at the psychology department of the University of McGill.

Britons spend £12 billion on children's hobbies: Cassandra Jardine, *Positive Not Pushy: How to Make the Most of Your Child's Potential* (London: Vermillion, 2005), p. 58.

Family meals promote language development: Based on 1996 research by Catherine Snow, professor of education at Harvard University.

National Merit Scholars eat family meals: Based on a twenty-year survey in the United States by the National Merit Scholarship Corporation.

James Boswell's grumpy report: Lawrence Stone, *Family, Sex and Marriage in England, 1500–1800* (London: Penguin Books, 1990), p. 276.

CHAPTER NINE: SPORTS: PLAY BALL

U.S. parents spend $4.1 billion sports training for kids: Taken from report by Velocity Sports Performance, a sports training center based in Chamblee, Georgia.

DAILY E-MAIL BULLETIN BY DOUGLAS ABRAMS: For more information e-mail AbramsD@missouri.edu.

STEROID USE TRIPLED SINCE 1993: Based on a 2003 study by the United States–based Centers for Disease Control.

GIVE US BACK OUR GAME: For more information, go to: www.giveusbackourgame.co.uk/.

CHAPTER TEN: DISCIPLINE: JUST SAY NO?

CONRAD SAM: Colin Heywood, *A History of Childhood: Children and Childhood in the West from Medieval to Modern Times* (London: Polity Press, 2001), p. 99.

TWICE AS LIKELY TO LIE, STEAL, OR DISOBEY AUTHORITY: Barbara Maughan, Stephan Collishaw, et al, *Journal of Child Psychology and Psychiatry (JCPP)*, vol. 45. Based on a twenty-five-year study of adolescent mental health published in 2004 by the Institute of Psychiatry at King's College London and the University of Manchester.

HIGH SELF-ESTEEM DOES NOT BOOST GRADES OR CAREER PROSPECTS: These are the conclusions of Roy Baumeister, a social psychology professor at Florida State University and one-time advocate of self-esteem, after reviewing 15,000 self-esteem studies on behalf of the Association for Psychological Science in 2003.

ROB PARSONS ON TAKING THE UNPOPULARITY HIT: Catherine O'Brien, "Never Letting Go," *London Times*, 9 July 2007.

10 PERCENT OF U.S. TWELVE-YEAR-OLD BOYS ON RITALIN: "Hidden dangers of failure to diagnose ADHD correctly," *New Scientist*, 1 April 2006.

ADHD DRUGS TRIPLED: Richard M. Scheffler, Stephen P. Hinshaw, Sepideh Modrek, and Peter Levine, "The Global Market for ADHD Medications," *Health Affairs*, vol. 26, no. 2 (March/April 2007), pp. 450–457.

COURTNEY LOVE ON RITALIN: Sue Palmer, *Toxic Childhood: How the Modern World Is Damaging Our Children and What We Can Do About It* (London: Orion, 2007), p. 17.

CHAPTER ELEVEN: CONSUMERISM: PESTER POWER AND THE WALKING, TALK-ING ATM

GIOVANNI DOMINICI: Lloyd de Mause (ed.), *The History of Childhood* (London: Souvenir Press, 1976), p. 204.

MARKETING SPEND 150 TIMES HIGHER: Juliet Schor, *Born to Buy: The Commercialized Child and the New Consumer Culture* (New York: Scribner, 2004), p. 21.

REVLON LEARNING MODULE: Schor, *Born to Buy,* p. 93

MARKET RESEARCH AT SLEEPOVERS: Schor, *Born to Buy,* p. 77.

INFLUENCE $700 BILLION OF SPENDING: Based on figures from James McNeal, a children's marketing consultant based in College Station, Texas.

DAVID BROOKS BIRTHDAY PARTY: "Another Marie Antoinette Moment," *New York Times,* 2 January 2006.

BIRTHDAYS CAUSE UPSET STOMACHS, ETC., IN PARENTS: Based on a survey conducted by Haribo in 2006.

QUINTILLIAN BEMOANS LEWD ANTICS: Neil Postman, *The Disappearance of Childhood* (New York: Vintage, 1994), p. 9.

70 PERCENT OF SEVEN-YEAR-OLD GIRLS WISHED THEY WERE SLIMMER: Hayley Dohnt and Marika Tiggemann, "Peer influences on body satisfaction and dieting awareness in young girls," *British Journal of Developmental Psychology,* vol. 23 (2005), pp. 103–116.

LINGERIE BARBIE: Susan Linn, *Consuming Kids: Protecting Our Children from the Onslaught of Marketing & Advertising* (New York: Anchor, 2005), p. 143.

CHAPTER TWELVE: SAFETY: PLAYING WITH FIRE

EARLY TEENS SUFFER MOST TRAFFIC ACCIDENTS: Based on findings in the Better Safe Than Sorry report published by the UK Audit Commission in 2007.

FULANI GIRLS FETCH WATER: Michelle Johnson, *The View from the Wuro: A Guide to Child Rearing for Fulani Parents* (Cambridge: Cambridge University Press, 2000), pp. 171–198

SMALL INCREASE IN PHYSICAL ACTIVITY REDUCES OBESITY: Andy R. Ness, Sam D. Leary, Calum Mattocks, et al., "Objectively Measured Physical Activity and Fat Mass in a Large Cohort of Children," *Public Library of Science Medicine,* vol. 4, no. 3 (March 2007).

SOARING ALLERGIES: Stanley Goldstein, "The Hygiene Hypothesis," *Allergy and Asthma Health Advocate,* Winter 2004.

Acknowledgments

I could never have written this book without help from so many people.

My agent, Patrick Walsh, paved the way with his usual verve and vision. My editors, Gideon Weil at HarperOne San Francisco and Michael Schellenberg at Knopf Canada, were the perfect tag team: patient, wise, engaged, meticulous, and always ready with words of encouragement. Ian Marshall, my editor at Orion UK, was a thoughtful and steadying presence throughout.

To make this a truly international book, I relied on people around the world to help with research and interviews. My gratitude goes to Chin-Hwa Lee, Steven Wong, Raymond Cheung, Maki Tanabe, Steve Trautlein, Sachie Kanda, Anna Fleischer. Along the way, I spoke to hundreds of families, teachers, and doctors and am grateful to all of them for taking the time to share their stories and insights. Only some are named in these pages, but every single interview helped to shape the book. I am also indebted to the many researchers and experts who patiently explained their work to me. A special thanks to Cathy Bache; Danny and Beth Bernstein; Jasmin Blunck; Mike Brody; Vincent Carpentier; Bill Doherty; David Eberhard; Arar Han; Kathy Hirsh-Pasek; Maurice Holt; Julie Lam; Levin; Marcia Marra; Annamaria Mucchi, Claudia Giudici, and everyone at Reggio

Children; Lena Nyberg; Tommi Paavola; Genevieve Pan; Denise Pope; Rachel Nixsieman; Vivian Numaguchi; Alejandra Rabuini; Gisela Rao; Uwe Schott; Heather Tansem; Eileen and Edward Tracy.

I would also like to thank my parents, and especially my mother, for helping to put the final polish on the book. As always, though, my deepest thanks go to my wife, Miranda France, for her patience, her way with words, and her knack for seeing the funny side of things. And for being such a fine mother to our children.

Index

Abe, Shinzo, 128
Abercrombie and Fitch, 234, 235
Abrams, Douglas, 183–84
ACL tears, 8
Adderall, 117
Adey, Philip, 119
adrenaline, 44
adults, 19–35; childcentric, 25, 165,
    177–78; competitive parenting,
    15, 25–35; overinvolvement in
    children's sports, 181–98
advertising, 4, 16, 27, 74–75,
    215–27
Advertising Age, 224
aggression, 44, 92
Alden, Margaret, 24
Alfano, Kathleen, 80
allergies, 252
Alzheimer's disease, 94
American Academy of Pediatrics, 15,
    103, 167
American Psychological Association,
    235
Anderegg, David, *Worried All the
    Time: Rediscovering the Joy of Par-
    enthood in an Age of Anxiety,* 243
animals, 40, 49–50
antidepressants, 10, 209–212
anxiety, 8–10, 246
Argentina, 77, 190
Ariès, Philippe, 20–21

Arizona, 96
art, 2, 3, 22, 49, 61, 64, 88, 171,
    262–63
Asda, 235
Assyrians, 200
Attenta, 209
attention deficit/hyperactivity dis-
    order (ADHD), 50, 92, 93, 139,
    209–212
Aurini, Janice, 156
Australia, 101, 135, 150, 176, 192,
    200, 235
Avian flu, 251
Axcell, Scott, 80

Baby Channel, 92
Baby Einstein DVDs, 40, 47, 76
baby sign language, 5, 45, 47
Bache, Cathy, 241
Backyard Sports, 193–97
Ballesteros, Severiano, 186
Barbie, 236
Barcelona, 94, 192
Barrie, J. M., *Peter Pan,* 19
baseball, 189–90, 191, 192
basketball, 182, 184, 187, 194–96
BBC, 27, 33, 85
Bebo, 99, 110
Beckham, David, 26, 194
Beijing, 150
Belgium, 224

Bernstein, Danny, 193–97
Bernstein, Leonard, 175
Bialystock, Ellen, 43
bicycles, 243
Bigelow, Bob, *Just Let the Kids Play*, 187–88, 189
bilingualism, 42–43
birthday parties, 227–32
birth rates, 15, 24; falling, 15, 26
Black, Dan, 7
Blake, Quentin, 2
Blake, William, 12, 64
block schedule, 130–32
blogging, 46, 99
books, 41; child-rearing, 37–38
boredom, 13, 54, 87, 217
Boston, 29
Boston Globe, 167
Boyce, Frank Cottrell, 221
brain, 50, 80; chemical imbalance, 210, 211; development, 26–27, 40–45, 54, 74, 80; multitasking and, 105–108; neocortices, 50
Brain, Cognition, and Action Laboratory, University of Michigan, 106
Brazil, 10, 51, 190, 191, 248
Brio train sets, 83, 85
Brody, Michael, 82, 218
Brooklyn, New York, 178
Brooks, David, 227–28
Bruer, John, *The Myth of the First Three Years*, 41
Buarque, Chico, 181, 191
Buckleitner, Warren, 97–98, 104
Buenos Aires, 18, 77, 190
bullying, 98, 119, 139, 201, 208
Burton, Carole, 81
Bush, George W., 76
Butler, Samuel, 248
Byers, John, 50

Cafaro, Claire, 117–18
California, 5, 9, 13, 17, 18, 67, 83, 108, 114, 117, 203, 229; schools and testing, 114, 117, 118, 129–32, 146, 158
camp, summer, 5–6
Canada, 13, 14, 28, 95, 117, 121, 153–56, 163, 176, 188, 197, 224, 250, 254; private tutoring in, 155–56
Canadian Pediatric Society, 104
Capriati, Jennifer, 186
Cargilfield, Edinburgh, Scotland, 152–53
Carroll, Lewis, 8
Cartwright, John, 190
celebrities, 9, 26, 27, 206–207, 217
cell phones, 5, 90, 91, 97, 102, 108, 110, 207, 224
Central Council for Education, 95
Channel One, 218, 223–24
Charlie Crow costumes, 225
cheating, 117–18, 119–20; sports, 185
Cheerios, 219
Chen Shui-bian, 15
child care, 29, 164
childcentric family, 25, 165, 177–78
childhood, 4; consumerization of, 215–37; in early twenty-first century, 7–18; history of, 20–24, 39, 165, 200, 209, 216–18, 231–32, 242; purpose of, 155
Children's Technology Review, 97
China, 5,6, 15, 28–29, 37, 42, 58, 100, 111, 188; homework, 150–52; preschool, 58, 68–70; schools and testing, 58, 68–70, 114–15, 118–19, 127, 150–52, 157–58, 259
Chinese International School (CIS), Hong Kong, 150–52, 153, 158

Christmas, 79, 216, 224; "brag letter," 25
clothing, 34; consumerism and, 233–36
coaches, 186, 190, 197, 259
Cobain, Kurt, 211
college, 6–7, 11, 12, 14, 16–17, 19–20, 99; brand-name, 113–14, 132–35, 147, 156, 173, 259; breakdowns in, 9; cheating, 117–18; costs, 33; sports, 183, 184
colors, 44, 64, 72
Colorado, 6
Commercial Alert, 223
community, 205, 244, 259
competition: academic, 113–43; parental, 15, 25–35; sports, 181–98
computer games, 89–90, 92, 93–105, 109, 111, 224
Concerta, 212
consumerism, 4, 16, 26, 31, 215–37, 262; advertising, 4, 16, 27, 74–75, 215–37; birthday parties, 227–32; brands and logos, 216, 217–21; clothing, 233–36; fighting, 223–37; food, 219, 222, 224, 233; in schools, 218–19, 223; television, 217–18, 219, 224
Coronation Street, 224
cortisol, 44
Cosby, Bill, 1
cost of raising a child, 33
Cowper, William, 233
creativity, 49, 50, 189
crime, 119, 244
Cruise, Tom, 6
Cumberland, Nigel, 52

Dahl, Roald, 2
Dale, Stacy, 134
Dangerous Book for Boys, 249

death, 24, 248; infant, 39; rates, 24
deMause, Lloyd, 21
Denmark, 60, 116, 252
depression, 8–10, 44
diabetes, 8, 252
dinner, family, 175–77
discipline, 119, 199–213; boundaries and rules, 206–209, 213; comeback of, 206–207; hyperactivity and, 209–212; lack of, 199–206
Disney-ABC, 219
divorce, 178
Doherty, Bill, 230
Domino's Pizza, 218
Doolittle, Hilda, 73
Dragon's Den, 85
drugs, 34, 246; ADHD, 209–212; performance-enhancing, 185; prescription, 10, 130, 209–212; side effects, 211–12
dual-income household, 29

"early MBA" program, 5
early years, 37–55; brain development, 26–27, 40–45, 54; developmental milestones, 38–39, 48; play, 48–55; stimulation, 40–45
eating disorders, 8, 34
eBay, 103
Eberhard, David, *Land of the Safety Junkies,* 244
economy, 31, 134, 216; consumerism, 215–37; global, 12
Edgeworth, Maria, 82
Einstein, Albert, 49, 113, 257
Elder, John, 153
elementary school, 110
e-mail, 90, 91, 92, 105, 108, 109
Emerson, Ralph Waldo, 82
Emotional Intelligence Quotient (EQ), 120

Eslite Bookstore, Taipei, 37–38, 74
etiquette manuals, 23
exercise, 8; lack of, 95
Exile, 109
extracurricular activities, 5, 16, 29, 161–79, 259, 260; cutting back, 169–79; overscheduling, 161–79
eye contact, 44–45

facial expressions, 44–45, 97
factories, 4, 232
farming, 4
Fauviau, Christophe, 181–82, 184
fertility, 26
fetal development, 4–5, 6
finances, 33
Finland, 18, 60, 122–26; schools and testing, 122–26, 142
fire, 239–40
Fisher, Dorothy Canfield, 163
Fisher-Price Company, 80, 84
Fixing Dinner, 176
flash cards, 41, 54
Florida, 229
Flynn effect, 94
Focalin, 209
food, 8; advertising, 219, 222, 224, 233; family meals, 175–77; junk, 224
football, 182, 184, 190
foreign languages, 42–43, 74, 171
France, 10, 14, 22, 26, 181–82
Frankel, Ruth, 163
freedom, 247
Frisch, Max, 89
Froebel, Friedrich, 53
Frog in the Hole, 86
Frost, Jo, 206
functional magnetic resonance imaging (fMRI), 107

Gainsborough, Thomas, 22
Game Boys, 85–86, 91, 111, 199–200
Garland, Judy, 217
Gates, Bill, 79
generational lines, blurring of, 34–35
genetics, 54–55
Germany, 42, 53, 148, 173–74, 200, 252
Ginsberg, Herbert, 52
Girls Intelligence Agency, 219
Give Us Back Our Game, 192
globalization, 12, 26
Goethe, Johann Wolfgang, 22
golf, 186, 187
Good Toy Guide, 81
Google, 108
GPS devices, 5
grades, 68
Great Britain, 1, 4, 5, 6, 9, 14, 16, 19–20, 23, 30, 47, 60, 73, 76, 81, 84, 90, 95, 98, 109, 116, 119, 169, 175, 176, 190, 192, 199, 201, 209, 222–25, 228, 232, 235, 236, 239–40, 243, 245, 248, 249; home education, 135–36; school and testing, 116, 118, 119–20, 126, 138–42, 147, 150, 240; Toy Fair, 84–88, 224–25
Greece, 75, 141, 224
Gregory of Tours, 21–22
growth hormone, 10
guilt, 28, 48, 75, 204–205, 258
Gunawardhana, Tina, 87–88
Gymboree, 57–58
gymnastics, 186

Hakim, Imran, 85
Halloween, 242
Hamleys, London, 73–74, 76, 83

happiness, 33, 116
Hartzell, Mary, 67
Harvard University, 9, 27, 114, 133, 156, 173, 175, 259
Hazlewood, Patrick, 138
headaches, 8
Head Start, 59
health, 8–10
Healy, David, 210
heart disease, 8
helicopter-parenting, 3–4
Hewlett Packard, 91–92
Highgate House preschool, Hong Kong, 68–70
high school, 8, 122, 211
hikikomori, 9, 10
history of childhood, 20–24, 39, 165, 200, 209, 216–18, 231–32, 242
hockey, 182, 183–84, 188, 197–98
Hoffman, Heinrich, *The Story of Fidgety Philip*, 210
Hoffman, Martha, 53–54, 55
homeschooling, 135–37
homework, 16, 60, 122, 142, 143, 145–59, 166, 175, 260; effect on academic performance, 148–50; history of, 146–47; surge in, 147–48; too much, 145–49; tutoring and, 155–59
Homework Myth: Why Our Kids Get Too Much of a Bad Thing, The, 150
Hong Kong, 18, 52, 118, 223; schools, 68–70, 150–52, 153, 156, 158, 259
hormones, stress, 44
How College Affects Students, 134
Humbar Valley Sharks, 197–98
Hyman, Steven, 9
hyperactivity, 209–212
hyper-parenting, 3–18

Iceland, 100
ice skating, 186
illness, 252
imagination, 81, 82, 84, 87, 153
India, 150, 156, 185
Industrial Revolution, 4, 232
Indus Valley, 75
infancy, *see* early years
infant mortality, 39
infertility, 26
instant messages, 92, 97, 105, 108
instincts, trusting, 104
Institute for Social Research, University of Michigan, 164
Institute of Child Health, 95
Interactive Toy Concepts, 101
International Association for the Study of Obesity, 8
International Play Association, 77–79
International Toy Research Centre, 81, 83
International Walk to School Day, 250
International Youth Sports Congress, 183
Internet, 3, 90, 97, 98–99, 102, 108, 109, 110, 224, 258; addiction, 100–103; bullying, 98; cyber tutors, 156; networking, 98–99
Iowa, 14
IQ, 94, 120; Flynn effect, 94
Israel, 149
Italy, 15, 18, 21, 217; Reggio preschool, 60–68, 122, 249
iTeddy, 85, 90

Japan, 4, 11, 95, 201, 233; *hikikomori*, 9, 10; preschool, 58; schools and testing, 58, 118, 120, 121, 127–28, 156; *yutori*, 127–28

Jews, 242
jigsaw puzzles, 76
Johnson, Steven, *Everything Bad Is Good for You,* 94
Jolie, Angelina, 31
Jones, Marilee, 16–17, 113–14, 116, 129, 172
Jordan, Michael, 187
Josephson Institute of Ethics, 185
Jump Up Internet Rescue School, 100

Kaasinen, Pekka, 124–25
Kaiser Family Foundation, 105
Khasminsky, Gene, 101
Kidsbeer, 233
Kidscape, 201
kindergarten, 14, 45, 58; first, 53; interview, 57; "redshirting" and, 14
Kindlon, Dan, *Too Much of a Good Thing: Raising Children of Character in an Indulgent Age,* 205
King's College, London, 95, 119
Kirova, Anna, 52
Kmart, 218
Krueger, Alan, 134
Kumon, 58, 156, 157–58

labor, child, 23–24, 165
lacrosse, 188
Ladies' Home Journal, 147
Lakeside School, Zurich, 71–72, 111
Lam, Julie, 68–70
Lambert, Sophie, 225–26
language, 39–43, 110, 175; foreign, 42–43, 74, 171
Lareau, Annette, *Unequal Childhoods: Class, Race, and Family Life,* 168, 169
Larson, Peer, 145–46
Latin America, 4

Latinos, 14
Latvia, 224
lawsuits, 30–31, 145–46
LazyTown, 100
League of Nations, 24
Leapfrog, 80
Lee Don-Hee, 129
Lego, 77, 78, 81–82, 87–88, 155, 216
letters, 52–53, 70, 74, 76, 93
Levine, Madeline, *The Price of Privilege,* 9
Levitt (Steven) and Dubner (Stephen), *Freakonomics,* 55
Lewis, Harry, 173
Little League Baseball International, 192
Locke, John, 22, 23, 54, 76, 217, 261; *Some Thoughts on Education,* 22
London, 1, 18, 31, 43, 47–48, 73, 84, 120, 158, 199, 221, 224, 228
Los Angeles, 13
Love, Courtney, 211–12
Lucretius, 37
Lynch, Stephen, 154, 155

Madonna, 207
Mahoney, Joseph, 167
Malaguzzi, Loris, 60–61, 66
mammals, 49–50
Mandarin, 28, 40, 42–43
Massachusetts Institute of Technology, 16, 113–14, 164, 172–73
math, 1, 2, 52, 110, 115, 119, 121, 122, 138, 143, 148, 149, 150, 153, 158
Matisse, Henri, 49
Mattel, 236
McCann, Madeleine, 30
McCarron, Mike, 197–98

McDonalds, 219
meals, family, 175–77
media, 15, 26, 27, 29–30, 167, 235; on child safety, 244–45
medication, 10, 130, 209–212, 261
me-first edge, 13–14, 205
meninos de rua, 51
Mennonites, 95
mental illness, 8–10
Meyer, David E., 106
Microsoft, 92
middle class, 4, 10
middle school, 110
Milwaukee, 121
Minjok Leadership Academy, South Korea, 129
Minnesota, 176, 230
Montaigne, Michel Eyquem de, 39
Montessori, Maria, 68
Montessori schools, 68, 70, 121
Mozart, Wolfgang Amadeus, 3, 41–42
Mozart effect, 42
multitasking, 105–108
music, 5, 40, 41–42, 43–44, 174–75
myopia, 92–93, 96, 149
MySpace, 98, 108

Nanny 911, 201
narcissism, 11–12, 99, 201–203
National Association of Toy and Leisure Libraries, 81
National Merit Scholars, 175
nature, 90, 110–11, 253
neuroscience, 80
New Jersey, 97, 117, 161, 186
Newsweek, 26, 62
Newton, Sir Isaac, 49
New York, 18, 67, 156
New Yorker, 162
New York Times, 217

New Zealand, 224
Nicklaus, Jack, 187
Nickelodeon, 219
Nintendo, 91, 111
Nintendo Wii, 100–101
Nishar, Dipchand, 108
Norway, 224, 241
numbers, 52–53, 58, 59, 70, 76, 93

obesity, 8, 95; television and, 95
object permanence, 39
Office of Christian Parents, 165
O'Hanlon, Jerry, 223
Ohio, 191, 207
Organization for Economic Cooperation and Development (OECD), 115, 125
overprotection, 245–51
overscheduling, 15, 161–79
Oxford University, 19–20, 117, 133, 259

Paavola, Tommi, 186
Palm Pilots, 5, 162
Paltrow, Gwyneth, 27
Paris, 14, 225
parks, 243
Parsons, Rob, *Teenagers: What Every Parent Has to Know,* 205
Pascarella, Ernest, 134
Pateman, Dave, 85–86
Pediatrics, 92, 93
pedophilia, 244, 245, 246, 248
peers, 55; pressure, 220
Pelé, 190
Persia, 75
Pester Power, 215–37, 262
Peter Pan culture, 204
Philadelphia, 59, 102, 184
Picasso, Pablo, 49, 170
Pitt, Brad, 26

Pizza Hut, 218
plastic surgery, 10–11
Plato, 20, 57, 93, 121, 231
play, 48–55, 193; early years, 48–55;
   preschool, 57–72; toys, 73–88
Playboy, 236
playground safety, 249
PlayStation, 102–103
politics, 31–32
pools, 30
Portugal, 30
praise, too much, 201–204
pregnancy, 4–5, 6, 26, 38
preschool, 57–72, 110, 120; as academic rat race, 57; early learning
   in, 57–59, 70; Montessori, 68,
   70; outdoor, 239–41, 251–55,
   260; play, 57–72; Reggio, 60–68,
   122, 249; toys, 74–76; Waldorf,
   68–72
Princeton University, 133
Programme for International Student Assessment (PISA), 115–16,
   122, 123
ProVigil, 117
Pupillus, Lucius Orbilius, 3
Puritans, 22, 35, 165
puzzles, 76, 77, 78

Quindlen, Anna, 15
Quintilian, 231–32

radio, 93
Raffi, 223
Rainer, Domisch, 123–24
Raven, 247
reading, 2, 58, 59, 60, 70, 121, 12,
   153
Ready, Set, Relax!, 162–63, 169–72
rebellion, 34
recess, 58

Reggio preschools, Italy, 60–68,
   122, 249
resources, 265–67
Reynolds, Joshua, 22
Ridgewood, New Jersey, 117,
   161–62, 168–72
Ripken, Cal, Jr., 191
Ritalin, 10, 117, 124, 209, 210, 211
Romantic movement, 22, 23, 232,
   261
Rome, 3, 21, 35, 75, 141–42, 232
Rousseau, George, 19–20, 22, 24, 35
Rousseau, Jean-Jacques, 22, 71, 115
Rule of Benedict, 21
Rylands, Tim, 109

safety, 5–6, 29–31, 239–55; fear
   and, 242–55; overprotection and,
   245–51; school, 243, 250
St. John's School and Community
   College, Marlborough, 138–43
Sam, Conrad, 200
San Francisco, 9, 229
Saratoga High, California, 129–32
SATs, 14, 120, 123, 130, 156
Scandinavia, 3, 71
Scarsdale, New York, 193–97
scheduling, 5, 25; infant, 45–47;
   overscheduling, 15, 161–79
Scheving, Magnus, 100
school, 41, 113–43, 259; ADHD
   and, 211; attendance, 23; block
   schedule, 130–32; brand-name
   colleges, 113–14, 132–35, 147,
   156, 173, 259; cheating in,
   117–18, 119–20; consumerism
   in, 218–19, 223; finding a good
   school, 137–43; Finnish, 122–26,
   142; homeschooling, 135–37;
   homework, 145–59; Japanese, 118,
   120, 121, 127–28; obsession with

academic achievement, 113–43, 155–59; parent-teacher meetings, 1–2; preschool, 57–72; safety, 243, 250; technology and, 108–12; testing, 113–43; tutoring and, 155–59; walking to, 250–51; *see also* college; elementary school; high school; middle school; preschool

Schor, Juliet, *Born to Buy,* 221–22

science, 110, 115, 121, 122, 138, 148

Scotland, 18, 152–53, 184, 208, 239–41, 252

Secret Garden nursery, Scotland, 239–41, 251–55, 260

self-harm, 8, 9, 34, 246

self-esteem, high, 201–203

Seneca, 21, 239

sex, 233–36; abuse, 248

Shakespeare, William, 116, 140

Shanghai, 5

Shanmugaratnam, Tharman, 127

shapes, 72, 94

Shopping Generation, 222

Showalter, Buck, 189–90

Singapore, 92, 127, 157, 174

Singh, Budhia, 185

skateboarding, 34

sleep, 44, 47, 204; deprivation, 96

Slow Down: Getting More Out of Harvard by Doing Less, 173

soccer, 182, 187, 189, 190–91, 192, 193, 259, 263

social class, 9, 67

social studies, 110

Society for Research in Child Development, 166

solitude, 13

Soranus, *How to Recognize the Newborn That Is Worth Rearing,* 21

South Korea, 89–90, 100, 172; schools and testing, 115, 119, 127, 128, 129, 156, 157; tutoring in, 156, 157, 158

Soviet Union, 26, 147

Spain, 7, 26, 94, 192, 247

Spartans, 35

speech, 39

spelling, 1

Spielberg, Steven, 130

sports, 5, 104, 170, 171, 181–98; adult involvement in children's sports, 181–98; college, 183, 184; early specialization, 186–88; eliminating pressure in, 193–98; injuries, 8, 185–86; organized, 181–93; private coaching, 182, 183; scholarships, 184, 185; win-at-all-costs ethos, 182, 188–90, 195

Sputnik, 26

Sri Lanka, 87

Starcraft, 89–90

Star Wars, 94

status symbols, children as, 26

stay-at-home twentysomethings, 11

Steinberg, Laurence, *The Ten Basic Principles of Good Parenting,* 206

steroids, 185

stimulation, 40–45, 84

Stockholm, 81, 187

stomach problems, 8

stranger danger, 248

street children, 51

street safety, 250

stress, 8, 130, 228; hormones, 44; -induced illnesses, 8–9; overscheduling, 161–79

Stressed Out Students (SOS), 129–30

Sudan, 4

suicide, 9, 10, 118–19

Supernanny, 11, 25, 206, 208

Svensson, Krister, 81, 82

Sweden, 13, 81, 83, 92, 111, 187, 224, 243, 244
Switzerland, 71–72

Taipei, 37, 111, 157
Taiwan, 15, 28–29, 37, 92, 111, 157–58
teachers, 55, 123, 124, 131, 139, 140, 154
technology, 5, 17, 31, 74, 89–112, 126, 229; addiction, 89–90, 100–103; balanced relationship with, 100–112; benefits of, 93–94, 109–10; multitasking, 105–108; schools and, 108–112; screen time, 89–91, 92–112; toy, 75, 77–78, 79–88; video games, 89–90, 92, 93–105, 111
teenagers, 9, 98, 99, 166, 227; suicide, 9, 10, 118–19
television, 11, 31, 90, 92, 93, 101, 102, 176, 201, 206, 244, 247; advertising, 217–18, 219, 224; limits, 103–104, 208; too much, 92, 95; violence, 92
Temple, Shirley, 217
tennis, 181, 182, 186
Terenzini, Patrick, 134
testing, 68, 113–43; Chinese, 114–15, 118–19; Finnish, 122–26, 142; homeschooling and, 135–37; tutoring and, 155–59
text messaging, 5, 91
Thrale, Hester Lynch, 257–58
Tianjin, 58
Time magazine, 146
Tintin, 232–33
Tiny Love Wonder Wheel, 74, 75
Tomlin, Lily, 145
Townsend, John, 23

toys, 73–88; educational, 76–77, 79–88; entertainment, 77–79; history of, 75–76; industry, 76; IPA experiment, 77–79; packaging, 74–75; play, 73–88; preschool, 74–76; technology, 75, 77–78, 79–88; wooden, 84, 87
Toys R Us, 219
trophy children, 26
Truman Show, 6
tutoring, private, 123, 155–59
Twain, Mark, 116
Tymms, Peter, 149
Tyndale, William, 232

ultrasound, 6
Ungar, Michael, *Too Safe for Their Own Good: How Risk and Responsibility Help Teens Thrive,* 247
UNICEF, 118, 122, 244
United Nations, 8–9
United States, 10, 14, 16, 18, 58, 59, 129, 176; *see also specific cities and states*
U.S. National Institute of Mental Health, 9

vacation, 178
Vancouver, 109
Vernon Barford, Edmonton, Canada, 153–56
Victorian era, 35, 51
video games, 79, 89–90, 92, 93–105, 111
Viertola, Vantaa, Finland, 124–25
violence, 92, 93, 119, 248
violin, 43–44, 174
Virginia, 30
vocabulary, 2, 41
VTech, 83, 84

Walcott, Theo, 187
Waldorf preschools, 68–72
Wales, 126
Wales, Jimmy, 99
Walker, Daniel, 151, 152
walking, 39; to school, 250–51
Wall Street Journal, 11
Wal-Mart, 224
wealth, 9
Web sites, 5, 6, 15, 31, 90, 117, 206,
    219, 224, 228, 266–67
welfare programs, 23
West Africa, 248
Whitnall High School, Greenfield,
    Wisconsin, 145–46
Wie, Michelle, 186
Wiese-Bjornstal, Diane, 184–85
Wikipedia, 99
Williams, Serena, 186, 194

Winnicott, D. W., 261
Wisconsin, 145
WombSong Serenades, 5
Woods, Tiger, 186–87
Wordsworth, William, 22
working mother, 29, 164
World Chess Federation, 117
World Health Organization, 9
World War II, 60, 147
writing, 2

Xbox, 101, 102, 183, 212

Yale University, 38, 133, 156
Yankus, Wayne, 168
yutori kyoiku, 127–28, 129

Zeta-Jones, Catherine, 27
Zurich, 71–72, 111